Advance Praise for *Presence-Based Leadership*

Presence-Based Leadership is a gift. Silsbee transparently shares his thinking, experience, and self. This wonderful volume actively cultivates the experience of presence in the reader. And, Silsbee articulates a strong case for presence as the core practice of consciousness in a world of polarity and complexity. We are fortunate to have this gift: listen as this book speaks!

—Robert C. Pianta; PhD, Dean, Curry School of Education, University of Virginia

For leaders in an age of overwhelming complexity, Silsbee offers deceptively simple guidance: a profound focus on the present. "Embodying what matters" gives leaders a dispassionate and actionable foundational understanding. This core insight, and thought-provoking practices throughout, is having a profound impact on how I show up as a leader and as a human being.

—Michael J. Anderson; Global Managing Partner; Leadership Advisory Business, Spencer Stuart

An expansive book for anyone in a leadership role, and for leadership development professionals. Silsbee integrates systems theory, neuroscience, somatics, mindfulness, complexity and leadership. His synthesis is accessible, yet challenges readers' ways of thinking, being and acting. This is a wise, insightful and intensely practical foundation for leading in ever-increasing levels of complexity.

—Bill Pullen; MCC, Co-Program Director, Leadership Coaching Program, Institute for Transformational Leadership, Georgetown University

The final book in Silsbee's must-read trilogy on leadership and coaching is the most important of all. In a crucial moment in history, Silsbee's book provides an exquisite guide for making meaning out of new patterns, "loosening the grip of outmoded habits" and leading at our best. This leadership model is brilliant!

—Pamela McLean; PhD, CEO, Hudson Institute of Coaching

The surge in healthcare complexity defies solutions. Yet in *Presence-Based Leadership*, Silsbee offers radical new perspectives and a pathway towards the answers we seek. Those answers are within us, emanating from our presence, our awareness, and the possibilities waiting to be realized through ourselves and those we lead.

—Sheldon Stadnyk; MD, Physician Executive, Leadership Development,
Former Chief Medical Officer, Banner Health

All of us in leadership encounter dilemmas that stymie our best efforts. Sometimes, we are able to pause and recognize that we are in a different game than we thought. Doug's third book offers experiences and powerful reflections about the personal and organizational transformations that can follow from these crucial moments.

—Bill Torbert; PhD, Emeritus Professor of Leadership, Boston College,
and author of 12 books

This book springs forth with the practical wisdom of a masterful leadership coach as we explore how to transform our relationship with the complex challenges we face. Here is practical guidance for harnessing the power of attention and presence to become a resilient catalyst for positive change. Be present with this work. Embody it, and watch your leadership evolve.

—Ginny Whitelaw; President, Institute for Zen Leadership, author of *The Zen Leader*

No leadership class nor treatise on the secrets of successful CEOs can teach you how to embrace the complexity, uncertainty, and shifting ground beneath your feet. Doug brilliantly and courageously reveals precisely where to find the clarity and resilience to access your skills and knowledge in those critical moments most vital to your success. This is radical new work at a crucial juncture in history.

—Marcia Reynolds; PhD, Former President, Global ICF,
and Author of *Outsmart Your Brain*

Presence-Based Leadership is an extraordinary resource. Working with individuals and teams across Africa, the Nine Panes provide me a wealth of resources and practices spectacularly relevant to leading in the face of intractable challenges such as climate change and protracted conflict.

—Heidrun Kippenberger; Leadership Coach and OD consultant,
CEO of Leadership Presence, Kenya

Oh, my! What an ambitious and beautifully-realized book! Challenging, revelatory, and provocative, the book itself will serve as a developmental catalyst for its readers, pushing us past the limits of our current sense-making. Here is a road map for developing the capacities necessary to effectively respond to the volatile and complex world in which so many of us find ourselves leading.

—Steve Heller; Former Program Director,
Georgetown University Leadership Coaching Certificate Program

Read this. Practice. Complexity will start to feel simpler. Doug's holistic approach has profoundly influenced the way I coach and work with senior executives as they struggle at the forefront of disruptive change. This is a practical go-to book that holds the essence of timeless wisdom.

—Johanne Lavoie; Partner, McKinsey & Company, Co-author of *Centered Leadership*

Here is a groundbreaking and comprehensive way to think about leadership in a complex world! These meta skills across every level of context will help you create the conditions for meeting your mounting challenges. Doug's years of experience, deep theoretical knowledge, and an honest and conversational style make this a joy to read. Life becomes the curriculum for growth; more successful organizations with happier people is the outcome.

—Jennifer Garvey Berger; PhD, CCO, Cultivating Leadership, New Zealand,
author of *Simple Habits for Complex Times*

Silsbee elegantly strikes a rare balance: profoundly illuminating and pragmatically instructive. In my complex world of public education, Doug offers rich experiments and practices for engaging in the authentic curriculum of our immediate experience. Well grounded in research, Silsbee transcendently integrates leadership and adult development theories into practical insights, examples and perspectives that will immediately strengthen your capacity for dealing with complex challenges.

—Kevin Foster; Superintendent, Valley School District, Valley, WA

PRESENCE-BASED LEADERSHIP

Complexity Practices for Clarity, Resilience, and Results That Matter

DOUG SILSBEE

Foreword by Kevin Cashman

YES! GLOBAL INC.

Author contact: dksilsbee@gmail.com
Website: http://ninepanes.org

Limits of Liability and Disclaimer of Warranty:

While the author and publisher of this book have used their best efforts in preparing this book, they make no representations regarding the accuracy and completeness of the ideas, examples, practices and experiments provided within, and specifically disclaim any implied warranties of merchantability or fitness for a particular purpose. Case examples are intentionally anonymized, and sometimes are composites, to more concisely convey particular learning points. No warranty may be created or extended by sales representatives or sales materials. The advice and strategies suggested herein may or may not be suitable for your situation; it is your responsibility to consult with a professional where appropriate.

The author and/or publisher shall not be liable for your misuse of this material. The contents are strictly for informational and educational purposes only. The author and/or publisher shall have neither liability nor responsibility to anyone with respect to any loss or damage caused, or alleged to be caused, directly or indirectly by the information contained in this book. Readers should be aware that Internet websites listed in this work may have changed or disappeared between when this work was written and when it is read.

Printed and bound in the United States of America
ISBN: 978-0-692-05334-8

Library of Congress Control Number: 2018900322

Table of Contents

Table of Figures and Callouts

(Note: Text-only callouts are not numbered. Numbered figures are referenced in the text.)

Table of Experiments and Practices

Acknowledgments and Lineage

IT TAKES A VILLAGE.

While the work offered in this book is a new synthesis, nothing is created from scratch. I am deeply grateful to the many leaders and teachers I've had the good fortune to learn from, directly or indirectly, over a lifetime of inquiry and exploration. Some have particularly shaped my thinking and my practice in significant ways; I hope that they would see this work as a worthy extension of their own lineage and contribution.

I want to extend specific appreciation to Irmansyeh Effendi, James Flaherty, Darya Funches, Barry Johnson, Robert Kegan, Peter Levine, Rod Napier, Nancy Spence, and Richard Strozzi-Heckler.

I am deeply appreciative of the countless clients and retreat participants who have brought their challenges and work to the table, thus providing me with the means to develop this body of work and fulfill my own sense of purpose. They, and their stories, are present throughout this book. Those that have been touched by this work in some way represent, of course, the continuation of lineages, some of which go back thousands of years. That these people chose to work with me in service to their own development has been a tremendous privilege. That I have learned far more from them than they have from me is a well-kept secret!

I am grateful to the many who gave me feedback along the way: Jennifer Garvey Berger, Carolyn Coughlin, Linda Ford, Sarah Halley, Bebe Hansen, Steve Heller, Bill Pullen, Linda Ford, Bob Silsbee, Walker Silsbee, Bev Wann, and Ginny Whitelaw. This project also benefited greatly from the efforts and talents of Catherine Adams, Bethany Kelly, Stefan Merour, and Frank Steele.

Four remarkable women were instrumental to this book; without each of them, this book would likely not exist, or would be greatly impoverished, so significant were their contributions:

- Bebe Hansen has encouraged me from the beginning to get this work out there, and has always showed up with both depth and precision in supporting me and in increasingly running many aspects of our business, freeing me up to write. She still saw where this was going sometimes when I was too far down in the weeds, and was gently insistent.

- Carolyn Coughlin has a deep understanding of adult development theory and complexity in organizational settings. She has been a rigorous sounding board for the ideas in this book, and a loving and candid reflector when my own habits showed up in the writing. My collaboration with her on designing and delivering multiple retreats around this content has been deeply satisfying. These retreats have shaped the book, and vice versa.

- Luckett Davidson created many of the graphics that we use in our teaching, and was gracious enough to spend far more hours on the graphic work for this book than she ever imagined. She has been a fun and creative collaborator with me in developing and communicating this work with graphics that support your learning in multiple ways.

- And, Walker. Need I say more? My beloved wife and life partner, who has stood with me for 35 years as we found our way through life, and who has been nothing but supportive of me writing this third book, simply because it was "mine to do." Her feedback, support, love, and fierce honesty and integrity have shaped me over decades; this book never could have been written without her.

In my world, I have close personal relationships and collaboration with many other professionals and firms, particularly with Cultivating Leadership and Strozzi Institute. If some of their vocabulary may have unconsciously slipped in without attribution because of shared lineage and countless conversations, I intend this as a blanket apology and as deep appreciation for their work.

Foreword by Kevin Cashman

THE PLANE IS DARK, THE SHADES ARE PULLED DOWN. My fellow passengers are mostly sleeping, an occasional flicker of movies spotting the cabin. It is a peaceful scene, a rare moment of pause for perspective after an intense weeklong trip to Europe to help a group of leaders in Austria access deeper purpose, self-awareness and resilience. Silence provides a potent and appropriate moment to pause and to reflect on both leadership and presence.

Interestingly, this jetliner is like the power of presence: a perspectival vehicle that integrates old with new, our deeper selves with our purpose, our minds with our hearts, our values with our actions, our organizations with a better world. Presence is the conscious, intentional awareness that connects our deepest heartfelt essence to the furthest reaches of societal contribution. Presence is the ever-present human potentiality to transform speed and transaction into significance and transformation.

In the world of leadership development, presence is too often reduced to a very surface definition and called *executive presence.* While executive presence can sometimes be a manifestation of deeper, essential presence, it is more often seen as an external behavior or style. Presence becomes a commodity, reduced to the ability of a leader to command a room and project a kind of assured confidence that is engaging, credible and charismatic.

Authentic leadership presence is so much more than this typical and superficial notion of executive presence. I have come to see presence not only as a deeper leadership dynamic but also as a fundamental meta-competency for leadership and life.

Leadership is essentially a human endeavor, and many would say humans are the most complex systems we know. It is no surprise that leadership is extremely complex. With considerable effort, Korn Ferry's research has narrowed down the list of leadership competencies to thirty-eight! With so many, we might well seek the most essential leadership competencies, the meta-competencies, the foundational aspects of what it means to be a leader. Self-awareness, emotional intelligence and learning agility have been validated as worthy of meta-competency status. I would add one more: presence. And, I will claim a special status for presence as possibly the most fundamental life and leadership competency.

So what is this thing we call presence? And, by the way, present with what? These are not easy questions. After three decades of observing leaders across the globe, and deeply considering these questions, I would suggest that ***presence is the real-time, simultaneous awareness of self, others, purpose, organization and society***. Leaders who can include these multiple levels in their awareness can bring forward the best in self and others to make a sustainable difference. They can "authentically influence to create enduring value," as suggested in *Leadership from the Inside Out*. Presence is the awareness that connects self to others and to enduring contribution. Presence is the awareness of self in self-awareness; it is the awareness of self *and* others in emotional intelligence; it is the awareness of learning in first-time situations; and it is the awareness of contribution in the biggest possible context. Presence is the meta-competency of living and leading in a socially responsible, sustainable and value-enriching way.

A requirement in today's complex world is transcend or be forced to transcend; be present or miss the opportunity-rich moment forever. When the only genuine shot at transformation is the presence, why do we so hyperactively avoid the pause and reflection required for this transforming moment? Our 24/7, caffeinated, ever-connected culture is perfectly designed to avoid taking a breath, let alone connecting to what is essential and important. As a result, we too rarely access the full potential of the present. Imagine a world-class athlete at the height of pressured performance yet with her or his attention elsewhere. The performance would fall apart, wouldn't it? Why should we be different?

Leaders are all engaged in a world-class undertaking of a different nature, one that is called to serve our loved ones, our teams, our descendants and our world. *Are we really present to this? Are we really attending to what is important?* A dear mentor of mine, Warren Bennis, counseled, "Leaders remind people what is important." However, how can we have a reasonable chance to remember what is most significant when we are too often consumed by speed, hurtling into a future before really having arrived here in this moment? Ultimately, pauseful, inside-out presence is the key to evoking a real and sustainable difference.

However, being present in the moment does not deal with the very challenging leadership paradox that leaders must be fully present in the moment *and* fully creating the future at the same time. Great leaders bridge this paradox; they have a sharp, localized awareness of the present moment while maintaining a broad, visionary context. Living in these two realities at the same time is the genuine challenge and opportunity of leadership presence.

Many of us can sense this state of highly developed holistic presence in great leaders—Nelson Mandela and Mahatma Gandhi come immediately to mind. When women and men are established in this state, no external event can shake them. Their presence is palpable to others, and they become a beacon for the rest of us.

Where do you go when times get tough for you as a leader? Do you go to a loved one, a trusted advisor or friend? Do you try to work through it while you exercise? These options are helpful, but where do you go when you need the deepest counsel and solace? Prayer? Meditation? Music? Learning to pause and to drop deeper into presence has never been more critical. As the British poet Lord Byron wrote, "The soul must pause to breathe." Authentic, presence-based leadership requires us to pause. Pause to breathe… pause to be… pause to create new value-creating futures.

Doug Silsbee's rich new book is not merely a book about leadership. It is a book about the inside-out presence that can enrich every interaction you have. Go slow with this one, reading with presence and awareness. Let this important work settle into your Being. Inquire deeply, rather than consuming it like intellectual candy. Practice BEING what Doug so beautifully describes. Practice presence as if life depended on it. *Be the book, rather than merely read it.*

Take a comfortable seat and immerse yourself in the experience of inside-out presence.

Kevin Cashman
Author, *Leadership from the Inside Out* and *The Pause Principle*
Senior Partner, CEO & Executive Development, Korn Ferry

Preface

AT TIMES, IN BOTH EVERYDAY LIFE AND IN SITUATIONS OF LEADERSHIP, *complicated* no longer describes the environment or the goal. *Complex* defines the day. What you have always counted on before—yourself, your skills, your proven methods—no longer works sufficiently. You need something new, you realize. But what?

This book seeks to offer some perspectives on this phenomenon—and on how to develop a deep and authentic leadership presence that is relevant to complexity.

In complexity, ***cause and effect are not predictable.*** Other people act in ways that don't make sense to us. Many interrelated factors affect what is emerging, and some things in the system affect others in ways impossible to predict. ***The harder we drive for results, the more the unanticipated side effects tend to multiply.***

In these kinds of environments, the usual ways of leading are often ineffective, even counterproductive. It can be liberating to recognize that we've been spending too much energy in approaches that actually don't work.

What if leading could in fact be both easier and more successful?

To scaffold new actions in our own complex leadership context, the condition of presence is foundational. ***Presence is an internal state: the awareness of immediacy, stillness, inclusive awareness and possibility.*** This state enables us to sense the world as it actually is and to sense ourselves as we actually are. A rigorous embrace of reality leads to clarity, resilience and results that matter.

Presence-Based Leadership is the commitment to, and practice of, these principles in situations demanding new solutions, new futures and even new understandings of self.

This has been the hardest, by far, of my three books to write. I've been experimenting with these ideas and practices for many years. This book has been asking me to write it for five. I've tried many ways to say what I wish to say: I wrote a complete first draft, put it on the back burner to simmer, then threw it out. Twice as many words as the contents of this entire book reside in my computer in deleted text files, like the marble a sculptor discards to finally reveal what lies inside the stone. If a sculptor's work is to seek what has always lain within, perhaps my work has been to sense my way into what I feel is so important to express.

I am aware that this material is itself complex and sometimes elusive. Yet, I'm also convinced that it is of profound importance. Accelerating the capacity of leaders to work through extraordinary complexity with clarity and resilience is one key to resolving the crucial issues of our times.

If I were writing this book three years from now, it would be a different book, just as this one is far different from what I was able to draft three years ago. I know it's not perfect, that it has holes and contradictions and vital pieces missing. I could spend more years refining it: literally every day new things occur to me that I want to add. But, perfect can be the enemy of good, and this is good enough. For now, this is what I know how to say. It's time to get this work out and let it do what it is to do. This book is my safe-to-fail experiment.

Ironically, in the very week I am completing this manuscript, I have received a diagnosis of advanced metastatic cancer. I have worked with everything in this book, in my personal and professional realms, for years. However, this now radically changed context immediately elevates my need to put what I espouse here into practice. You, reading this in what is my future and your present, will likely know more about how this journey plays out for me than I can know now. What I do know now is that my condition presents me with a world-class opportunity to practice.

Oh, by the way. I am white and American. I'm sixty-three. I have a degree in geology. Both my parents have PhDs. I grew up in the era of cheap oil. I am male, basically liberal, and come from a relatively privileged background that has enabled opportunities for travel, education, and meaningful and rewarding work. I'm a husband, a father, a grandfather, and a cancer patient among many other designations.

I offer this brief list (which could be much longer) not at all to establish my qualifications for offering this work. Nor as apology for the limitations that my history and demographics certainly impose on how I view and interpret the world. I offer it simply as disclosure and transparency.

I, like you, write and lead and love from an embodied history that reflects a particular set of circumstances that provide me with both generous capabilities and real limitations. This of course is the human condition.

It is my hope that I can speak into our shared human condition in a way that will be useful and empowering to fellow humans who have different backgrounds and histories than I do.

It is my deepest hope that this work is of some service in a suffering world.

Introduction

*In a time of drastic change it is the learners who inherit
the future. The learned usually find themselves equipped
to live in a world that no longer exists.*
— Eric Hoffer

*Successful leaders embrace the reality that their models
may be wrong or incomplete. Only when we admit what
we don't know can we ever hope to learn it.*
— Ed Catmull

Y OU, THE INTENDED READER OF THIS BOOK, ARE A LEADER.
You may have senior-level responsibilities in a corporation, university, or
nonprofit. You may be a coach or other intermediary who leads by helping
others bring out the best in themselves. You may be an entrepreneur with a
product, a service and a lot of energy and commitment. Or, simply a human
being seeking to lead a life of value and service to those you care about—a leader
for community betterment.

Whatever the specifics of your leadership context, you are almost assuredly
daunted by **complexity** in some form. While you care passionately, game-
changing disruptions make it impossible to plan, distractions abound, and
tedious must-do's siphon your attention from what's really important. You are
experienced enough to see countless choices and savvy enough to recognize

that, while every decision solves some problems, it also creates others. You likely experience some frustration that you, as a competent, smart achiever, are not able more consistently to manage the unruly people and forces in your world towards better outcomes.

These difficulties can feel personal. They are not.

Complex situations destabilize us. They are unpredictable. They do not follow cause-and-effect logic, nor lend themselves to classic cause-and-effect solutions. But this complexity is far larger than the situation you face as a leader. Our entire world intensifies around us. Historical stability seems to vanish. Globalization, intensified competition, the need to do more with less, disruptive technologies, climate change, resource scarcities, economic disenfranchisement, macroeconomic sea changes, and political paralysis can give rise to a real sense that the world is hurtling towards chaos. Navigating these enormous challenges together to to build a healthy world that works for all requires extraordinary new leadership across all levels and sectors of society.

All this is simply to point out: You have assumed the mantle of leadership at a critical turning point in history. The scale and complexity of the challenges that we collectively face are increasing exponentially, and your training and preparation are insufficient preparation for what you face. The bad news is that it sometimes feels as if you are being asked to be a leader you have not yet become.

The resulting gap between the needs of the moment and your ability to create a new future only means that, realistically, you face conditions different from those you prepared for or could possibly anticipate.

Producing results that matter requires doing things differently—perhaps even radically differently. Learning new ways to do the same things more effectively will not be enough. Rather, it is time to reimagine what leadership itself can be, and to step up in ways that you can't yet see, bringing your whole self to your challenges.

The good news is that complex problems can be seen as powerful catalysts for your ongoing development. Approached wisely, obstacles often accelerate growth. This book intends to focus the energies of those catalysts into fundamental shifts in how you approach your own learning and development. You will develop new ways to perceive and to engage with yourself, allowing you to confront the complexity that already exists, but to do so with less angst, more clarity and greater resilience.

Meta-competencies and Why They Matter

At some point in your career, you began to recognize your limitations.

Since then, you have read books, gotten coached, attended leadership seminars and studied the latest theories and methods. Potent and majestic frameworks like Robert Kegan and Lisa Laskow Lahey's *Immunity to Change*, C. Otto Scharmer's *Theory U*, Bob Anderson's *Leadership Circle*, and Richard Strozzi-Heckler's *Embodied Leadership*[1] are but a few of the excellent resources that you may well have integrated into your leadership vernacular.

You are serious about self-improvement, but you've also noticed that every leading-edge approach or tool over time begins to seem partial and incomplete. Change has accelerated, which is one reason why new models appear frequently and with great promise—and the *next* big challenge still seems to overwhelm our preparedness.

We yearn for something deeper: a bigger view that can help us navigate into the future. Rather than relying on one model, we must draw fluidly from many frameworks in order to discover our own path and to make meaning in ways most helpful for our unique situation. We must deepen our access to innate core capacities that lie deeper than any model or method, rather than hoping for the just-in-time emergence of the just-right tool.

Artist Pablo Picasso had a career spanning decades and artistic periods. He anticipated and revolutionized artistic styles; somehow, he always seemed just ahead of the newest development. While some artists are known for their skill in sculpture and others for watercolor, Picasso moved fluidly from paint to print to clay to collage to mixtures of them all. Like Picasso choosing among many media to best express a truth, the adept leader chooses among numerous models and approaches, yet remains true to an authentic core even while serving diverse constituencies and agendas.

Picasso's search for expression pushed him to experiment and explore. Though he was gifted at many forms of expression, his allegiance to unfettered self-expression was his meta-competency.

A meta-competency is a capability that underpins everything else that we do. It becomes deeply woven into the fabric of who we are and how we organize and respond to our world. A meta-competency includes and enables other competencies. It is a way of being as much as a way of doing.

This book will help you develop three such overarching meta-competencies. These represent three core processes of organizing ourselves and responding to the world: *Sensing* (the way we take in information about our world and about ourselves),

PRESENCE-BASED LEADERSHIP PROMISES

As a result of understanding the meta-competencies in this book and by working with the exercises and practices, you will:

- Increase your capacity to move fluidly among a set of rich and complementary *perspectives*,

- Explore how *Complexity* challenges your very *identity*, blinding you to possibilities,

- Discover the universal road map that has always shaped your process of lifelong *development*,

- Increase your capacity to *observe and self-regulate* your internal state,

- Deepen your *resilience*—your capacity to stay *creative* and *resourceful* no matter what's going on around you,

- Choose and *embody* commitments to what you care about, acting in *congruence* with them,

- Develop your *leadership presence* and the resulting connection and resonance with others, and

- Act in *Complexity*, discerning high-leverage actions that scale awareness and create the *conditions* for what you care about.

Being (our inner condition as we process this information moment-by-moment) and *Acting* (what we think, say, and do, all of which arise out of this internal experience).

Whether you are aware of these fundamental, ongoing processes or not, they are always and actively occurring, including in this very moment. They are constant, never-ending, reliable and life-giving. *Presence is in large part about bringing awareness and attention to these core human processes.* While they occur in every sentient being, it's one of the many marvelous benefits of being human that you can become aware of these subtle and implicit processes. You can direct your attention to them. And you can intervene in the usually automatic nature of their functioning.

In a leadership context, the inherent human capacity both to direct and to observe your attention itself is immensely pragmatic. With the awareness you are building, you can consciously develop the meta-competencies of:

- *Sensing* yourself and your context in ways that produce *clarity*,

- *Being* so as to invite the inner state of *presence* in service to your *resilience*, creativity and fluidity, and

- *Acting* in order to invite new conditions (both internal to you *and* external in the world around you) that encourage *results that matter*.[2]

Our Road Map

Exploration of the three meta-competencies of *Sensing, Being*, and *Acting* will be our road map for exploring Presence-Based Leadership. *These three meta-competencies, applied at three levels of scale—Context, Identity, and Soma*—provide nine distinguishable perspectives on our moment-by-moment experience of the domain that is called **Complexity**.

Each perspective, or *Pane*, is a window into your situation. Each Pane informs a set of perspectives, actions, practices and approaches rich with opportunity for engaging with an out-of-control world in potent and generative new ways.

Each is an important but partial view; each renders your understanding more inclusive and complete. Taken together, they provide a powerful and integrated way for accelerating your development as a leader and for accessing an ever-increasing range of your innate capabilities in service to what you care about.

I have organized this material into four parts.

In Part One, you will understand in profoundly important ways how you became the leader you are. And, what's wonderful about that and what's problematic. This will orient you on your personal map of the developmental journey.

- Chapter 1: *The Territory of Complexity* offers a simple set of stepping stones—navigation and support aids—for recognizing the domain of Complexity when you are in it and normalizing your reaction to it. You explore the ingredients of new and pragmatic approaches to addressing the demands that Complexity places on you.

- Chapter 2: *Embodiment, Identity and the Bell Jar* unpacks the lifelong process of development as an unfolding of identity, how your learning has always been shaped as a set of responses to changing conditions and requirements. We introduce the metaphor of the Bell Jar, and realize how our development to date has imbued us with wonderful strengths and inarguable limitations.

- Chapter 3: ***Realization and the Developmental Edge*** looks at your development as a series of stages. By exercising the muscle of attention, you begin to recognize the pervasiveness of invisible habits that have made you successful but also limit you. This awareness prepares you for the meta-competencies of ***Sensing, Being and Acting***.

- Chapter 4: ***The Nine-Paned Leadership Model*** adds three levels of scale—***Context, Identity, and Soma***—to your exploration. Overlaying the three meta-competencies on three levels of scale reveals the nine Panes, illuminating unconventional possibilities for your creativity and resourcefulness.

In Part Two, ***Sensing*** takes center stage. This meta-competency makes visible the very ways you take in information about your world and about yourself, a process so automatic that you are unlikely to have examined how you do it. With this awareness comes new clarity for shaping your response to the world.

- Chapter 5: ***Observe the System*** provides you with new distinctions for observing the world around you, the Context, in new ways. While the unpredictability of a complex world doesn't lessen through this Sensing, a more discerning perspective makes it reassuringly more knowable.

- Chapter 6: ***Recognize Identity at Stake*** challenges you to acknowledge how Complexity confronts your sense of who you are. Reflexively defending your identity during these moments of confrontation obscures the clarity of your view of what is going on around you. You work to transform that interplay so you can use it for your development as a leader.

- Chapter 7: ***Attend to Experience*** puts awareness of your inner experience front and center, observing your body in the constant process of defending your identity. Directing attention into your internal experience allows you to recognize and intervene in the very impulses that precede behavior, and thus to choose new actions.

In Part Three, the meta-competency of **Being** facilitates direct engagement with your own internal state, the basis for every action you take. You will discover principles and methods for shifting your inner state, accessing your innate creativity and resilience, and embodying the very commitments you care most deeply about. Directing your attention where you choose produces presence-based **resilience** no matter what is going on around you.

- Chapter 8: **Regulate Inner State** invites you to experiment with how directed attention affects your own nervous system. You will experience how the quality and focus of your attention opens radical possibilities for self-mastery.

- Chapter 9: **Decouple State from Context** invites you to direct your attention to serve resilience itself. Staying present with your experience and shifting your inner state out of reactivity and into resilience liberates you from the constraints of what is going on around you. The resulting freedom supports everything you care about most.

- Chapter 10: **Embody What Matters** explores a fundamental act of leadership: your embodiment of an intended future. Declaring a future that you care about makes it far more likely. And, you will create the conditions for this future through internal congruence with what matters.

Acting has always been the expression of your inner work into the world. However, in Part Four, **Acting** is redefined in deliberate ways. Now, after your work with Sensing and Being, it arises out of a stable and resilient set of inner conditions that you have actively cultivated. Rooted in Being, your Acting is less to **drive** results and more to **create the conditions** for the results that matter most—to bring creativity and presence to relationships, to scale awareness, and to accelerate the development of your capacity for the rest of your life.

- Chapter 11: **An Attitude of Curiosity and Experimentation** invites you into a different attitude of practice: one of curiosity. Rather than the oppressive overfocus on problem-solving and results, an approach often ineffective in Complexity, you explore a brief and simple set of stepping stones for safe-to-fail experiments. You then act out of this attitude of curiosity.

- Chapter 12: **Connection** works with exploring the conditions of connection and differentiation. You explore the field that connects you with others, with leadership presence as the key to collaborating, inspiring and influencing. Connection becomes an organizing principle in the system.

- Chapter 13: *Fluidity* explores how your own internal fluidity can scale into your relationships and the culture of your context. In conjunction with the continued cultivation of experimentation and curiosity, your embodiment of fluidity evokes more fluidity in your situation.

- Chapter 14: *Stability* acknowledges a core paradox: the very future you intend requires both conditions of fluidity and also of stability. In a crazy world, finding sources of stability, first within yourself, and then in your relationships and the context in which you lead, are essential prerequisites for the results you care about.

An *Epilogue: Paradox and Integration* takes a perspective on the deep context within which you act. You see that your development requires that you simultaneously develop and surrender an identity, a paradox like none other. You recognize the impermanence of the very things that you cherish most and thereby come to appreciate the preciousness and limited control inherent in what you do.

Five *Appendices* include a glossary of terms, a summary of the core realizations of Sensing, Being and Acting, examples of safe-to-fail experiments on three levels of system, a resource for those of you applying this work in a coaching context, and a bibliography for those who wish deeper dives.

Getting the Most out of This Book

If you and I do our work together well, this book will prove a pragmatic guide to leadership in situations of Complexity. You will see the world and yourself differently. You will have a coherent map of how leaders grow and develop, some direct experiences that validate and ground that map, pragmatic ideas for how you can accelerate your own development, and safe-to-fail experiments to tweak the situation in which you are leading. All of this advances your leadership towards what you care about most deeply.

I have provided many *examples*. Some are from business, some from non-profit or educational sectors. Some are personal and others from well-known public figures, and together they cover many levels of scale. This diversity is intended to convey the universality of these principles and strategies. In every sector and at all levels of scale, leaders need Complexity practices for navigating perilous times.

The vast majority of examples are drawn from my client work over several decades. Because development work can be so very personal, I have anonymized client examples by changing particulars. Several are composites, drawing from multiple clients to more concisely illustrate the principles and practices in the book. I am grateful to the human beings in these examples; I have learned far more from them than they from me.

Graphics are included at the front of every chapter, and occasionally in other places. The graphics are intended to convey information in a different way, bypassing the language-based left brain to register in the more metaphorical, image-sensitive right brain. Engaging both sides of the brain in meaning-making is more holistic and inclusive, and for many years we have found graphics instrumental and powerful in landing some of the key distinctions in our coach training work. The graphics provide both whimsy and orienting signposts for what might seem a serious, confusing and circuitous journey.

Scattered throughout the book are what I call *Presence Pauses*. Think of these as micro-experiments: invitations to stop reading for, say, thirty seconds and let the information settle in you. Some will be accompanied by more specific directions, but for the most part, Presence Pauses simply serve as reminders to feel and sense what is being discussed and to experience what it triggers in you, what possibilities open, and what you resist. I want you to take the ideas into your body, inviting important and nuanced linkages between your cognitive understanding and your felt sense of the territory. This simple practice will go a long way towards allowing the book to become multidimensional.[3]

You also will find *experiments* throughout. *Experiments* are generally one-time events through which you work with some questions to make new meaning, to inquire into your own experience, or to try out a new behavior to see what happens. The spirit of curiosity and experimentation is central to this book; it greatly amplifies your own internal conditions for learning.

A journal or notebook in which you can write brief reflections will be very helpful for these experiments. Yes, writing by hand may seem old-fashioned in this era of devices, but in my experience it is far more fluid, honoring of both sides of the brain. Plus, it's that much more personal, and sidesteps at least some of the distractions enabled by technology.

Practices are intended to be repeated over time as a way of building capacity; their value specifically derives from repetition and consistency. It has been said that the "half-life of an insight is short and getting shorter."[4] Reading will change you but a little. Practice is how you became who you are, and it is the only way to become who you choose to be. There is no shortcut to embodied learning.

Test everything, take nothing at my word. Validate it for yourself. Do the practices. They will change you at the core.

A WORD TO COACHES

This is not primarily a coaching book. Those who are familiar with my coaching books or who have studied Presence-Based Coaching may find this curious or may assess that this is a departure from previous work. That's not my sense of it. The process of developing ourselves to coach others has always occurred to me simply as a specialized application of developing ourselves to lead others.

Coaching is an act of "meta-leadership": leadership in service to leaders. This book is the third in a developmental trilogy, each building upon the previous. Here, leadership principles, previously implicit and background to coaching principles, now take center stage. Coaching goes into the background, a specialized application of this material. Yet everything herein applies equally to the art of coaching as well as to the leadership work that our clients, and we ourselves, are engaged in.

Coaches who want some suggestions for translating this into their work with clients will find some pragmatic suggestions in Appendix D. Please know that the entire book is also written for you as a coach, in service both to your own development and to the development of those you serve through the leadership act of coaching.

AN INVITATION:
NAME YOUR OWN COMPLEXITY CHALLENGE

One more thing, and not a little one. To reveal the greatest opportunities from this book, it is imperative to treat this neither as a purely cognitive exploration nor as a series of experiential experiments linked by a narrative. Rather, I encourage you to approach this entire book as a deeper exploration of the unfolding of your own story.

To do this, it will be most helpful for you to choose a specific undertaking: a significant professional or personal challenge you are currently facing. Your *Complexity Challenge* should be something deeply important to you and that confronts you in a variety of ways. It should require you to become a different person than you are now. You should sense that your practiced ways of Sensing, Being, and Acting have somehow become rather inadequate. The outcome should be uncertain, the process of moving forward emergent, the territory unknown and perhaps unknowable. And, the results should matter significantly to you.

Examples might be: You're writing a book. You have a significant new responsibility. You are challenged by leading without authority, but are also accountable for results. You have a significant leadership challenge, and are failing. You are launching a new product or service or business that's never been done before. A competitor has just disrupted your business model, and your organization is scrambling.

If you can identify such a context, you are in the right place, and this is the right book.

The experiments and practices that follow have been written with the assumption that you are deciding, at this very moment, to enter with this mindset.

Take a moment to consider what you are in the middle of.

Decide.

≈ PRESENCE PAUSE ≈

Welcome. And thank you for joining me.

Now, take a few minutes and write down this Complexity Challenge as you see it right now. Simply describe what you know about it, what you know about yourself in it, and what feels complex about it. Take the time to put down some words; the concreteness and focus of this will be most helpful as we move forward together.

PART
ONE

Foundations

The suffering and happiness each of us experiences is a reflection of the distortion or clarity with which we view ourselves and the world.

– The Dalai Lama

W E CAN SENSE THAT THE WORLD IS CHANGING IN DEEP AND FUNDAMENTAL WAYS. It's easy to throw up our hands and say, "Hey, this is bigger than my pay grade. It's out of my control. My job is to hunker down and do what's in front of me to do." True enough. And, wholly insufficient.

The complexity of the world and of the macro conditions for which we are all witnesses—global warming and rising sea levels, the rise of authoritarian regimes, growing economic disparities, displaced populations, and violence, to name just a few—impact all of us. The trickle-down effects of these and other disruptions affect everything. We are connected, whether we like it or not: What affects some of us affects all of us.

We each have a part to play in our particular time and location in the scheme of things. Here's an example:

California suffered a five-year drought of historic proportions that came to an official end for most of the state in April 2017 after prodigious rains and a deep snowpack in the Sierras. Governor Jerry Brown had declared a water emergency through a series of executive orders, mandating twenty percent across the board reductions in consumption, Water Department contingency plans, and the replacement of grass lawns with arid landscaping among others.[5] By most measures, the efforts were reasonably successful.

Yet much of California remains vulnerable, and future droughts are predicted to recur with increasing intensity, making complacency dangerous.[6] California's population is growing consistently, and water resources are stretched even in the best of conditions. A state initiative to require budget-based regulation of local water usage ran into fierce opposition from local utilities. As a state water official remarked, "People get tired of being told they have to do more, they have to do more."[7]

This is a perfect storm of Complexity. Rising global temperatures, increased aridity, growing population, political resistance to regulation, public apathy and fatigue, reduced water supplies and increased demand for a scarce resource.

Lots of interconnected moving parts! This is Complexity. And it affects everyone, from farmers making investments in crops based on assumptions about water for irrigation, to residents facing lifestyle and budget decisions, to local water boards trying to influence cultural and behavioral norms, to state regulators seeking to rally political support for legal measures, to environmental leaders trying to reduce habits of consumption backed by a sense of entitlement.

How might each of these human beings seek to reconcile personal interests with even their own perspectives on other interests? How might interests collide? How might this complex and dynamic situation be navigated wisely and together?

However tempting it might be, it's insufficient to bury our heads in the sand or to say it's up to others. We all face real limitations on our power and influence. And we all make a difference in our own spheres. As leaders, we are players in our relationships, in our families, in our teams and in our organizations and communities.

Reality offers no guarantees, either for well-being or for success. The challenge is to move past our comfort zones and to engage with our present conditions in radically creative new ways that generate a future worth having.

My fundamental premises, each explored in Part One, are that:

- We live in extraordinary times with perilous and complex consequences for business as usual.

- We are wired for business as usual.

- Not only are we inadequately prepared for this Complexity, but Complexity itself triggers us into responses that are both natural and counterproductive.

- We need the accelerated development of a critical mass of leaders who can respond to Complexity in new and generative ways.

- And those leaders need an understanding of the nature of development itself to do this well.

You are one of those leaders.

What lies ahead...

The Territory of Complexity

*It is almost banal to say so it needs to be
stressed continually: All is creation, all is change,
all is flux, all is metamorphosis.*

– Henry Miller

*When we experience the world as too complex
we are not just experiencing the complexity of the world.
We are experiencing a mismatch between the world's
complexity and our own at this moment.*

– Robert Kegan

THIS IS A BOOK, IN LARGE PART, ABOUT HOW YOU LEAD IN COMPLEXITY. At the outset, it's helpful simply to recognize that when you are mired in Complexity, it's difficult to recognize it as such. The work in front of you will consist of shifting your relationship with Complexity by first learning to recognize it, and second using Complexity itself as a catalyst for developing yourself to meet it in new and resilient ways.

Five stories will get you started in recognizing the challenges inherent in the terrain of Complexity. Together, you and I will revisit and expand each story later in the book. These leaders each faced overwhelming situations for which they felt unprepared. Each will show us something about how to move skillfully as human beings in contexts we were not designed for.

1) Rachel was the newly promoted CEO of a regional health-care company, replacing a notoriously difficult predecessor who finally retired after years of low morale and lost market share. Rachel was a kind person and well-respected. She welcomed the challenge of restoring trust and a positive culture, which played to her strengths. However, the business results were not following the employee-friendly changes she had quickly made. The business was in real trouble, and the way Rachel knew to lead was not producing results. *What organizational need was she not able to see? Or, perhaps she just wasn't the right person... After all, she was trying as hard as she could!* **What we are not yet able to see lies just past the edge of our development. Rachel's story sheds much light on the underlying process of how we grow as leaders.**

2) Luz was the newly hired dean of an architectural research institute housed within a major West Coast university. While the institute had a strong international reputation, it was also in decline and not keeping up with the strong trend towards more environmental designs. Luz's charge was to revitalize the culture, rebuild an entrepreneurial and accountable world class faculty, and reposition the institute as a major green design hub. From the start, however, Luz underestimated the resistance to change, and found herself frequently under attack for initiatives that seemed common sense to her. *How could Luz begin to see the dynamics differently, including how she was reacting to the resistance and the impasses?* **Sensing is the meta-competency of how we access information; bringing awareness and choice to this is essential to navigating the terrain of Complexity.**

3) Rajeev was the head of development for an international nonprofit spearheading a bold new micro-loan initiative. He felt very much on the line on this project, staking his personal reputation on its success in a very high-profile way. Yet his team wasn't stepping up to the challenge. Worse, if they weren't unified, it would be very difficult for them to create alignment across a complex global organization with conflicting priorities. Seeing his team's shortcomings wound Rajeev up, but the harder he pushed to get people on board, the more passive they became. *How can Rajeev settle his internal state so that his anxiety and tension don't exacerbate an already difficult situation?* **Being is the meta-competency of self-regulation and mastery of our internal state, developed in service of resilience, creativity and resourcefulness.**

4) Susan was the new minister at a traditional church. Membership and financials had been declining for years, and most of the major contributors

and lay leadership of the church had been there forever and didn't want things to change. Susan was brought in to revitalize the church community and to attract new members. She had a lot of ideas about participatory leadership and experience-based spirituality. At the same time, it was a mainstream church; rocking the boat felt risky. Susan was between a rock and a hard place. Don't change and the church continues to decline. Change too fast, and the financial pillars and long-standing leaders of the church were likely to leave. In either direction lies failure. *Caught between a rock and a hard place, what moves can Susan make?* **Acting is the meta-competency of extending our inner state outwards to create the conditions for the results we care about most.**

5) The fifth story is yours. Your **Complexity Challenge** is actively unfolding in this present moment. While you are not entirely in control (if you were, it wouldn't be complex!), you influence it through how you engage with your world. By the time you finish this book, your challenge will have changed in ways that you can't possibly foresee as you read these words. Your situation will have changed both because of things that happen "out there" and because of the shifts you invite within yourself and through new actions you choose to take.

I am quite confident that you face unprecedented challenges. Your world is not so predictable, and some of the very people you count on most are not doing what you need. Others are behaving downright strangely or even actively working at cross-purposes to you. The situation seems to be asking you to be someone you're not: more courageous, more flexible, more... something!

These realities present you not only with unknown territory but also with the opportunity, indeed the imperative, to discover your own creative potential in circumstances not entirely of your making.

In your own Complexity Challenge, consider:

- How might the way you are accessing information be limited? What would be different if your Sensing could produce clarity out of murkiness?

- How does your inner state become stressed and reactive? And what would change if your Being was essentially resilient?

- How might your current actions be counterproductive in ways that you can't see? How might Acting with presence and awareness change the conditions in your situation?

Take a moment to reflect, and sense, where you are in this particular moment with your own challenge.

꾸 PRESENCE PAUSE 꾸

THE GAP

Let's explore what these stories, including your own, have in common. And begin to seek stepping stones for how to face, and navigate, these perplexing and often urgent callings.

First and most importantly, we are all hurtling headlong into the future. Our world is changing at light speed, ever more unpredictable and complex.

You and I are not changing at light speed.

That's the headline.

"Every system is perfectly designed to get the results it gets."[8] This Zen-like business aphorism invites us to look underneath the results we don't like, to the way every system *self-organizes* in order to get precisely the current results. From the perspective of each of the leaders in the five examples above (including yours), there are results not to our liking. We can push harder for the results we want. But perhaps it might be wiser first to learn how the system is working to create the results we are already getting.

Everything that arises does so in response to then-extant **conditions**. Conditions are like a garden: Depending on the soil, rainfall, and organic content, certain plants will thrive, while others will perish. This notion of conditions will turn out to be important, both in recognizing the dynamics of Complexity and in understanding the leadership challenges of helpfully responding to Complexity.

Like it or not, we are not only a part of the system, but crucially, the only part of the system that, in theory, we actually have some control over! We are embodied creatures with a nervous system that evolved hundreds of thousands of years ago as a well-adapted response to the conditions that existed then. But, those conditions did not include the Internet, complex matrixed organizations, multiple languages, and vast global economies. We are biological organisms, designed for survival in a world that no longer exists.

Because we aren't programmed for the world that we actually live in, we tend to rely on what has worked in our personal history. Our nervous system is designed to recognize conditions that seem familiar, and then to default to the strategies that previously have made us successful. We are wired to use what always have been our strengths, but we are not at all wired to notice when those strengths have somehow become limiting.

This combination virtually guarantees an experience of lagging behind, as well as a persistent gap or inadequacy between who we are and what our current conditions ask of us.

Since we are unlikely to be able to reduce the complexity of what is coming at us, this book offers an approach to using Complexity as a catalyst for developing ourselves to meet it in new ways.

The first is to recognize the nature of Complexity itself.

RECOGNIZING COMPLEXITY: THE CYNEFIN FRAMEWORK

Before we can change our relationship to Complexity, we need to be able to recognize and name it when it is affecting us.

To this end, let's build some language together. This will not be an exhaustive treatment; please look to other work[9] for a detailed description of Complexity theory as it's applied to leadership. We are grazing the surface here because, while these distinctions are essential for our journey, we are also headed elsewhere.

David Snowden[10] proposes four domains. His Cynefin framework describes how we might be experiencing the context in which we are leading. Depending on which seems the best fit, various approaches to leading might be indicated.

These domains begin to build a vocabulary of distinctions. Differentiating them supports our observation of and navigation through a reality radically different from what we have been prepared for. They reveal new ways to organize ourselves as leaders.

These domains are:

- **Obvious** (Snowden uses the term "simple"). This is the domain of predictable, straightforward action. Cause and effect is known, and we can safely assume that if we take a certain action, our desired results will follow. *Changing the tire on the car, delegating a project to a competent direct report, sitting down to a family dinner.*

- **Complicated.** Here, cause and effect is predictable, but we don't necessarily know how to do it. With the right expertise (which we can presumably find), we can find the right solution, but there are lots of interrelated elements in a solution that have to be optimized for the best results. *Diagnosing a subtle engine problem, prioritizing tasks in a complicated workflow, planning an elaborate menu for a dinner party knowing several guests' dietary preferences.*

- **Complex.** In this domain, cause and effect are not predictable. There are many interrelated factors that are unknown, and some things in the system affect other things in ways impossible to predict. The harder we drive things, the more unanticipated side effects tend to appear, and other people act in ways that don't make sense to us. *Driving through rush hour when accidents and traffic patterns and construction mean that the best route is constantly changing, building commitment in a team to a new and challenging project when they are already overextended, planning seating for a family reunion under difficult circumstances where some of the people heartily dislike each other.*

- **Chaotic.** Here, events are disconnected and seem to appear at random. There is no apparent cause and effect at all, and phenomena come at us faster than we can react or make sense. There's no time to process, and patterns are not visible. *A truck runs a red light in front of us and we careen to avoid it, a fire breaks out in the plant during a strategy meeting, a fistfight erupts at the family reunion.*

Leadership behaviors, perspectives, and ways of acting in the situation vary greatly depending on what domain we are operating in. For example, if we need to build team commitment to a challenging project (Complex) but treat it as if it were simply a matter of reprioritizing tasks (Complicated), we will be rightly seen as tone-deaf, controlling and simplistic. If we log onto a GPS app to obtain crowdsourced traffic flow to drive to the store on a Sunday morning with no traffic (responding to an Obvious context with a Complex solution), we are probably worrying more than we need to, and our tech-savvy kids will think we are dinosaurs.

Nearly everything we are exploring in this book applies to all four of these domains in some way. It is crucial to be able to differentiate in which domain(s) our primary challenges lie. Together, we will focus mostly on the Complex domain.

For leaders, Complex is a useful label for much of the terrain that we are living in. Of the four domains, it is most front and center, the most different from what we are wired and trained for, and the most challenging for our nervous system to engage with in new and creative ways.

SIX STEPPING STONES FOR COMPLEXITY

In contrast to humans, nobody has to tell an acorn how to be an oak. The acorn has within its DNA the potential and the design template to develop into a majestic oak tree.

This is not simply a metaphor. You also have within you the impulse and the design template to become the leader you will need to be for the unimaginable challenges and opportunities thrown your way. All you need is the right catalyst (conveniently provided by your Complexity Challenge identified above!), some guidance, and stepping stones along the way.

Here are six stepping stones for Complexity, to be discussed further below.

- Notice and embrace the complex nature of your external context

- Shift your language to support new observations

- Access and utilize multiple perspectives

- Make meaning of things in new ways

- Practice new capacities

- Cultivate presence, that awareness that opens the door to the equanimity and resilience of your own inner state.

As you read further, consider how each of these might be relevant to your own Complexity Challenge.

Notice and Embrace the Complex Nature of the External Context

The world will always show up. It is unrelenting, inarguable and real. It is absolutely reliable. You can count on people not acting in the ways you wish they would. Whole cities are threatened by rising seas while aquifer depletion parches others. Elected officials prioritize reelection over solving long-term problems; tides of desperate refugees overwhelm well-intended hosts. Macro forces have local impacts that affect each of us. This is just the way things are: reality can absolutely be counted on to keep showing up!

There is good news in this. Your situation already provides precisely the right conditions for your growth! Reality, as it is rather than as you wish it were, is already a worthy crucible for your development.

What is unknown? What is interesting? What are you being asked for? Who must you become in order to respond? These are juicy, central questions about what it means to be a leader, to be human, in your unique context. Sometimes, as leaders, we have little control over what's coming at us. But we can always change our relationship to our context.

This begins with observing it in different ways.

Shift Your Language to Support New Observations

The Bible begins with the words: "In the beginning… God saw that the light was good, and He separated the light from the darkness… God called the light *day*, and the darkness he called *night.*"[11]

With this opening, the author of Genesis created a ***distinction***: a set of labels with which we distinguish one thing from another thing. Distinctions allow new observations, refining what we are able to notice. Through the differentiating power of language, we distinguish light and dark, day and night. We can differentiate poodles and golden retrievers. Boss and direct report. Threat and opportunity. Bold and timid, complex and simple, authority and responsibility, power and love.

Further, we can communicate these observations to others. If I say to you, "It's night," or "It's blue," you know what I mean, because we share this linguistic distinction. The commonality of language shapes our understanding of our world, makes it more knowable, and provides the basis for communicating with others. This builds a shared understanding of the world from which we can take action.

Developing our language through new distinctions means that we make the world more knowable. Language enables us to observe, comprehend, and communicate about the world.

Access and Utilize Multiple Perspectives

Our *perspective* is our vantage point on some phenomenon. It defines the relationship between us (the observer) and that phenomenon (the observed). It also constricts that relationship.

Young children, looking at opposite sides of a piece of paper, cannot imagine that the other side of the paper is a different color than what they see. In the United States, in 2017, many people simply cannot "get" the point of view of people on a different place along the political spectrum.

Yet in both of these examples, a more useful and complete understanding of the reality of that piece of paper or the precarious state of our democracy actually requires being able to step into, and accept, multiple perspectives.

The truth is that we tend to organize our seeing the world according to a particular perspective, and we filter out information that doesn't fit with that understanding. When we talk about it in this way, it seems narrow-minded, even myopic, and this would be true. And it's also true that this is the way we humans tend to work: We actively construct our world through the particular perspective we inhabit and the data that we thereby unconsciously include and exclude.

Reality is always more complex and dynamic than we can possibly imagine. When we comfortingly confuse our perspective with truth, we over-simplify reality, sometimes to our peril. By increasing the range of perspectives available, we actually access a clearer and more integrated view of reality itself. This begins with the realization that perspectives are both subjective and changeable.

Realizing, deeply, how automatically we react to and shape our worlds opens the door to consciously responding differently.

Make Meaning of Things in New Ways

Equipped with new distinctions, and with the awareness that we are likely to have a particular and limited perspective on our context, we begin to understand that we are naturally wired to take in information, unconsciously organize it into frameworks, and then make meaning of this information.

Acquiring more refined perspectives on the territory we are navigating as a leader is enormously helpful. Seeing things clearly begins with *differentiating* them so that we can observe them, and then *connecting* the differentiated parts so that we have clarity about how they are related to each other.[12] Differentiation and connection allow us to integrate our Sensing so as to open up new possibilities for action. They support new **meaning-making**: our innate capacity to construct meaning with the information we selectively take in.

Our meaning-making includes how we interpret and understand the world around us, and our role and place in that world. It determines our sense of self and the actions that make sense to us as leaders and as humans. It is important to see that this understanding, this meaning-making, is not an objective and fixed view of how things really are. Rather, it is an active and dynamic process of constructing, moment by moment, a personal working model of reality that defines who we are and our purpose, providing a basis for everything we do.

This meaning-making process, while automatic, is also flexible. It can be made visible and it can be changed and developed. This leads to a more nuanced meaning-making that often reveals possibilities that were previously unavailable.

STEPPING STONES IN COMPLEXITY

- Notice and embrace the complex nature of your *external context*

- Shift your *language* to support new observations

- Access and utilize multiple *perspectives*

- *Make meaning* of things in new ways

- Practice new *capacities*

- Cultivate *presence*

Practice New Capacities

As leaders, we get skilled at holding specific perspectives and acting in particular ways. We get reinforced and validated for these skills, which over time become embodied. Our body is an extraordinary learning machine. When we do something on a regular basis, we get better at it.

The good news? We're remarkably proficient at what we've practiced. The bad news? Our very proficiency narrows the range of perspectives available. It narrows, too, our potential responses to what is coming at us.

Building new proficiencies in a complex and unpredictable world means practicing new things. We can practice observing differently. We can practice taking new perspectives. We can practice working with our inner state to stay calm and settled no matter what's going on around us. And we can practice new and generative behaviors and actions.

Cultivate Presence

In order to respond more nimbly, collaborate better and lead more appropriately, we must loosen the grip of outmoded habits. We must access a greater proportion of our inherent resourcefulness, inviting fluidity and creativity in our responses to what's coming at us. This requires an internal loosening: a willingness to be uncomfortable and creative and resourceful all at once. To be available for what is new and for what might emerge.

This is where presence comes in.

Presence is an internal state. It is the inclusive awareness of stillness, possibility and immediacy. It is the precise awareness of our present-moment experience. It means being fully here, rather than hanging out in regrets about the past or planning for the future. Presence enables us to sense the world as it actually is, to sense ourselves as we actually are. It means being fully present with reality as it is, not as we would like it to be.

Presence is not about hanging out in a nice blissful state, as commercialized by photos of lovely blonde women sitting in the lotus position in front of a pile of stacked rocks waiting for their spa appointment.

Rather, it means being present to whatever is happening. It means staying and tolerating whatever is showing up. Perhaps this is joy and gratitude. And, perhaps it is rawness, vulnerability, a sense of inadequacy, or rage. These unpleasant experiences, too, are reality.

Presence requires us to stay with even what is uncomfortable, so that it becomes tolerable and so that we can organize ourselves towards what matters, rather than away from discomfort.

It's impossible to overstate the importance of presence if we are to develop ourselves to meet new and complex challenges. Presence is the underlying internal condition for doing all the rest of this stuff well and consistently. It is the very foundation for resourcefulness in Complexity.

Presence is how we:

- Stay with whatever is arising in this moment

- Recognize and inhibit old habits, allowing new choices

- Access multiple perspectives

- Settle our inner state to be calm and creative when our context feels challenging

- Extend that calm resourcefulness to others

Cultivating our own leadership presence means first stabilizing presence within ourselves as an internal resource. Then and only then can we express this externally in order to connect with others in service to collaboration and results that matter.

Applying the Six Stepping Stones to Your Complexity Challenge

With the stepping stones outlined above, you are now ready to begin to engage with the complexity of your challenge in new ways.

This section invites you into a perspective shift—a first taste of applying one of the stepping stones—on your immediate challenge. After this taste, I will offer an experiment: a brief tour of how all six stepping stones might prove relevant and enabling as you face into your Complexity Challenge from this new perspective.

Please try on this perspective. You have a set of challenges in front of you. You see these challenges as problems to be solved, and you are motivated because the problems are inherently uncomfortable. Naturally, you look around for the tools and perspectives that will help you solve the problem. When the problem is resolved, it will be a relief, you'll take a deep breath, and there will be others knocking at the door. You'll move on to the next, and the next, and the next... learning as you go. You will be successful through persistence and an ever-greater capacity to anticipate and resolve these issues as they arise.

By the way, this is a perfectly fine perspective and one that is probably rather familiar. *It's just not the only one available.* Here's a different one.

You have a set of challenges in front of you. You see these challenges as problems to be solved. *You also welcome them as catalysts for your development as a human.* To this end, you reach beyond the skills and actions you're already good at. As you begin to use your six new stepping stones to observe, make sense, and practice differently, you include a longer-term view of your own development process. You choose to invest in your underlying capacity not only to address this immediate challenge but also to meet a never-ending flood of future challenges with optimism, equanimity, and resourcefulness. You welcome—indeed, you actively choose—this adventure.

Notice that both of these perspectives are true. One is tactical and oriented towards the resolution of immediate problems; the other more forward looking. ***However, they are not in conflict.*** You can shift back and forth between the two. And with practice, both are available.

Take a moment to reflect or journal on your Complexity Challenge from both of these perspectives.

PRESENCE PAUSE

The practice of perspective-shifting develops a flexibility of mind and strongly supports empathizing with others, reconciling disparate points of view and entrenched conflicts, understanding the roots of complex problems, staying married after the honeymoon period, and many other worthwhile endeavors. In other words, it cuts across the domains of life.

Granted, you still have to solve immediate problems, and your urgency can focus you narrowly and exclusively on what's in front of you. When you do so, you react to short-term needs and never get around to the long game: the deep preparation for futures that you can't yet foresee.

I'm proposing that, in facing your Complexity Challenge, you place this preparation at the center of your attention.

You develop yourself to meet your challenges. And you take on challenges in order to develop yourself.

PRESENCE PAUSE

Experiment 1.1:
Stepping Stones for Your Complexity Challenge

Take some time to consider your Complexity Challenge in light of the stepping stones. I suggest that you handwrite notes in a journal to aid reflection.

This is an initial exploration. Please note any impulse you might have to arrive at immediate and actionable insights. This impatience is both understandable and symptomatic of the first perspective above; it's also anti-helpful in Complexity.

Instead, see if you can inhabit the second perspective above, the longer-term view of your development, in the course of this exploration. Hold these questions as if you are trying on new clothes at the store and seeing how you feel in them. Be curious what might open from each; you can change the questions if a different slant calls you.

- *External context:* What changes if you simply recognize that the context is what it is, and you accept this?
- *Language:* What new ideas and distinctions from the text so far are relevant to your challenge and have enabled you to see it differently?
- *Perspectives:* What perspective is available to you about your Complexity Challenge that changes your relationship to it?
- *Meaning-making:* What is your understanding of how this challenge, however difficult it might seem, actually might be preparing you for something unforeseen in the future?
- *New capacities:* What new capacities as a leader can you imagine would be helpful in this challenge?
- *Presence:* How might staying with your present-moment experience be supportive of you?

CHAPTER SUMMARY

The territory of Complexity is enveloping you, and your own challenges most certainly contain significant elements of this Complexity. I'm inviting you into the perspective that your own Complexity Challenges might actually be welcomed as nourishment for your ongoing developmental journey.

The core realization of this chapter is that Complexity is both pervasive and normal; as such, you can name it and recognize it. Navigating Complexity first requires recognizing and accepting it. And, it requires creating the internal conditions for Sensing, Being, and Acting in Complexity-adapted ways.

You explored six stepping stones for this new territory, each of which can tremendously enable and accelerate your capacity to respond in resilient, creative ways to seemingly intractable situations:

- Recognizing and accepting the perverse and complex nature of your external context
- Developing and shifting your language, through new distinctions, in order to observe your world and yourself in new ways
- Exploring multiple perspectives, fluidly shifting between perspectives being a crucial meta-competency for development
- Making meaning in new ways, since we can actively construct meaning through maps and lenses of our choosing
- Practicing new capacities to develop new leadership muscles, rather than falling back on what's worked before
- Cultivating presence so as to meet any situation as it is, and with greater internal equanimity and resilience.

In the next chapter, you will take the perspective of looking at the overall arc of human development.

After all, how you came to be the leader that you already are has everything to do with how you can become the leader you intend to be.

Our world is a bell jar; what lies outside is fuzzy or unseen....

Embodiment, Identity and the Bell Jar

*By using a shared vocabulary we continuously assure
ourselves and each other of what makes sense. With every
word uttered, we reinforce the shared conceptual map
of our world. We use language to identify the concrete
objects and events around us and to tell the stories of
our group and of ourselves. [We are] conditioned by
the available interpretations in our environment...
throughout our lives and in all realms of experience.*

– Susanne Cook-Greuter

ECOGNIZING THAT COMPLEXITY IS EVERYWHERE CAN COME AS A BIT OF A RELIEF, as can the recognition of pragmatic stepping stones for navigating the territory.

It is, however, sobering to also recognize that everywhere you go, your personality also goes! Who you are as a leader is seriously all tangled up with the unfolding dramas around you. Knowing how your personality was formed, and how tenaciously it now seeks to perpetuate itself, is the next step on your journey.

What follows is a personal Complexity example. I include this in part so that you get to know me better as we embark on this journey. And also to emphasize the point that the dynamics of identity, development, and Complexity appear everywhere, not just in organizations and boardrooms.

A personal Complexity story

In 1996, my wife Walker and I bought a sixty-three-acre farm in the mountains of North Carolina. We both saw the potential of the old tobacco barn as a gathering place for people seeking to come together, learn and develop themselves. As an organization consultant, workshop facilitator, and developer of leaders, I sensed the possibilities for what could happen in a well-crafted and inspiring space. Walker's energy came alive more from the possibility of applying her limitless creativity to the design of the physical space itself and its integration with the land around it. We decided to renovate the fifty-year-old barn, creating a beautiful residential retreat space. Bend of Ivy Lodge.

I had significant previous building experience; Walker had a strong sense of design but had generally deferred the project management and technical aspects to me. Neither of us had done a project of this scale before. Walker became the primary driver of the project: the architect, the general contractor, the painter, the person who made it happen.

We were stretched financially, and the project was a major leap of faith that required a second mortgage on our home and my taking on insane amounts of work and travel to keep the cash flowing. I was gone a lot, and Walker was stressed by the project. She was coordinating and directing legions of craftsmen, engineers, backhoe operators, and governmental authorities, among others. All men.

She'd never done this before, and she truly came into her own on this project. But at the time I didn't yet fully trust her capabilities. When I came back from my business travel, I would visit the project. With the best of intentions, I often gave direction to the builders. I had legitimate expertise to offer, and I had taken real pleasure in building in the past. Renovating a fifty-year-old barn of course came with challenges. It was evident to me that Walker and the carpenters could use all the support they could get, and I was eager for some kind of involvement and contribution other than simply keeping the financial ship afloat.

However, my well-intended contributions made interpersonal messes on the job site. Dropping in from nowhere to offer direction undermined Walker as the authority on the job, sometimes even contradicting aesthetic considerations or decisions she had already made. These cross-currents were confusing to the craftsmen on site. She resented my muddying the waters on her project, especially when she was already working hard to establish her authority. Some of the men had never taken direction from a woman on a construction site.

With hindsight, my behaviors, well-intentioned as they might have been, were unskillful and produced unintended consequences for my wife and the builders. At the time, I was unable to take their perspectives, or to inhibit the urges to be helpful that sometimes overrode my better judgments. The angry feedback from my wife was painful, and in turn I felt unappreciated for my efforts.

I was unable to recognize the dynamics of the situation, the unconscious drivers of my behavior, or the impact those behaviors were having on my beloved wife and a project I cared deeply about. I was simply blind to the larger picture of what I was doing: I could only be the person I was. Without helpful stepping stones and different perspectives, new choices (obvious in hindsight) were simply not available to me.

It is crucial to bring presence and awareness to how we became the leader that we currently are. This offers the perspective of our development as a lifelong process, upon which we embarked long ago, and which will continue into the unforeseeable future.

Recognizing how we got here in the first place, and using the stepping stones that in every moment reveal new choices, will be of tremendous value as we seek to become the leader we are now asked to be.

Embodied Learning

We begin our exploration of human development at the beginning.

Experimentation: Three Aspects of Development

As babies, we were born experimenters.

We learned what produced pleasure and safety. When we were hungry, deep instincts led us to root around for the breast. When we needed something, we cried. There was urgency in this genetically endowed and impulsive drive for survival. This underlying imperative, and our own directly experienced needs, led us to trial-and-error learning.

What worked for us, we did more. What didn't work, we stopped. As children, we got more skillful. We learned through a powerful combination of genetically endowed instincts, natural imitation of others, and a persistent, overwhelming, and creative urge to try new things.

This learning process begins before birth, as our brain and nervous system grows. The natural unfolding of the development process eventually boots up a largely unprogrammed network of many billions of neurons with more potential connections than there are stars in the universe. Over many years, our experiences become encoded into this network as patterns of associated neurons that represent our experiences and capabilities. (This process is popularly described as "neurons that fire together wire together."[13]) When some behavior produces pleasure or safety, our nervous system stores it in long-term memory, and we generally don't have to relearn it. Our bodies have a phenomenal capacity for retaining learning from experience.

Three primary aspects shape our development process:

- The *development impulse* drives us towards creativity and experimentation. It arises as urges, cravings, desires and survival instincts. Some people have a strong desire for learning and growth; others are more content with the status quo.

- *Embodied learning* is the internalization of learning into the built-in, readily available reservoir of our capabilities. This is enabled by our nervous system's astoundingly efficient mechanisms for internalizing and automatizing what it has learned, freeing processing bandwidth for new experiences and new learning. The *embodiment* of learning means that what we care about, and the drivers of our meaning-making and our behavior, become biologically rooted and supported.

- The *context* in which we are living and leading sometimes is undemanding and sometimes complex and insistent. When our embodied learning is adequate for what the context is asking of us, development isn't needed. However, when our embodied learning is inadequate for understanding what we face, or for taking skillful action to get the results we intend, we are challenged to develop to meet those challenges in new ways.

> ## THREE ASPECTS OF DEVELOPMENT
>
> Development proceeds at the intersection of:
>
> - Our *development impulse*: the drive to learn, achieve, seek aliveness and stimulation
>
> - A *context* that reveals opportunities that trigger our aspirations
>
> - The *embodiment* of capabilities that provide a psychobiological foundation.
>
> Our development is largely dedicated to constructing and perpetuating a solid *Identity*: our sense of who we are in the world.

There is a constant interaction between our development impulse and our context. This dynamic process—driven by curiosity and experimentation and learning—ensures that our body-based development, and the meaning-making and behaviors that result, unfold over time as we and our situations become more complicated or complex.

Our social context (peers, community, schooling, teachers, other adults in the neighborhood) shaped us. Our gender, race, socioeconomic circumstances, sexual orientation, nationality, and numerous other factors all shaped the explicit and implicit messages we internalized about who we were and who we could and should be.[14]

Collectively, we call the impact of these shaping forces **conditioning**. Our conditioning eventually becomes concretized as a unique personality, a way of being, a way of seeing and making sense of the world and finding and preserving our place in it.

Psychobiology

One of the many miraculous aspects of our precious human body is its capacity to remember. Experiences become embodied, particularly when they are repeated, have strong emotional content, and are related to our well-being or survival.

Our *psychobiology* is the embodied structure of this lifelong learning. It is the product of a lifetime of experiences that have conditioned the raw, impressionable piece of meat that is our nervous system. It takes the form of a unique, miraculous, semi-permanent and tenacious physiological structure that is the physical corollary of our Identity as leaders and as humans.

Figure 2.1 reveals this underlying structure. Everything

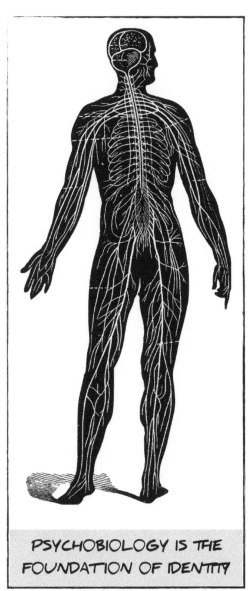

PSYCHOBIOLOGY IS THE FOUNDATION OF IDENTITY

Figure 2.1

that we are and everything that we experience and do is possible because of the embodied structures of our psychobiology that encode and scaffold our personality.

We can witness this psychobiology as it manifests in our **habit nature**: the unique constellation of behaviors and meaning-making and reactions that we have embodied along the way and that have now become characteristically us. We can see, even, that our sense of self, our identities, are rooted in these psychobiological structures. In fact, our personalities and our physiology are inseparable; they are simply two different perspectives on the same phenomenon.

A conditioning story

As the eldest of three boys in my family, and as a prime leader of the roving pack of young males in our neighborhood, I was often the instigator. I was easily bored and always initiating adventures: exploring the vast woods behind our house, getting the boys together for a farm-pond hockey game, pushing the limits of sledding down steep icy runs on banked curves we built deep in the forest.

I loved building things, creating things with my hands. I built a beautiful home in which my wife and I lived before we built the retreat center. I did much of that work myself, including the carpentry, plumbing, electrical and tile work, and everything else. While many others contributed energy and expertise, I also knew intimately every piece of wood in the place and took considerable pride in this accomplishment.

I say all this so that you can see the formation of the personality that showed up on the Bend of Ivy project site. Through my years up to that point, I had become deeply identified with my ability to initiate action, build things, create things that had never been before, and thereby earn validation and approval from others for the things that I knew how to do. Seeking validation of my identity had become embodied in my psychobiology to the extent that it was invisible to me.

Yet this conditioned personality was driving my behaviors. In my own mind, those behaviors were justified by the narrative that I was being helpful. My psychobiology was skillful at manufacturing justifying stories for myself about why "this time" my involvement would be okay.

That I persisted in these behaviors even after the irate feedback from my wife was a wake-up call. I was simply blind to how my embodied narratives and psychobiology ran the show.

It is important to see this example as representative of the unfathomably intricate processes through which we all have come to be who we are. Everything we have experienced has taken up residence in our bodies—in our bones, our sinews, all the way down into our nervous system.

None of this is visible to us, of course. Changing this blindness—by bringing awareness and light to these internal parts of ourselves—is a central offer of this book.

The Construction of Identity

Our personal history endows us with particular ways of making sense of the world. As we experience this world, our unique psychobiology constantly and automatically scans for opportunities, threats, challenges, openings and closings. The particular way we do this is integral to our individual personality, supporting who we believe ourselves to be.

Identity is our self-image. It is a self-representation that resides in our psychobiology. We may have an Identity as a compassionate person, as a competitor, as a go-getter, as a creative problem solver. This Identity is deeply reassuring. When our Identity is being reinforced, we feel confident, assured, seen by others. We have a solid sense of selfhood.

On the other hand, when our Identity is challenged, we are shaken. We act to protect this Identity by hiding, lashing out, or defending. Left to its own devices, our psychobiology will do nearly anything to preserve the sense of self that we have developed.

For better and for worse, this means that we are quite capable in familiar situations: Our psychobiology has adapted to these circumstances, and our embodied competencies are sufficient to preserve our Identity and to do what we need to do.

However, embodiment also means that we are much less flexible and resourceful than we need to be in unfamiliar situations. Since our embodiment results from learning over time about what works and what doesn't in a particular context, our embodied capacities are responses to the demands of the context. Embodiment lags behind changes in the context. Unfamiliar situations (e.g., as in Complexity!) reliably challenge what we have learned in previous situations. We are on our developmental edge.

Here's an example of how this is played out in a leadership context.

The Trap of Identity

Let's come back to Rachel, the protagonist of one of the stories at the beginning of the last chapter. We will follow Rachel across the next three chapters, as she has much to teach us about the nature of development itself.

Rachel and the good and bad news about Identity

Rachel was the new CEO in the brief story at the beginning of Chapter 1. As you recall, she was recently promoted from director of operations to lead this regional home health-care company. The organization had been losing market share rapidly under her alpha male predecessor, an unpopular, cold, and manipulative leader. Rachel inherited a demoralized organization, primarily women who really wanted to contribute but who also felt afraid to speak out about what they saw. Rachel had to heal a culture of fear.

Rachel's Identity had been built from an early age. The oldest of three, she was the only girl. She had learned her lessons well. In a family with an absentee father and a kind but stressed-out mother, Rachel often was the one in charge, the one to console and take care of her brothers, the one to buffer the younger kids from the erratic behavior of their mother. She became a care-taker and felt responsible for the well-being of others.

Rachel was kind, caring, and well-respected, and immediately instituted a number of employee-friendly policies in an attempt to improve the climate: flex times, social events, liberalization of the dress code, etc. These were appreciated, and after six months, people reported better morale. However, the organization's poor financial, market, and service performance remained unchanged.

Over the course of my work with Rachel and her leadership team, it became clear that Rachel's strong suit was being supportive and changing the culture. On the other hand, she shied away from holding people accountable and confronting ubiquitous performance issues. She was eager to reassure her people that she was the antithesis of her predecessor. In a challenging situation, she led from her strengths: warmth and an orientation towards people.

However, when asked, her people wanted both a supportive culture AND a performance culture. While they found Rachel's leadership approach a refreshing change, they also wanted to be successful again, and to rebuild an organization in which many had previously taken deep pride.

Rachel's well-intended but unconscious default left a major blind spot. Acutely aware of the wounds of the past, she conflated support with not confronting performance issues. This was a limitation visible to others but not to herself. She was simply incapable of recognizing her own discomfort with holding people accountable, and she believed her own narrative that confronting performance issues directly would reinforce the cycle of morale and decline that she was so committed to turning around.

Meaning-Making: Constructing a World

We can see how Rachel's history created a leader who, in some ways, was the perfect person to take over a wounded organization. The staff loved and trusted her, and she was a welcome reprieve from what had preceded her.

Rachel faced a developmental challenge. She was naturally attuned to what her psychobiology had been trained to seek: opportunities to care for people. This helped her make sense of the world, particularly to find a perfect and reassuring fit between her Identity and what was needed. It also justified the convenient narrative that her new CEO role was primarily one of restoring safety and caring for people. She told herself, and others, that performance would follow trust and camaraderie. Of course, this actually served her own Identity needs, playing to her strengths and validating her sense of herself as a kind, caring person.

However, the organizing principle of caring for others, while desperately needed, was insufficient. She was unable to see what she had not been conditioned to see: that holding people accountable and confronting performance problems were also needed for the organization to heal.

This understanding was beyond what Rachel could readily access under the stress of her onboarding. The considerable strengths she led with were welcomed by the organization, but the excitement of this change also blinded her to other possibilities, especially those inconsistent with the Identity she had always sought to project.

Rachel unconsciously made sense of the world through lenses that both derived from her Identity (her psychobiology was trained to seek certain data but not others) and reaffirmed it (the selected data reaffirmed her sense of herself in the world). This is the very definition of meaning-making: Rachel was actively constructing a role for herself with the information she selectively took in. And, she was unable to see that she was doing so.

We can see, in this example, that Rachel (like all of us) inhabited an actively changing world. Yet her meaning-making about this complex world was, paradoxically, both determined and limited by her go-to strengths and Identity. Like most of us, Rachel had successfully adapted her way through a less-than-perfect childhood and emerged with a drive and set of strengths that led to success. Yet when the circumstances demanded something other than what her natural tendencies led her to do, she was lost at sea.

We'll come back to Rachel again. To her credit, she became able to expand her meaning-making and lead in ways less driven by her Identity, and therefore much more effective.

THE BELL JAR OF IDENTITY

The *Bell Jar* is a metaphor for our unique constructed world that supports our Identity and allows us to see some things but not others. The Bell Jar metaphor helps us visualize the gap between the realities and possibilities of the world and our preparedness to approach and engage them.

We all live in a Bell Jar. While we mostly don't see how we construct our particular Bell Jar, we are actively constructing it every second of our life. Rachel lived in a Bell Jar, as did I in the Bend of Ivy Lodge story earlier. As do you.

And, of course, everyone else that we interact with (and sleep with!) also lives in their own Identity-based Bell Jar. Bell Jars admit certain kinds of information and filter out contradictory information. We live and dance together through a kind of Bell Jar Ball, in which the constant interactions between constricted Identities exchange partial information, create reassuring agreements about how reality is, and base actions on untested assumptions.

Recognizing the limitations of your own Bell Jar is a primary stepping stone to becoming a more embodied leader in Complexity.

Living in a Bell Jar

The way we perceive the world is subjective and trained into us by our history. The effects of living in a Bell Jar are apparent in my own story, shared earlier in this chapter. And in how Rachel, the new CEO, unconsciously organized herself around her Identity as a caretaker, one who could restore trust and camaraderie in a broken organization. Yet, from inside her Bell Jar, she was unable to recognize the yearning in her organization for accountability, for performance, and for coming together around a mission. And how this itself would also be healing.

The shape and composition of our Bell Jars represent our view of the world and our place in it. They represent the Identities we have so carefully cultivated over many years. Our Bell Jars determine what we can and can't see around us. They determine our default reactions to stress and challenge, and they drive the very habits that get us into trouble as we become caricatures of the more agile and resourceful leaders we are actually capable of being.

Recognizing our own habit nature, our Bell Jar, is the central move of the process of developing ourselves.

Challenges as Developmental Catalysts

Like Rachel, we see our worlds through a kind of Identity-driven myopia. We are instinctively drawn to situations in which our capabilities might prove relevant and useful and thus further validated. Success breeds more success, and the strengths that have made us who we are become embedded more and more deeply into the architecture of our psychobiology. We fail to see, or we actively avoid confronting, challenges to our Identity. Our Bell Jar is reinforced by the circumstances that we choose.

This limitation becomes a default, especially when the context we are leading in inevitably no longer matches the context within which our strengths developed. We usually revert to what has historically worked well for us, rather than pursue the new and difficult that will push and transform us.

Much of this book will explore how to engage differently with this conundrum. For now, let's simply posit that intractable challenges in Complexity Contexts are "happy opportunities" for us to stretch in new ways and to acquire new capacities. Rather than working harder, or doubling down on what has worked before, these challenges serve as catalysts for our development. Rather than providing comforting reassurance that we, in our established way of leading, still have the chops, developmental challenges provide an edgy crucible that crucible that reveals our Bell Jar for what it is.

In this crucible, we can feel that our very sense of who we are is at risk. We put our Identity on the line, potentially expanding this Identity to include new elements that we never imagined possible. And along the way, we may have to let go of who we thought we were in order to become someone new.

A simple example illustrates.

An engineer faces the edge

Rick was an outstanding engineer. He loved problem-solving, had personally led the design of some very innovative new control systems in the power plant in which he had worked for twenty years, and held several patents. Given Rick's experience, seniority, and track record, it was inevitable that he would be offered a promotion to manager of the engineering department.

However, the skills, capabilities and Identity of a manager were very different from that of an engineer, and Rick's engineering prowess and self-confidence didn't automatically translate to his new role. In fact, he found himself constantly getting pulled into details, being a lover of solving design problems. It was very difficult for him to give feedback or do performance reviews (these were his friends; he'd worked with some for many years. It felt uncomfortable to have authority over them). And he was not accustomed to managing up to get resources, nor to prioritizing and delegating work.

The things he found deeply satisfying about work were no longer in his job description. What was required of him as manager were things that he had little experience with and didn't find interesting or rewarding. He was an engineer. This was his Identity. While Rick was plenty smart and could have learned the new job, it would have required a wholesale shift in Identity from that of a designer and problem-solver to that of a developer of people and an organizer of workflow and priorities.

After three months, Rick took a pay cut and went back to his individual contributor role. He was much happier.

The moral of this story is neither that Rick was a failure nor that he should have read this book before taking the new job. Working with the edge of our own development is a thing that nourishes some and not others. Rick knew he could have been successful in the new role, but chose not to. Shifting Identities to let go of the very things that have been satisfactory to us in the past is not an easy thing, even when success with the new requires it. The affirming Bell Jar of Rick's Identity as an engineer was just fine for him.

We can lower our risk by navigating away from developmental challenges. We can do the best we can with what we've got, persisting in doing what we're already good at. Most of the time we'll be able to get by; we can fool enough people enough of the time that we'll be okay.

In this mindset, we meet challenges that confront us with the inarguable limitations of our capabilities. But continuing to be the same person we've always been is likely to become increasingly problematic. We have the choice to deny this reality, or we can step into these challenges, knowing that they will require us to become literally a different person. For some, working with the edge of our own development is enlivening, as well as pragmatic.

How is your Complexity Challenge asking you to become a different leader?

≈∾ PRESENCE PAUSE ∾≈

Please take a few minutes to ground the material from this chapter in your own leadership challenge.

Experiment 2.1:
Name Default Tendencies and Habits

Blind spots are, by definition, impossible to see. Yet we can get curious about what we might not be seeing. We can begin to recognize our defaults and where we might be missing crucial information.

- What strengths do you bring to your Complexity Challenge?
- What habits do you recognize in this: things that you perhaps do automatically?
- What behaviors do you tend to repeat but that sometimes produce unintended and problematic side effects?

This kind of reflection—taking a balcony view for a new perspective on yourself—is consistent with our stepping stones from the previous chapter. It will run as a consistent thread throughout this book.

CHAPTER SUMMARY

In this chapter, you took a long view of the lifelong process through which you became the leader that you are and through which you will continue to develop.

The core realization of this chapter is that your development has always unfolded according to principles of embodiment and learning. Your Identity has always driven the train, but this has previously been mostly invisible to you. Leveraging the realization of the nature and pervasive influence of your Identity on everything you touch will help you meet immediate challenges in new ways.

Stepping stones for this process include the realizations that:

- You live in an Identity-based Bell Jar: a set of habitual ways of making meaning and of acting that preclude clarity on the realities and possibilities that might lie right in front of you.
- Your Identity, together with the conditioned habits and meaning-making that hold that Identity in place, are embodied as psychobiology.
- Your Identity has an internal stability that actively resists changing; you are a creature of habit.

- External challenges to your Identity are disruptive; you're pretty attached to maintaining your Identity!
- Challenges provide essential catalysts for development; these require recognizing and negotiating with your Identity and its imperviousness to change.

You began to appreciate the gift of embodied learning, while also glimpsing how it might blind you to the very things most important to see. Hopefully, you have a sense that there are as-yet unseen perspectives and distinctions that might prove immensely valuable in engaging your Complexity Challenge.

With our stepping stones in mind, I invited you to make this personal by naming some of your own habits. I'm hoping that you are beginning to recognize, in yourself, a habituated Identity that was formed in the crucible of your history and which has become embodied. You are, in fact, the only person you could be given this history. Presence allows you to see and recognize this reality as it is.

And I'm hoping that you are also recognizing the possibility that the very challenges you now face may be inviting you to become literally a different person—to surrender aspects of your hard-earned Identity in service to something new and emergent.

If you suspect this to be true, you and I are on the right path together.

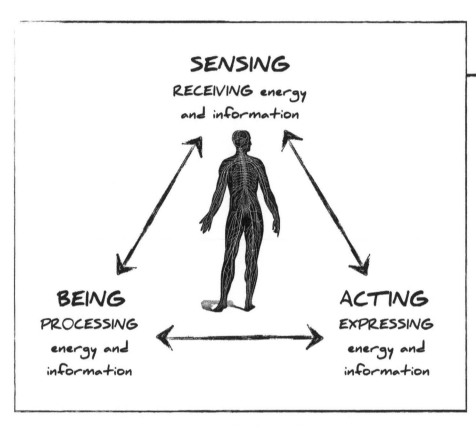

Three processes for being human...

Realization and the Developmental Edge

*Faced with the choice between changing one's mind
and proving that there is no need to do so, almost
everybody gets busy on the proof.*

– John Kenneth Galbraith

*And the day came when the risk to remain tight in a bud
was more painful than the risk it took to blossom.*

– Anais Nin

N THE PREVIOUS CHAPTER, you explored how your Identity was formed over time within an evolving set of conditions, as well as how embodiment stores remarkable capabilities that you now have the luxury of taking for granted.

At the same time, since your Identity has become habituated and embodied to the point where it is largely automatic and you can't even see it, changing conditions will inevitably reveal the limitations of what you have embodied.

How might you as a leader begin to make these crucial but subtle Bell Jar dynamics visible? How might you wake up to the active workings and construction of your Identity so as to approach your complex challenges with more success?

In this chapter, we address these very questions, making visible what was previously invisible. This is the core shift in perspective. This shift enables us to adapt and to develop to meet new challenges in ways that are creative and responsive to reality as it actually is, rather than respond with legacy behaviors appropriate for the historical contexts in which we developed our current defaults.

When have you had the sense of a startling *realization*? Have you ever felt recognition that the world wasn't the way you thought it was? Realization is the direct experience of both the cognitive understanding that comes from new information *and* the felt sense of energy and clarity as we glimpse a reality that we had previously been blind to.

For instance, there was the time when, reflected in the mirror of a hotel lobby bathroom while I shaved, an elegantly dressed woman walked past me on her way to the stalls. In a flash, I realized I was shaving in the women's room! Or, take the time I approached a group of three-year-olds in Thailand with my children. I hoped they'd play together; instead I discovered that the kids were playing with a putrid dead puppy.

When have you realized with a start that *you* weren't who you thought you were? Several years ago, I had to turn back, humbled and sad, from a climb of a glaciated peak in the Canadian Rockies at three in the morning because I didn't have the stamina, while the rest of the party that I had primarily organized went on to the spectacular summit. In the previous chapter, I shared an example of my giving well-intentioned directions to our crew on the Bend of Ivy Lodge construction site. My wife angrily upended my comfortable belief that I was helping her out by telling me I was undermining her authority and confusing the carpenters. In both of these situations, the world was different than I had seen, and it was startling and disruptive to realize that I was not at all who I believed myself to be.

These moments of realization are a significant shift, a jolt out of a comfortable status quo, and a startling expansion into a new experience. They reveal gaps—the gaps between the world that you thought you inhabited and the world that exists in reality.

Stepping into these gaps with curiosity accelerates your embodiment of capacities that are suited to the world that actually exists.

Realizations are often coupled with a sense of *presence*: an internally experienced state of immediacy, inclusive awareness, and possibility. This experience of presence, as we shall see, is a doorway into accelerated development and new ways of leading. It's not always pleasant—but it's real, raw, and new.

Life at the Edge

The startling realization that we even have a Bell Jar immediately shifts us into a more inclusive perspective.

To sense a bigger reality means that something previously invisible and implicit has become visible and explicit, even obvious. Bringing awareness to what has previously been invisible is what allows us to move past the edges of our capabilities to access greater creativity and resourcefulness. It is the central task that enables us to meet Complexity from new ground.

Buddhists, for thousands of years, have taught about stepping back as witness to ourselves. This kind of self-awareness is throughout the leadership literature, as well as wisdom traditions from the world over.[15]

We need to turn what has been automatic—the construction of our Bell Jars and Identity—into something considered. This fundamental move, the thrust of this entire book, is the developable foundational capacity to take what was invisible, and to witness and observe it, in the present moment.

 PRESENCE PAUSE

Developmental Stages and Transitions

Development, as detailed in Chapter 2, proceeds from the tension between the *development impulse*, always within us as curiosity and aspiration, and *embodiment*, where newfound skills and capacities become internalized, incorporated into our Identities, and largely unconscious. This tension exists within a certain environment—an environment we call a *Context*.

The tension is dynamic. Sometimes the Context allows us to be complacent. Things feel stable and our embodied capabilities are a good match for what is needed.

Other times, we are on our *developmental edge*. The realities of the world confront us with the yawning gap between our capabilities and what is actually needed. On this edge, we feel a rawness and vulnerability. This is both uncomfortable and revealing of an opportunity for awareness and development.

The lifelong process of human development largely consists of the interplay of continually running up against the limits of our Bell Jars—our meaning-making, behavioral, and Identity-preserving defaults—and transcending those limitations to access greater capacities.

When the Context inevitably confronts us with the limitations of our Bell Jars and Identity, we are playing at the edge. This is the opportunity for a transition. Like a baby learning to crawl, or Rachel facing a new Context as CEO that she was only partially prepared for, the edge can feel difficult, elusive and frustrating. These transitions can be a bear in the moment!

Stages and the Arc of Development

It is reasonable, given the rigor this journey seems to require, to want a sense of where it leads. Where does a commitment to development take us?

Just as in the motor development of a child through crawling, walking, and so forth, our cognitive capabilities unfold with a particular directionality. Developmental theorists such as Kegan, Cook-Greuter, Gilligan, Wilber, Torbert, and others[16] have researched a fairly predictable sequence of stages of development through which we all tend to progress:

1. We act impulsively in service to our own interests.
2. We recognize the societal imperative to conform and play by the rules; we seek to fit in.
3. We work within these rules to create what we care about.
4. As that fails to suffice, we rewrite rules and author new ways of interacting with the world.
5. When this stops producing what we care about most, we re-author ourselves, examining and transforming the very Identity that governs our ways of Sensing, Being and Acting.
6. As this work reveals perspectives and possibilities beyond what we know, we increasingly relinquish our hard-earned Identity to be in the service of something larger than ourselves.

The underlying directionality of all stage models is remarkably consistent, no matter the terms and labels used. We have been following this directionality ever since we were born. Our process of development is, at core, a repeated and ceaseless process of recognizing our Bell Jars, discarding them only to slip into the next one, bigger and more spacious, yet still a Bell Jar with limitations that restrict what we can sense and act on.

For us, the names and descriptions of developmental stages are not so important. There are many ways of assessing these stages, and this can be very useful and pragmatic. However, we are much more interested in the moment-by-moment practice of realization. It is realization, after all, supported and facilitated by presence, that is the fundamental move of development. And realization that is the catalyst for new learning.

Development largely happens on its own. It is an organic and natural growth process. Yet, on the edge, it's up to us to create the conditions that can ease and facilitate this natural process. That is our work here.

Transitions: Including and Transcending

Stepping out of a comfortable Bell Jar into bigger territory can feel terrifying and disorienting. But this isn't the end of the story. We don't have to discard anything when we recognize a Bell Jar. Yes, the new realization expands or shifts our perspective. Presence arises with the immediacy of this realization, and our new perspective can strongly affect our meaning-making about ourselves and about the world.

Much of the previous structure remains, however. Stages of Identity and meaning-making are cumulative. Like a child retaining the knowledge of how to crawl after he learns how to walk, the range and capacity of our meaning-making also increases, as does our range of possible perspectives and actions. This is a moment of addition, not replacement.

In each of our stages, new capabilities are first demanded, then learned, and finally embodied. When faced with situations that are beyond our understanding, we stretch and grasp to make sense of them. And, when we have some breakthrough, when we find some new perspective or new understanding, this becomes internalized as part of our meaning-making capabilities. Our meaning-making has expanded to *include* the new understanding. And, in doing so, it has *transcended* the limitations of the previous stage.

Our lifelong process of development is largely a continual process of *including and transcending*[17] prior capabilities in new and more complex capabilities. Each stage transcends the previous stages, consolidating new learning into a more complex and capable Identity. This map is universal, describing the underlying template for how we became the person we are.

Nested Bell Jars: The Making of a Leader

Let's revisit Rachel, the too-nice CEO from the previous chapter. As you recall, she came into her new role facing a significant culture problem. Her unrecognized Identity—her current Bell Jar—led her to default to employee-friendly, trust-building initiatives while neglecting performance and accountability. Let's look at some of the stages she passed through on her career to that point. Thanks to Rachel, we can learn much about stages and transitions.

To start, as I would learn through our coaching conversations, Rachel grew up in a less-than-perfect family. She was the source of stability with a kind but erratic mother and a father who was often gone. She was the responsible oldest child, with all the expectations for nurturance and care for others that the female gender is often burdened with. She became responsible for others from a very early age.

Upon adulthood, Rachel entered a new stage of development. Drawn to care-taking, she trained as an RN. Her first job was in a hospital, and after two years, she hired on with a home health-care company, delivering nursing services to homebound elderly. She loved the responsibility of caring for "her" patients. *In this new stage she **included** caring for others as a profession, **transcending** this sense of responsibility for her family members.*

Later, Rachel became a supervisor, responsible for one team's delivery of services. Here, her concern was taking care of both the patients and her small team of nurses. *At this stage, she **included** supervision and caring for her staff, while **transcending** pure patient care.*

Five years later, she became director of operations, responsible for operating performance measures, coordinating multiple teams, scheduling, managing hiring/firing/promotions, etc. *In this role, she **included** overall management of complex business operations, while **transcending** an exclusive focus on one team. This required a new kind of meaning-making about what was important.*

On her predecessor's retirement, she became CEO, responsible for overall performance of the entire organization, the culture of the organization, and restoring morale. She understandably focused on employee-friendly initiatives. Her new role **included** *overall planning and strategy and culture,* **transcending** *an exclusive focus on operations.*

At every stage of this process, there was a developmental shift. Some Bell Jar—a restricted way of Being—was recognized and lifted, and Rachel was able to make new sense of herself and her world in a transcendent fashion. Through this series of realizations, her Identity as a caretaker, and the corresponding meaning-making about what was worth caring for, evolved over time. While at each stage transition she had a more inclusive view of her world, there were also things she remained blind to. Each include-and-transcend shift opened into a new view from a larger and more expansive, but still limited Bell Jar.

We can see a strong conditioned tendency running throughout: Rachel's caring and responsibility were deeply embodied. Yet each shift along the way required recognizing the Bell Jar that she had been in and then revising her sense of her own Identity to include both a broader span of caring and new capabilities. These Identity shifts were intertwined with specific new behaviors required of her, generating meaning-making and interpretive maps of the world that helped her organize herself in an increasingly complex world.

Your History with the Edge

Let's now turn to you. You have been passing through such developmental shifts since before you were born. This book places your capacity to access and facilitate these developmental shifts squarely at the core of what is required to lead in Complexity.

Because of this, it can be helpful to reflect on your history of successfully moving through these shifts, these include-and-transcend moments. You actually are, though you may not yet recognize it, quite good at this!

Experiment 3.1:
13, 25, Now?[18]

This experiment invites you into direct experience of your own *edge*: the frequent experiences we have all had in our lives as our meaning-making shifts and develops over time. Use your imagination for this, or speak into a simple audio recording device, which can make such reflections more spontaneous and authentic (even if it's only a device that's listening!).

Remember back to when you were just entering adolescence; say, age thirteen. Now, invite your thirteen-year-old awareness and thirteen-year-old physical shape to come alive in you.

Take the time to really settle into the feeling of being thirteen again. Recall what you were doing, who you were with, what was up for you.
- Speaking from the *felt sense* of your thirteen-year-old self, what can you see clearly?
- From this shape, what can you not yet see?

Then do the same for your twenty-five-year-old (or whenever you began to feel like a real adult) self.
- What can you see clearly?
- What can you not yet see?

Then do the same for your *now* self.
- What can you see clearly?
- What can you not yet see?

Reflect:

- What did the *edge* feel like?
- What was it like to be up against your own Bell Jar, knowing there was something you couldn't yet see?
- What opens when you see that this *edge* is a place you have been before?

SENSING, BEING, AND ACTING

When we become self-aware about how our Identity and Bell Jar construct meaning-making about ourselves and about the world, we are in a prime position to leverage awareness to seek new information and understanding.

Realization is where Bell Jars dissolve and new capabilities emerge. The experience of this can be liberating and energizing; it can also be overwhelming or disorienting as we release the comforting illusion of the Identity-based Bell Jar. It's helpful to normalize this, seeing these disruptions simply as part of the journey.

To ease and facilitate these transitional opportunities for emerging new capabilities, an attention to our experience of ***presence*** can make all the difference.

Lifting the Bell Jar

Again, presence is an internal state. Presence is expanded awareness, within which we sense the world as it actually is and sense ourselves as we actually are. Enabled by present-moment awareness, the ***realization move*** of development is the key to expanding the limits of our meaning-making.

Realization happens when what has been invisible to us becomes visible. We recognize phenomena as separate from us. Every time we do this, we experience the realization of a more complete and inclusive perspective. By recognizing that we even ***have*** a Bell Jar, by making our Identity-based way of Sensing itself visible, our perspective opens and we Sense reality itself with greater directness and immediacy.

Realization brings a sense of ***clarity***. This clarity is more than simply a sharp understanding; it's viscerally felt, a sense of truth. As if we were seeing something revealed that we've never seen before.

REALIZATION: LIFTING THE BELL JAR

Figure 3.1

Figure 3.1 shows a world revealed with far greater clarity by the lifting of the Bell Jar. What was murky is now sharp; previously invisible distinctions are now observable. We might not know how to navigate this territory, but it is newly in focus, and we have a clarity of Sensing that was unavailable when reality was obscured by our Bell Jar: our Identity-based filters, interpretations, and limiting assumptions.

Sometimes realization just happens. It could be forced on us by events or by necessity. At every stage transition for Rachel, we can see (as could she, if only with hindsight!) that as she included new things and transcended the old, what she was previously unable to see became visible.

Rather than waiting for serendipity or forced circumstances, I suggest embarking on a deliberate path by practicing the intentional movement of things from the invisible to the visible. Continually lifting the Bell Jar so that we can see what is outside.

This lifting is never easy, but doing this work is simpler when built on appropriate distinctions. Language and names for things actually enable us to observe them as phenomena.

Realization and Our Three Human Meta-Competencies

Through the metaphor of the Bell Jar, we can begin to make active and productive use of the three meta-competencies revealed in the Introduction. Presence-Based Leadership is built upon the three human processes of *Sensing, Being and Acting*. These fundamental processes are both mundane and omnipresent. Our meta-competencies are the means through which we respectively *take in*, *process*, and then *express* the *energy and information*[19] that *are the currency of all our relationships and all our interactions with the world*.

The potential for realization that these three offer is always available, thus also nearly always invisible. Because we are engaged in all three constantly, they disappear into the background, taken for granted. Precisely because we don't recognize them, Sensing, Being, and Acting comprise the very fabric of the metaphorical Bell Jars that define the separation between our present capacities and what is being asked of us.

The distinctions of Sensing, Being and Acting thus provide an always-available vehicle for realization. By differentiating these three simple verbs, we make possible *transcending* our habitual ways of Sensing, Being and Acting to *include* entirely new ways. *In this way, we accelerate our own development towards a level of complexity appropriate to the circumstances.*

- *Sensing*: attending to and refining the multiple channels through which we take in energy and information about the world and about ourselves in it. *We gain **clarity** with the realization that our Sensing is a dynamic human process involving perspectives and distinctions to which we can bring awareness and choice.*

- *Being*: regulating our inner state as we process energy and information in order to remain creative and resourceful no matter what's going on around us. *We build **resilience** through the realization that our Being, our inner state, is a dynamic human process to which we can bring awareness and choice.*

- *Acting*: taking actions that express internal energy and information into the world for the sake of making our preferred futures more likely. *We evoke **results that matter** through the realization that our Acting, our expression of ourselves into the world, is a dynamic human process to which we can bring awareness and choice.*

We make these meta-competencies explicit by bringing our attention and awareness to each of them. We discover real choice in each such moment, and we gain the real possibilities of a presence-based approach to leadership.

Sensing

Sensing is how we invite the outside world, along with our internal experience, into conscious awareness. With new language (distinctions), we can sense the world in new ways, rather than in the habitual ways that tend to produce the same reactive behaviors that worked in the past.

We can also learn to Sense the pull of our Identity, particularly because high-stakes situations feel risky precisely because they challenge our Identity. The anxiety we often feel reflects our automatic and deeply rooted concerns about what will happen to our Identity if things don't go according to plan. As we witness the ways we protect and defend our Identities, we decrease the power that these embodied habits have. We become less "triggerable."

Sensing is also how we become present with ourselves. Directing our attention into our interior experience provides access to clarity.

The realizations of Sensing allow us to:

- Recognize the inherently subjective process of constructing our worlds

- Increase the range of the body of distinctions that enable skillful observing

- Increase our access to a wide range of perspectives and mental models

- Hold our views lightly as subjective, tentative, and partial

Being

Being refers to our inner state. When we begin to pay attention to our state, we notice our mood (e.g., resentful, resigned, excited, optimistic, etc.). We notice our sensations. We notice our thoughts. We begin to recognize that these phenomena have their own process and that they are "not us." We recognize and witness our feelings and thoughts and sensations as we have them, and we discover that through our witnessing, they change and shift on their own. We observe ourselves in the granular and intimate process of metabolizing energy and information.

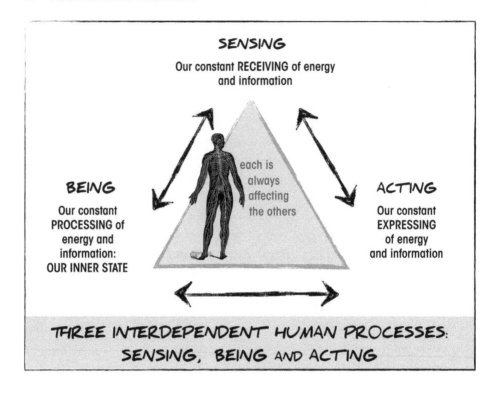

Figure 3.2

We recognize that we can build a relationship with our inner state. We can cultivate and embody states of our choosing. As a result, we are not doomed to continually internalize the crazy systems of which we are a part. By decoupling our inner state from the conditions of our Context, we discover freedom and resilience.

Being, aligned with this presence, leads to embodying what we care about in a way that the future we intend is available in us now.

With the realizations of Being, we:

- Witness our own internal thoughts, emotions, and internal sensations as crucial information

- Decouple our inner state from our Context, not taking on the craziness of the system so we can actually be useful as leaders

- Discover that we can regulate our mood and our inner state through our attention

- Access the fullness of our capacities

- Become a living embodiment of the very things we care about most

Acting

Acting, of course, is central to leadership. The traditional view of leadership is being out in front, inspiring, creating a vision for where we're going, being the hero. However useful heroic behaviors might occasionally be, more often than not they are driven unconsciously by our own Identity needs. And, we don't have to look too far to find examples of where they have catastrophic consequences.

The realization of Acting means bringing presence and choice to all we do. It means slowing down to Sense our Context and ourselves in it. It means taking the time to access resourceful inner states and extending attention and intention with others and into the systems around us. Only then can we act with leadership presence and an embodiment of what we care about and the direction we intend.

When we act in this way, we invite results that matter. We do so when we:

- Embody an attitude of curiosity and experimentation

- Extend our internal congruence and leadership presence into every action

- Invest in the ongoing cultivation of our self

- Cultivate conditions for collective resilience and creativity

Realization Is Pragmatic

When we introduced Rachel in Chapter 1, she was in a bit of a pickle. Her Bell Jar, despite intentions, blinded her to essential aspects of what was needed as new CEO. In this chapter, we learned how her history had been a reflection of a series of developmental stages, each becoming more complex as she moved to greater and greater responsibility. But she was still rather stuck.

Rachel works with Sensing, Being, and Acting

A number of months after becoming CEO, she had come to see that simply building a kinder, gentler culture was not automatically going to lead to performance. Even during the initial honeymoon period, fault lines began to surface. While people appreciated her kindness, the organization was still losing money and market share, and people were increasingly frustrated.

Rachel was wise enough to recognize that she needed help. Through coaching and organization development support, she worked skillfully with our three meta-competencies.

Through working with Sensing, Rachel listened more to what her direct reports had been trying to tell her: She had been exclusively focusing on caring while neglecting performance. She asked others what she was missing. Rachel also discerned her own reluctance and discomfort about holding people accountable for performance "until trust had been restored." She also sensed the downward trends in key metrics, which had continued unabated for the first three months of her tenure.

Through Being, Rachel practiced regulating her state to remain visibly calm and confident in the office. She recognized the stress in the environment and worked with holding people accountable. And she became increasingly visibly optimistic about the direction and the future.

In the domain of Acting, Rachel began to track her interactions with others when performance and accountability were central. She invited others to experiment with new ways of sharing results and of building commitments towards a more positive direction for the business.

*In this new stage of Rachel's development, after a rough start, she became successful in **including** a new and rigorous attention to performance, lofty goals, and accountability and in **transcending** a primary focus on caring and rebuilding morale. Rachel's meaning-making changed and she saw that, even in these difficult times, accountability and caring were actually complementary. Over the next six months, the company regained two major customers, the ledgers began showing a profit, and the company leaders took considerable pride in holding each other accountable in ways that they had never done before.*

Your practicing and your presence, if you work with these three meta-competencies over time, will lead you to cultivate internal self-correction and to become a positive organizing principle in the system that will catalyze the larger system to practice self-correction and resilience.

Experiment 3.2:
The Three Meta-Competencies and Your Challenge

Take a step back. Consider yourself: a rather successful Identity in the midst of navigating an unsettling situation. This situation presumably puts you on the edge somehow, or you would not have identified it as a Complexity Challenge in the first place.

Here, you are invited to witness yourself in relationship to this Complexity Challenge through the lenses of this chapter.

Sensing and your Complexity Challenge
- What are some things you believe you understand about this challenge and yourself in it?
- What are some things you really can't see about this challenge and yourself in it?

Being and your Complexity Challenge
- What do you notice, in the present, about your inner state in this challenging situation?
- What inner state would be helpful to be able to maintain?

Acting and your Complexity Challenge
- What actions do your historical strengths predispose you towards in this situation?
- What paradoxical or unintended consequences are you seeing to these actions?

CHAPTER SUMMARY

In this chapter, you explored development as a series of stages through which you naturally unfold.

The core realization of this chapter is that the constraining habits of your meaning-making and behavioral drivers are largely invisible to you. The central move of development is the recognition and witnessing of this "Bell Jar," together with the continual waking up to self-awareness to how your Identity and meaning-making are being constructed each and every moment. This waking up, through practicing realization, facilitates and accelerates the natural process of development.

Specific stepping stones and realizations will anchor your understanding of meaning-making and development:
- Development is a natural process of unfolding through identifiable stages. Each has specific capabilities and limitations.

- The arc of your development trends towards a greater capacity to work with Complexity, to extend care and compassion, and to hold a more inclusive perspective.
- Recognizing and transcending your habits—seeing your own Bell Jar—is the central move of development. We call this experience of awakening *realization*.
- You are always engaged in Sensing, Being and Acting. These three fundamental activities of the human condition, when illuminated through awareness and attention, can be the very objects of realization.
- You can observe yourself in the very process of Sensing, Being, and Acting, building your capacity for meaning-making in new, creative, transcendent ways. Your moment-by-moment awareness of these activities is the key to making what was invisible explicit.

This is presence: bringing awareness to the moment. Presence, and the realizations provided by our three meta-competencies, can shift your relationship with whatever is going on around you.

The moment-by-moment realizations of Sensing, Being and Acting are the doorways into presence. As you will discover in Parts Two and Three of this book, they invite the internal conditions through which you can engage Complexity with clarity and resilience. And, in Part Four, the internal and external conditions for results that matter.

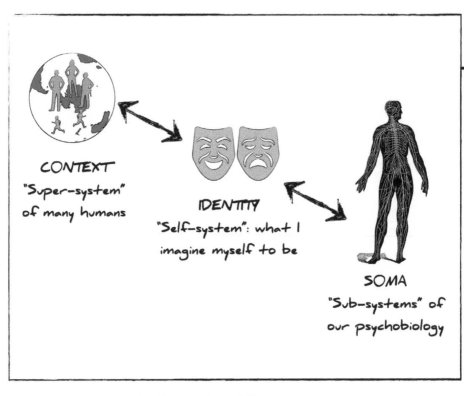

CONTEXT
"Super-system"
of many humans

IDENTITY
"Self-system": what I
imagine myself to be

SOMA
"Sub-systems" of
our psychobiology

In the midst of dynamism...

CHAPTER 4

Nine Panes for Leadership

Our theory determines what we can observe.
– Albert Einstein

The map is not the territory.
– Alfred Korzybski

B RINGING AWARENESS AND PRESENCE TO THE META-COMPETENCIES OF SENSING, Being, and Acting, and recognizing the inherent limitations of your Bell Jar, will begin to reveal a vaster range of possibilities than you ever knew was possible. Within this expanded range will inevitably lie many choices for how to engage in new and creative ways with your Complexity Challenges.

In this chapter, you will add one more key set of distinctions to our overall framework. As a leader, you influence the systems around us. However, you are often blind to the multiple nested levels of system that are present in every situation, influencing you even as you myopically focus on the limited data that your Bell Jar allows you to see.

As a leader, you must not only engage with the ***Context*** system in which you lead. You must also acknowledge and negotiate with the automatic and incessant drives of your own ***Identity*** system within that Context. And, you must learn to direct awareness into the ceaseless dynamism of your ***Soma*** (body) system as it self-organizes to respond to the world and perpetuate your Identity.

Whoa! Three different systems, all part of this Complexity. What's a leader to do? Right now, this may seem esoteric, but like Rachel—and like me, when Walker and I were creating Bend of Ivy Lodge—it's a safe bet that you are at this very moment missing significant data on less-obvious levels of system that could radically inform the way you lead.

This will prove both pragmatic and relevant. Hang in there.

CONTEXT, IDENTITY AND SOMA

Let's look more closely at the distinctions of Context, Identity, and Soma, which have been mentioned many times, beginning with the introduction, but have not been foregrounded until now. The differentiation of these three levels of system will play an important part in our meaning-making in Complexity.

Nested Systems

If we look around, we can easily find countless examples of ***nested systems*** of things.[20] For starters, think of the classic hierarchical structure of an organization. Or the design of governance in a representative democracy.

Now, switch your imagination to the physical. Imagine one of the marvelous sets of Russian *matryoshka* dolls. A tiny doll at the center is contained within a larger one, which is in turn contained within a still larger one. At home, I have a gorgeous set of ten nested dolls, and they are made with up to seventy.

Now, imagine the following nested system. Subatomic particles combine to form atoms. Atoms bond to form molecules. Get enough of the right molecules together and arrange them properly, and you get a human cell. ***Include*** other cells and ***transcend*** the single cell, and you get a heart, a neuron, a bone. Include and transcend again, and you have a living, breathing human. Put a group of humans around a table, and you have a team (or a family). Put teams together and you have an organization. Keep going, and you get to industries, cultures, nation-states, a species, a planet. (Sounds simple on paper, but it took the creative forces of the universe some 13.8 billion years to discover how to do this!)

You can easily see that, in this nested system, every level has an influence on the levels above and below it. Cells exist in dynamic interaction with the organs of which they are a part; each level influences the other. Leaders influence, and are influenced by, the

Context in which they lead. Component parts on any level exist not only in relationship with other parts on that level, but also in relation to the levels above (in which they are included) and in relation to the levels below (of which they are comprised).[21]

It is important to recognize that *the present-moment reality of any Complexity situation in fact exists on multiple, simultaneous levels of a nested system.* The interactions and interdependencies between levels are an inherent part of the complexity of the overall system. As leaders, recognizing and leveraging these interactions has a profound impact on our understanding of how the whole system actually works, and therefore on our capacity to produce results that we care about.

Emergent phenomena on any level of a nested system are determined by interactions and dynamics in the levels of system below it. What happens in a human system (Context) is produced by interactions between the people that make up that system. And, how each individual (Identity) acts is determined by complex and invisible interdependencies within his or her psychobiology (Soma).

Following this logic, we arrive at a radical new realization. Understanding the functioning and causalities of any complex human system requires a new and non-negotiable awareness. To begin to understand a system, we must include, in our Sensing and perceptions, the conditioned driving forces embodied deeply and invisibly in the Somas of the individuals that make up that system.

Yet, most of us cannot see or access the information and perspectives inherent in the scales of system either bigger or smaller than we are trained to observe. Mostly, we have been rewarded for paying attention to the external Context that immediately impacts us. Other levels of system that absolutely shape our reality remain invisible, obscured by our myopic attention to the Context immediately outside and surrounding us.

This is another Bell Jar. We are blind to the multiple levels of system, which, in their dynamic interdependence, produce everything around us. Recognizing and lifting this blindness will be crucial to our Sensing of Complexity.

A new set of distinctions is emerging here. Let's make the levels of this nested system explicit and describe them so that we can get better at recognizing the complexity of the dynamic and adaptive multilevel system of which we are a part. Thus, we will access a deeper understanding of the system that will, in turn, inform how we create conditions for what matters.

Context

The system occurring around us is our human *Context*. This can include many levels of scale, but whatever naturally comes to mind for you is probably the right starting point for your Complexity Challenge. Some readers are leaders in a team, others in a university, marriage, family, nonprofit, company or community. Context, for our purposes, is the level of human system within which you consider yourself a leader.

Context, of course, also could include the larger ecosystem and economies in which you play a part. It could include the health of the planet, and the macro systems that we read about in the news but that we imagine have impacts elsewhere but not on us. Of course, we are directly or indirectly affected by all of it, and presence relentlessly deepens our connection to these larger views.

As we examine what is really important to us, it is important to consider the biggest possible view that we can choose to organize around. That said, on a daily basis, we focus most often on the level of Context that is the human system in which we consider ourselves a leader, and that's mostly what we will address here.

Our Context is the most obvious level of system to see. It is the level to which we've been most trained to pay attention, and it is what we naturally organize around and attempt to act upon as leaders. However, it is only one level; we ignore others at our peril.

Identity

As unique individuals, we function as an *Identity* system. Our Identity is our individual personality, our sense of our self in the world as an entity with particular characteristics that are uniquely ours: strengths, ambitions, skills, awareness, choice and free will.

As with Rachel, and with me at Bend of Ivy, it is a human tendency to make meaning of our Context in ways that are Identity-driven. We seek to protect and affirm our sense of who we are in the world. We are, each one of us, a *self-system* that is in the business of self-organizing to perpetuate itself and to maintain the illusion of a secure stasis.

Our Identity system is also a component of various super-systems (our teams, organizations, communities, nation-states, etc.). These super-systems include other humans, each of whom is protecting and affirming their own sense of who they are in the world. Our identities are strongly affected by these larger super-systems; we might feel enlivened or threatened. Either way, we can sometimes react in ways that aren't helpful. And, the ways in which we respond in turn affect that super-system.

Soma

Similarly, each of us is comprised of sub-systems (our nervous system, muscles, bones, endocrine system, heart, etc.). These have been conditioned by our life experiences as a psychobiology that provides both the physical basis for life and the biological substrate of personality. Our **Soma**[22] refers to this set of psychobiological structures, as well as the conditioned functioning through which these structures preserve our Identity and produce our subjective experience.

Our internal *somatic* sub-systems collaborate rather elegantly to keep the physical body functioning, as well as maintain the psychobiology that underpins and encodes our sense of who we are. They are strongly affected by what our Identity is experiencing (particularly when it is threatened!). They are trained to act consistently and automatically to defend and perpetuate the Identity system that we imagine ourselves to be.

Somatic literacy is the essential capacity to be present with our own intimate internal dynamism as we respond to and generate our worlds. It is the essential entry point to Sensing, moment by moment, how our somatic sub-systems interact to express thoughts, emotions, sensations, urges, internal states, and ultimately actions.

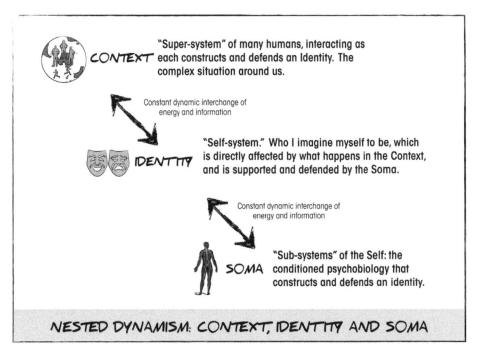

"Super-system" of many humans, interacting as CONTEXT each constructs and defends an Identity. The complex situation around us.

Constant dynamic interchange of energy and information

"Self-system." Who I imagine myself to be, which IDENTITY is directly affected by what happens in the Context, and is supported and defended by the Soma.

Constant dynamic interchange of energy and information

"Sub-systems" of the Self: the SOMA conditioned psychobiology that constructs and defends an identity.

NESTED DYNAMISM: CONTEXT, IDENTITY AND SOMA

Figure 4.1

Because all thought or behavior arises from conditions in the Soma, information from our Soma system reveals previously invisible but mission-critical influences in the overall multilevel system in which we hope to lead.

Nested Systems as a Lens on Complexity

What is enabled by seeing this multilevel nested system as a lens upon our Complexity situations?

Each of these levels of system—Context, Identity, and Soma—is an integral and critical component of the overall situation in which we intend to lead. The conditions and tendencies of each level have profound influences on the others, as well as on the whole. Yet, some of those effects are simply invisible to us. Because these dynamics are not obvious and take energy and attention to recognize, we miss crucial pieces of information about how the whole system in which we are leading is functioning. This information could profoundly influence our choices.

Let's look at what happened with Rachel with these three levels of structure as a lens. With the stepping stones of our new distinctions, hindsight reveals intricate dynamics of Context, Identity, and Soma. All were present during Rachel's brief honeymoon, the dawning realization that the ship was still sinking, and the turnaround process.

For Rachel, the growing awareness of how her Identity was entangled with the Context, along with how her Soma automatically acted to protect and defend her Identity, became instrumental in the turnaround. These enabled fresh approaches for Rachel to both observe and intervene in the Context itself.

Rachel recognizes the interdependencies of Context, Identity and Soma

Initially, when Rachel stepped into the CEO slot after the resignation of her predecessor, the entire organization breathed a sigh of relief. The Board as well as other leaders were appreciative and encouraging. To a person, they told her that her kind and caring manner would be important for restoring trust and getting the company back on its feet. *We can see, with the benefit of hindsight, that there was a lot of energy in the **Context** that supported Rachel's emphasis on culture and people. This, of course, resonated with Rachel's **Identity**-based tendency to rely on well-practiced strengths. Rachel's **Soma** responded with excitement, energy, and a sense of optimism, all of which reinforced her meaning-making that she could make the difference.*

After several months, it became increasingly apparent that the company wasn't out of the woods. Staff appreciated more flex hours and Friday afternoon social events. But another major customer went to the competition, and the quarterly financials were terrible. Staff felt that they were entitled to some good treatment, but many started asking what Rachel intended to do to turn the ship around. The fun atmosphere began to seem forced and artificial, and people became stressed and impatient. *Plenty of evidence in the **Context** indicated all was not well. Rachel's **Identity** and confidence were being challenged. She recognized trouble and was beginning to doubt if she really had the guts, vision and skills to turn things around. Equipped with new **Somatic** distinctions, she recognized a continual sense of weight on her shoulders, persistent anxiety, knotted shoulders and an instant urgency to put positive spin on bad news. All this contributed to the atmosphere of anxiety she was trying to change.*

Rachel reached out for help, engaging a coach who could also work with the entire leadership team. Intensive work for her, and off-site work for the team, led to a multipronged collaborative effort on rebuilding trust, building shared accountability around performance, and going after some of the customers that had been lost over the past couple of years. *Rachel saw her developmental edge. Her go-to behaviors were both useful and incomplete. She saw that her **Identity** needed to include driving rigor and accountability, while transcending her natural focus on care-taking. She built the skill of paying attention to her inner **Somatic** experience. Rachel learned to spot, in the moment, her internal urges to duck difficult conversations about performance in the guise of "trust-building." In-the-moment awareness enabled Rachel to intervene in her own automaticity and to bring forward new actions. Rachel's broader range of leadership behaviors inspired and energized others in her **Context**, engaging staff in new collaborative processes that produced shared ownership.*

As I hope that you are beginning to see, excluding any of the three levels from awareness means we miss crucial information about the operation of the whole system in which our Identity and our Soma play vital parts.

Experiment 4.1:
The Nested Levels of System and Your Challenge

This is an initial opportunity to name and acknowledge the three nested levels of system that are most certainly present in your Complexity Challenge.

Context and your Complexity Challenge

- What is the scale of Context most apparent to you in this situation?
- Who are the primary stakeholders who strongly influence the dynamics?

- Who are the less visible, or even invisible, stakeholders who influence the long-term outcomes?

Identity and your Complexity Challenge
- What is at stake for you personally in this situation?
- Who would you be if this challenge is resolved successfully?
- What would you tell yourself *about yourself* if you were not successful?

Soma and your Complexity Challenge
- As you answered the previous questions about Identity, what did you sense in your body?
- What do you sense in your body right now?
- What do you sense in your body most frequently as you engage with this challenge?

INTRODUCING THE NINE PANES

Realizing the fluidity of the territory of Complexity, and also cultivating the stability of stepping stones for a pathway through it, is our premise.

In Chapter 3, we introduced into our Presence-Based Leadership model *three meta-competencies:* Sensing, Being, and Acting. By attending to these through *presence*, we cultivate present-moment realization of these three core human processes, making visible what is normally invisible. These three meta-competencies influence each other in ways both profound and subtle.

Now in Chapter 4, we have introduced into our model *three levels of a nested system*: *Context, Identity, and Soma.* Each represents a different level of scale. Context is the scale of the situation. Identity is the scale of our personality, the sense of self in that Context. Soma is the scale of the embodied habits and psychobiology that holds our Identity in place. Taken together, these three dynamic and interdependent levels of scale represent a more complete understanding of reality than if any were excluded through our own blindness.

Each level of scale contains information and dynamics upon which our three meta-competencies can operate. Each is fodder for *realization*. Yet, the myopia of our Bell Jars and our single-minded dedication to Identity preservation keep us blind to much of what would otherwise be readily available for us.

How, then, might we remove our blindness?

I propose that we do so systematically through the lens of the Nine-Paned Leadership Model. This model takes our three meta-competencies, on the one

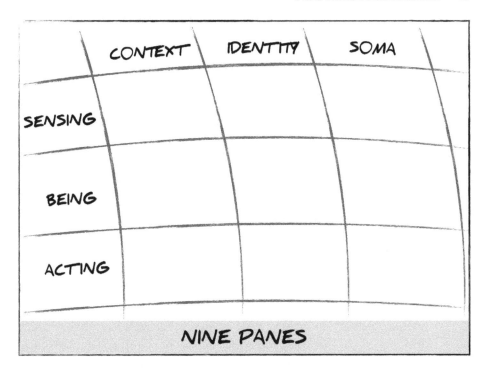

Figure 4.2

hand, and the three nested systems, on the other, and combines them. Three times three equals nine. The result: nine different Panes, or "windows," or perspectives, into any given situation.

By viewing reality through each of these differentiated Nine Panes, we can fluidly shift our perspectives, access previously unavailable information and practices, and realize more of how reality is truly operating. We become present to what is and more able to lead with clarity and resilience towards results that matter.

Three Meta-Competencies at Three Levels of Scale

Overlaying *Sensing, Being, and Acting* onto *Context, Identity, and Soma* provides a new meaning-making framework. Each Pane is a unique perspective that integrates an omnipresent meta-competency with an omnipresent level of scale.

This grid is three by three. These are the Nine Panes. We could name other meta-competencies, as well as both bigger and smaller layers of the nested system. The grid, theoretically, could be four by four, or eleven by six. It could include anything else we decide to throw into the kitchen sink.

In my experience, however, these three simple meta-competencies and three levels of scale are a gold mine. I am not claiming that this model is either complete or rigorously scientific. My chief concern is pragmatism. The Nine Panes are always "on," always available. As such, the nine views are accessible and useful. They are places to look, providing unconventional and high-leverage ways of working with difficult situations.

Here's a promise. In the swirl of your Complexity Challenge, each of these Nine Panes offers you:

- A unique *perspective* on some of the critical vectors that influence your immediate situation and that are likely invisible to most people without these distinctions

- A set of *distinctions* that allow you to observe yourself and/or the situation in more inclusive and precise ways, making visible what has previously been invisible to you. These realizations will increase your clarity and understanding of what is true in the moment. They enable new *meaning-making*.

- A set of *practices* that can dramatically increase your present-moment awareness of the choices that are available to you as a leader. These practices will, with some consistency and dedication, produce real and pragmatic embodied capacities for awareness, your way of being, and the actions that are available to you.

- *Core realizations* that are rather universal, and provide a powerful source of clarity and stability for any situation that you may find yourself in

The Nine Panes are particularly powerful when leading in conditions that feel elusive and "stretchy" and new, requiring adaptive learning and development. When the leadership cookbook inevitably fails us, here are nine places to look for new, present-moment understanding.

Co-Arising: Distinct and Interdependent

It's tempting to see these as nine distinct areas of focus. After all, they are always present, always in operation, always accessible just for the looking.

	CONTEXT Super-System around the Self	**IDENTITY** Self-System	**SOMA** Sub-Systems of the Self: Our Psychobiology
SENSING RECEIVING Energy and Information	**Observe the system** Complexity is normal and interesting. Accepting and observing it produces clarity.	**Recognize Identity at stake** Complexity challenges us; it is natural to respond with habits primarily designed to defend Identity.	**Attend to experience** Recognizing and staying present with internal experience increases information and choice.
BEING PROCESSING Energy and Information	**Decouple state from Context** Liberating inner state from outer conditions provides resilience and choice.	**Embody what matters** Building internal congruence with a future that matters provides an organizing principle for leadership.	**Regulate inner state** Directed and focused attention regulates, stabilizes, and shifts inner state.
ACTING EXPRESSING Energy and Information	**Scale awareness** Complexity-adapted capacities are cultivated through shared experimentation.	**Extend leadership presence** Internal congruence, expressed externally, invites resonance and collaboration with others.	**Tune the instrument** Sustained development results from the practice and embodiment of new capacities.

NINE PANES OF PRESENCE-BASED LEADERSHIP

Figure 4.3

Each would seem neat, complete, and straightforward, and we might think we can master each and employ them appropriately. And, to some extent, we will explore them as distinct areas of inquiry.

While this isn't wrong, it is a limited view. It is a Bell Jar that could support the reassuring belief that working through the Nine Panes, step by step, would result in a reliable road map that tells us how to use each perspective in the right amount and in the correct order to produce certain results. Sorry, reality doesn't work like this.

Rather, these nine areas of attention *co-arise*. What happens in any Pane affects each of the others. The Nine Panes are dynamic, interdependent, co-arising phenomena.

The bad news about this is that we can't take one Pane and work with and fix it in isolation, as we might replace a broken pane of a window.

The good news is that because of this interconnectedness, action or change in any Pane will necessarily affect others. This interdependence is actually intrinsic to Complexity, and so the dynamism of the model appropriately reflects the dynamism of the interdependent systems we are seeking to engage.

It can be astonishing how a nudge in one place begins to influence others, often in completely unpredictable ways. A major takeaway for leading in Complexity is that we get to experiment and see what happens!

An Integrative and Creative View of Leadership

The subsequent chapters will offer enough to understand what each of the Panes might open for you. I invite you to see the Nine Panes as a *set of lenses through which to engage your own Complexity situation with fluidity, inventiveness, and creativity.*

They are neither a methodology nor a nice, neat process to smooth the ever-shifting emergent process of leading. Rather, the Panes are partial and pragmatic lenses on reality. They are available descriptions that can help us identify areas for attention in navigating this territory.

Taken separately, they offer new distinctions, perspectives and practices. Or, taken together, they are a radically new view of leadership in Complexity. Ultimately, I invite you to embody an artistic, spacious and integrated view of the Nine Panes as a whole. I invite you to practice integrating the parts in new and innovative ways that create the conditions for what you care about to emerge.

For now, with the benefit of new distinctions and equipped with 20/20 hindsight, we can use Rachel's new responses to complex challenges to glimpse some of the leverage points and possibilities that had always been available to her but were previously invisible without these distinctions.

Rachel's leadership is clarified by the Nine Panes

With coaching support, Rachel began to see that turning around the company was not simply a matter of building a compassionate culture, nor even figuring out the "right" places to intervene in the system. Rather, it required a creative process for developing herself as a more aware leader, embodying and committed both to compassion and to performance. Rachel's Identity was as much of a change project as the organization itself!

Through working with the Nine Panes across the meta-competencies and levels of scale, Rachel became more able to observe and describe the intricacies of the dynamics within her organization, as well as how she was blinded by her own Identity needs.

Rachel practiced staying present with herself. She began to recognize the internal sensations of avoidance when a strong move was needed. She learned to settle herself to be both direct and compassionate. Working with her inner state to build resilience became both enjoyable and powerful as she expanded her leadership presence to include a broader range of leadership moves that supported both performance and compassion. She no longer saw these two qualities as being in conflict, and she believed, in fact, that she could be the embodiment of both. She expressed this consistently in her conversations and relationships with others.

Small experiments across the organization engaged many people. Paying attention to positive results began to build trust and confidence in Rachel and her people. She saw that through new practices, her own leadership style and the range of moves enabled by awareness were changing in ways that surprised even her. Her confidence and assurance grew in parallel with the organization's success in collectively creating a culture that embraced both compassion and accountability.

Rachel's development as a leader was both intricate and exquisite. Her own change process had not been a separate undertaking from the company's change process. And she was both happy and relieved at the growing realization that leadership didn't all rest on her shoulders, but was rather a wholehearted and human participation in a complex and emergent process. Rachel marveled at how much had changed in six months!

Consider, for a moment, what opened for Rachel through this process. And consider what possibilities might be waiting, not yet visible, for the light of day in your own Complexity Challenge.

≈∽ PRESENCE PAUSE ⟋≈

In subsequent chapters of this book, we will explore the Nine Panes in detail. For now, I invite you to take a first look at your own situation through these panes.

Think of this experiment as an entry point. I encourage you not to expect solutions or answers; your understandable desire for certainty is actually ***anti-helpful*** in Complexity—worse than only neutrally unhelpful, it is actively counterproductive.

Rather, I want you simply to practice being curious. Please assume, for now, that the Nine Panes might later reveal currently dormant, invisible opportunities. For new realizations to emerge, simply being curious is the best starting point. So, fill in what you can. And, really, don't worry if nothing comes up for now.

Experiment 4.2:
An Initial Nine Panes Perspective on Your Complexity Challenge

Divide a large sheet of paper, in landscape orientation, into a three-by-three grid. If you have a large piece of paper (flip chart or poster board) use that. Label the rows and columns per Figure 4.3 (on page 77). Then, fill in what you can for each Pane.

This is not a test; you are just getting started. Still, it's helpful to build connections between your developing understanding and your real-life Complexity Challenge. Don't worry about completeness or "getting it right." This is really about jump-starting your curiosity rather than finding clear answers. In each pane, write down some brief high-level bullet points for each question. You might refer to Figure 4.3 (on page 77) for a reminder of what each Pane reveals:

- What is the relevance of this Pane to your situation?
- What do you suspect you already know about this Pane?
- What do you suspect you might not yet know?

CHAPTER SUMMARY

In this chapter, you looked within your situation to recognize three nested levels of system. You live and lead as an Identity, within a Context that you seek to influence, and as a Soma (a set of psychobiological sub-systems) acting in concert to construct and perpetuate that Identity. These three nested systems (Context, Identity and Soma) comprise the most accessible and relevant levels of the whole of the situation you are facing.

As you map these three nested levels of system against the three meta-competencies of Sensing, Being, and Acting, you get nine combinations. Like a nine-paned window, each of these Panes looks out on the same landscape. Yet, each offers a unique perspective on the system and its functioning.

The core realization? You have available a fluid and accessible set of perspectives on the overall reality of your Complexity Challenge. These complementary views can be taken one at a time, or taken together, to make a whole range of phenomena explicit and actionable.

Being present to all nine of these perspectives is stretchy and liberating. With presence, you can easily and fluidly shift between them, accessing what is most relevant and pragmatic at any given moment. Each offers a different way of making meaning. Each offers intervention points and opportunities for a different kind of engagement with Complexity. Each provides a stepping stone for realization and clarity.

And, paradoxically, they are also an integrated whole. They co-arise, and a change in any affects all. Collectively, these Nine Panes comprise a radical new view of Complexity and of the leadership opportunities Complexity offers.

PART
TWO

Sensing

Every system is perfectly designed to get the results it gets.

– Paul Batalden, after Arthur Jones

Not everything that is faced can be changed, but nothing can be changed until it is faced.

– James Baldwin

THE FIRST PART OF THE BOOK LAID THE FOUNDATION FOR THE TERRITORY INTO WHICH OUR JOURNEY TOGETHER LEADS US. You explored the nature of Complexity and some stepping stones for engaging with it in new ways. You experienced the sense of realization when the Bell Jar is lifted to make visible what was previously invisible. You saw how realization continually supports the arc of development, accumulating into more inclusive and complex stages for making meaning about the world and your place in it.

Next you saw how the distinctions of our three meta-competencies (the human processes of Sensing, Being, and Acting) when overlaid on three levels of scale (Context, Identity, and Soma) provide nine *differentiated and connected* perspectives: the Nine Panes.

The Panes are *differentiated* because each offers unique realizations and practices. You can double-click on any one of the Panes to open up new perspectives and approaches that shift your relationship with Complexity in significant ways. You can compartmentalize, using an individual Pane as an entry point for exploration. This will be a primary approach of this book.

However, this parsing and double-clicking approach is only one way to engage with the Panes. Seeing them as distinct is also partial and misses the crucial perspective that the Nine Panes are *connected* and interdependent. The Panes are dynamically related, each affecting the other. They are a whole, and focusing myopically on any part misses the dynamism of the whole.

You will be working with this tension between differentiation and connection throughout. Like Complexity itself, everything makes a difference, and a shift in one place produces shifts elsewhere in the system.

Part Two of the book focuses on Sensing, the first of our three meta-competencies. Sensing is the fundamental human process of bringing into awareness *energy and information* from both outside and inside ourselves. Sensing is a prerequisite for engaging with the world as it actually is and for engaging with the world as you actually are. Sensing is about receiving reality as it is. No whitewashing, no varnishing. Just truth.

The realization of Sensing—choosing wisely where you direct your attention, and therefore the information that becomes available—produces clarity. You recognize that you can wisely choose the distinctions and the lenses through which you make meaning.

While reality will always be more complex than you can possibly understand, Sensing allows you to discern ever more deeply both what the world is up to as well as what is being asked of you. The curiosity to keep Sensing into what you don't yet understand will carry you a long way towards identifying leverage points for making a difference.

In Part Two, you will explore Sensing on three levels of scale: Context, Identity and Soma. One chapter for each. In that specific sequence.

Context is the easiest entry point for Sensing. Like all of us, you have in large part already been trained to look outwards at your environment in order to find ways to fix things and shape things to your liking. Developing yourself begins with getting out of the fixing game and into the understanding game. Full disclosure: This will make your world neither predictable nor controllable.

At least you will understand why it's not predictable! Naming and describing the complexity you see around you provides reassuring clarity.

Next. If, like me, your Identity is largely organized around feeling competent and getting stuff done, then you're probably decent at predicting and controlling. Sensing your Identity helps you understand why you get rattled when Complexity jeopardizes your well-laid plans and, by extension, your comforting sense of who you are. Like me, you sometimes unconsciously defend this Identity with reactive behaviors that exacerbate the very conditions that created the challenge in the first place. And, because of your own Identity-based Bell Jar, you don't see that you do this; you only experience the collateral damage which astonishes and dismays you. This is the human condition. The no-fault realization that this is so explains a lot, and it can be a real relief.

Third, you will begin to Sense your interior in new ways. You begin to Sense the inner workings of your body, your Soma, in the moment-by-moment dynamic process of metabolizing energy and information in order to construct and defend your Identity. Directing the spotlight of your attention into your own present-moment experience reveals a wealth of information. You will experience, directly, the felt urges that precede previously automatic reactions. Directly sensing your psychobiology as it interacts with your situation is an excellent starting place for unwinding the Gordian knot of causality.

The realizations of Sensing offer a fuller experience of how you are actively taking in information and making meaning about the world and your place in it. The clarity that results is the foundation for what follows in later parts of the book: the possibility of intervening in your internal condition, habits and reactive behavioral patterns. You will choose new and generative possibilities for action that were always present but that perhaps you have never seen.

This is what opens from presence. Presence enables us to sense the world as it actually is, and to sense ourselves as we actually are. This rigorous embrace of reality, of the truth of this immediate moment, produces clarity.

Acting in new ways in a complex world paradoxically begins with slowing down enough to Sense reality as it is.

	CONTEXT	IDENTITY	SOMA
SENSING	OBSERVE THE SYSTEM		
BEING			
ACTING			

Sensing Context: Observe the System

> *We see the world, not as it is, but as we are—or, as we are*
> *conditioned to see it. When we open our mouths to describe what we*
> *see, we in effect describe ourselves, our perceptions, our paradigms.*
>
> – Stephen Covey, elaborating on quote from the Talmud

> *Reality does not take breaks.*
> – A. H. Almaas

YOU BEGIN THE EXPLORATION OF THE NINE PANES WITH SOME NEW DISTINCTIONS FOR SENSING YOUR COMPLEX CONTEXT. You long for distinctions that bring clarity to murkiness. As stated previously, you are used to looking externally, so this might feel like a natural starting point.

Luz, who you met briefly at the beginning of Chapter 1, was up against a wall in her efforts to bring about change.

Luz's Context fights back

Luz[23] was the newly hired dean of an architectural research institute housed within a major West Coast university. Proud of a historically prestigious brand, the institute was in decline. Luz was an outsider recruited for her academic reputation, driven personality and proven fundraising ability. Her charge was to revitalize promotion and accountability systems, build financial viability, rebuild an international reputation and rebrand the school as a green-architecture hub by attracting pioneering academicians in environmentally responsible urban design.

Her background led her to think of things as Complicated (needing detailed planning and efficient execution) rather than Complex (meaning unpredictable and emergent and paradoxical). In Luz's world, things could be figured out, change could be orchestrated, and people behaved in sensible ways and followed structure and order. The changes she was to implement were obviously the right things for the institute; after all, she had a mandate from the university leadership and expected success.

But Luz had also inherited a complacent bureaucracy. Many faculty were biding their time until retirement. Others had leveraged the institute's brand for lucrative personal consulting and design contracts. Most weren't interested in more accountability, new performance metrics or working harder.

Luz was astonished at how her usually successful directness and enthusiasm seemed to only alienate others, when the benefits of the change to faculty were obvious. The harder she pushed in faculty meetings to position the change process and sell the benefits of this for all, the more toxic the pushback became. Several loud and obnoxious faculty seemed to be getting support from others she had thought were on board. The tone had become rather personal, and people either ignored decisions that she thought had been made in meetings or actively acted in ways counter to them.

When the attacks became more personal, Luz had to step back and acknowledge that she had underestimated the power of an entrenched system to resist a change process that was so patently beneficial for both the institute and the faculty. She wasn't sleeping well and was working long and tense hours. The job seemed very different from what she had been pitched. She actively wondered if she'd made the biggest mistake of her career, and whether she had the chops to deliver.

Like Luz in her new academic environment, you are likely also dealing with a system around you that behaves in ways that are unpredictable, even perverse. Your actions sometimes provoke responses that make no sense, or a frustrating lack of any response at all. With Luz, a long track record of success had conditioned her to seek to orchestrate change through a series of policy decisions driven from above, with a modicum of input and involvement from faculty. Yet the responses of people in the system simply didn't fit with her assumptions, nor did they seem to follow any logic she could discern. Instead, her organization seemed to be conspiring against her at every turn. The job had two certainties: its unpredictability and its power to overwhelm.

Learning to Sense your Context will better prepare you to counter the overwhelming unpredictability of Complexity situations. It offers you new means for observing and describing what's going on around you.

While observation and description will by themselves not make things predictable, new realizations about the system begin to fundamentally change your relationship with Complexity itself. Realization provides the clarity and relief to see *why* things aren't predictable, igniting a curiosity about how you can partner with Complexity for learning, rather than trying to wrestle it to the ground as if it were a problem to be solved.

REALITY DOES NOT TAKE BREAKS[24]

Relentless onslaughts of change confront us, along with an emergent reality we could not possibly be prepared for. We are seeking perspectives and practices that are helpful in these Contexts.

In fact, simply naming the unpredictability of our environment and recognizing it as Complex can be a palpable physical relief. Normalization and acceptance provide a different place to stand in a world a-swirl.

Our education was not at all designed to prepare us for a complex world. And, our traditional narratives about success implicitly (and often explicitly) teach us that we should be able to largely control and direct things according to our wishes.

In school there was generally a right answer that, with sufficient study, we could arrive at. Executive MBA programs charge a lot of money to teach leaders that with the right sophisticated analysis, illuminated by benchmarking of what has worked elsewhere, we should be able to derive a strategy that will likely produce success.

But we also notice with increasing frequency that doing the right things doesn't necessarily produce the results we expected. In fact, there's a greater and greater dissonance between the world we have prepared our entire lives to act upon and the world that actually exists. There is a yawning chasm, too, between our learned and reasonable expectations that we should be able to determine what happens, and the mounting and disturbing evidence that we can't control much at all.

It is natural, though exceedingly unhelpful, to cling to the illusion that the world is as we have trained to see it. Our sense of well-being rests on an assumption, alluringly easy to make, about the inertia of reality. We are unconsciously and deeply wired to produce results in the belief that *this* action will produce *that* result. Of course, this requires that the world be knowable and relatively deterministic. There are laws that determine cause and effect. Or, at least, there's some benevolent force that assures that things will work out okay.

These belief systems are strong and mostly invisible to us, and unable to see reality as it actually is, we experience confusion. We exert tremendous efforts to respond in ways that sometimes make our intended outcomes less likely, not more.

Further, we can feel that it's our fault somehow. We can think we only need to tighten down. Work harder. Build our leadership or technical competencies. Get more power so we are finally in charge. Then, somehow, the ship will right itself and we'll be able to sail more or less on course to what James Flaherty calls "the island where everything works out."

Doing what has worked previously is understandable. It's a predictable reaction to a new and mysterious set of conditions. And it's wrong.

A radically new way of leading requires developing a new way of Sensing the world. We begin by recognizing and acknowledging that we are struggling, accepting that we want things to be simpler and more predictable than they actually are, and that we are at an impasse as to how to navigate.

This acceptance invites *presence*, freeing us from attachment and illusion. We begin to see, and marvel at, the nature of Complexity itself, rather than only seeing our Context as a set of obstacles to our agenda. Though it is ultimately impossible to be free of our constructed meaning-making, distinguishing and building familiarity with the underlying dynamics of Complexity moves us in that direction.

MAKING COMPLEXITY ITSELF VISIBLE

We've been trained to look at our Context, but the lenses we use tend to be implicit. We don't see the lens through which we are looking, and most often don't even recognize that we are looking through a lens at all. We mistake our conditioned and filtered views of reality for reality itself, taking false comfort in the reassuring illusion that we are in possession of the facts.

Having new distinctions to increase the objectivity of our Sensing is crucial, particularly as the stakes become higher and/or when what is happening in our Context becomes less familiar and more complex. New distinctions—new language to support our new observations—are stepping stones that inform our decision-making. They help us come to accept that there's no way we should be expected to control, or even navigate, this complex world smoothly.

In the rest of this section, we will differentiate some common elements of Complexity. Being able to recognize and differentiate these elements might not make things predictable, but it does help us get a grip on why change in Complex systems is so elusive, often producing resistance and perverse consequences.

Here are seven very helpful elements of this vocabulary.[25]

- *Stasis*: a state in a Complex system in which conditions persist in a relatively stable form over some period of time

- *Emergence*: the process through which unpredictable macro phenomena result from complex and often invisible interactions between smaller phenomena

- *Feedback loops*: a dynamic where one element of a system creates change in another element, which in turn leads to change in the first element

- *Disruptors*: an emergent force that upsets stasis, with consequences experienced throughout connected systems

- *Organizing principles*: values, people, directions, or cultural norms that have an organizing power within a system, either positive or negative [26]

- *Polarities*: pairs of values or organizing principles that, in the short term, appear to be in conflict with each other but in actuality are both important to acknowledge and take care of in the long term[27]

- *Stillness*: a condition of unsettledness or indetermination in which *what is next* is unknowable but also subject to influence

Each appears in all levels of system. They are elements of Complex systems in general, identifiable wherever we look: in the functioning of galaxies, ecosystems, organizations, and human bodies. However, in this chapter we will explore these primarily as they appear on the level of our leadership Context. I will introduce each of these distinctions with brief descriptions, some illustrations from various levels of system, and an example of how each element affected Luz's experience as the newly appointed dean.

Stasis

In *stasis*, conditions persist in a relatively stable form over some period of time. There may be change, but it is slow and relatively predictable. In stasis we have a reassuring sense that change is incremental and that our situation is characterized by greater stability than may actually be true. Stasis is generally supported by balancing feedback loops (discussed below) and by boundaries that limit change.

Five-year strategic plans are often based on assumptions of stasis; anticipating how to respond to unanticipated disruptions makes such planning difficult at best. We make investments in lifestyle and home improvements based on confidence that our current income level will continue. Retirement plans assume some level of stasis. Global warming is proceeding slowly enough that some can rationalize their way out of believing it's a crisis.

Our own internal stasis shows up as an overconfidence that we can meet the challenges that we currently face with the skillsets and knowledge built from our past. Stasis assumes that the future is fundamentally an extension of what we have faced before rather than something qualitatively different. This may or may not be true.

> *Luz, in fact, made tacit assumptions, underestimating the complexities of the culture she faced. (In fairness, the search committee had also understated these complexities for their own reasons, but this often happens.) Luz was hired, in fact, because stasis had become a core problem facing the institute. The world was changing, green design was a crucial emergent trend, and the institute was acting as if it were not. The administration knew that something different was needed, but not how resistant to change the institute would turn out to be.*

Emergence

Emergence is all around us. It is the process through which phenomena with new properties unpredictably appear out of the interactions between smaller and often invisible phenomena. In Complexity, emergence can disrupt or delight us, depending on whether we like the nature of the surprises. Because the causalities that produce emergence are largely invisible to us, it is impossible to fully control the process of emergence.

We can work backwards from emergence to investigate the underlying conditions and causalities in the sub-systems that might lead this particular phenomenon to emerge. Rising tensions in a team break out in arguments in meetings. Someone quits. The rise of a climate-denial sector of the public. The breakout of mob violence. The Velvet Revolution and the fall of the Berlin Wall.

What emerges in the Context of a human system is the result of complex and dynamic interactions between the Identities that make up that system. What emerges as behaviors and actions of those Identities is the result of complex interactions below the level of awareness: the workings of the Soma. Emergence in a human system always arises from the psychobiologies of the people in the system.

And, we can learn to Sense and to shape the conditions within which emergence takes place.

The emergence of passive-aggressive resistance to Luz's change initiative resulted from complex interactions and causalities. There was a lot of history of which she'd not been a part. A number of unskillful interactions between Luz and faculty, personal dynamics between faculty leaders, and the sheer coincidence of the timing of Luz's arrival with changes in career plans of certain key faculty were just a few of the many moving parts in this system. And, the personalities of all the players were driven by what they had embodied.

Feedback Loops

Feedback loops result when a change in one component of a system creates secondary effects that then influence the original change, either dampening or accelerating that change.

Balancing feedback loops limit change: The feedback effects dampen the original change. For example, team meetings become inefficient, members voice frustration, and together they work to improve meeting processes and facilitation. Deviation from an agreed-upon range of measures triggers corrective action. The population of a species increases until it reaches the limits of the environment to support the population, and then it stabilizes or dies back until a new stasis is reached. Employees are promoted until the reach the limits of their capabilities.

Reinforcing feedback loops feed a virtuous, or vicious, cycle of escalating effects. One action produces an effect that in turn encourages the original action. Arms races, or any kind of zero-sum competition for scarce resources. When leaders motivate followers by fear, morale and performance tend to decline, creating more apparent need for motivation. Melting polar sea ice increases absorption of sunlight by the darker water, which warms the water, which increases the rate of melting. The cycle of mistrust in a marriage. Not exercising makes exercising harder, which reduces motivation to exercise, which leads to less exercising. You get the idea.

*Luz's predecessor had encouraged faculty to publish more and to co-brand truly innovative design projects with the institute. He also backed off pretty quickly when faculty ignored or complained about requests from the dean's office that were perceived as inequitable or that implied faculty were not doing enough for the institution. This was a **balancing feedback loop:** the previous dean was conflict-averse, and the faculty became accustomed to being able to do what they wanted. Any efforts at change triggered quick pushback. **Stasis** was more comfortable for everyone, and the cycle of decline continued until the financial and brand data was irrefutable.*

*However, when Luz began to instigate change, complacent and powerful faculty accused her publicly of strong-arming them and not engaging faculty in a collaborative process. The more she drove the vision, the stronger the voices of concern became. This was a **reinforcing feedback loop**. Luz's pushing for change invited resistance, which invited Luz to raise the tone of her pitch, which invited more resistance, and so forth.*

COMPLEX SYSTEM ELEMENTS

Recognizing some of the common elements in dynamic complex systems increases clarity. These (and other) system elements appear at every level of system:

- Stasis
- Emergence
- Feedback loops
- Disruptors
- Organizing principles
- Polarities
- Stillness

Disruptors

A *disruptor* is some emergent force that upsets the appearance of stasis and slow, evolutionary change; consequences ripple throughout connected systems. Sometimes a disruptor emerges from within a system; sometimes a disruption comes from outside the system. Either way, the system is perturbed, sometimes dramatically, and has to change as a result.

Donald Trump's ascent to power. Apple and Google and Uber and Airbnb. From a larger temporal perspective, the appearance of humans on earth. Receiving difficult feedback. A major health crisis. A competitor's innovation.

*Luz was brought in as a **disruptor** when her predecessor finally retired. The university knew they needed someone who could initiate major change, and Luz had the credibility and passion to upset the stasis. She had a clear mandate for change and the personality to drive it.*

Organizing Principles

Pervasive forces, specific people, or cultural conditions can have a strong organizing power within a system. These strong influences can be so embedded that they are invisible, yet they guide individual and collective behavior in pervasive ways.

Organizing principles is a broad term, and we will explore a number of different forms that they can assume:

- Broad **conditions** of the system can become embedded in organizational culture to the extent that they are invisible. For example, conditions of **connection**, **fluidity** and **stability** are **organizing principles** that run throughout the book. We will work extensively with these conditions in Part Four.

- The **direction** in which we intend to lead the system is a different kind of organizing principle. Leaders can declare, and foster, directions in Complexity that become an organizing principle. Chapter 10 will look at how we can embody a future direction in our leadership.

- Our own **inner states** can also become an organizing principle both personally and for others.

Examples of organizing principles in the systems around us are everywhere. A cultural focus on customer service has given rise to legendary stories of FedEx drivers taking heroic measures on their own authority to deliver packages under extraordinary circumstances; the organizing principle is to take care of the customer, no matter what.[28] An organizing principle of tech-driven radical innovation, on the other hand, can resist "old school" policies and procedures necessary for scaling an organization.[29] Unquestioned cultural assumptions about entitlement impede making the collective sacrifices needed for a stable climate. For me, the drive for success and achievement sometimes has overridden my commitment to home and family. In the Part One example, Rachel's strong focus on employee-friendly initiatives and a culture of care was an organizing principle that also blinded her to other needs.

Organizing principles at Luz's institute included an entrenched reward-and-tenure system that was working well for many individuals, even as it dis-incentivized change, and a culture of prima donna architects that pursued lucrative consulting and design contracts that leveraged the institute's brand for personal gain but returned little money or prestige. A central task of organizational change consists of disrupting stasis and shifting the organizing principles that drive behavior in the system. As Luz discovered, the organizing principles were deeply embedded.

Polarities

Polarities are a common dynamic in complex systems, whether intrapersonal (e.g., the tension between time for work and time for family) or organizational (e.g., product launches often require trade-offs between time-to-market and product quality). Polarities are present when two important values or *organizing principles* (poles) appear to be in conflict with each other, but are actually both vital and important in the long term.

Who would say that time for work and time for family are not both important? Yet the tension between these is difficult, even painful, for nearly every leader I know.

In an organizational Context, a leader driving one pole while ignoring the other will often be surprised by how intransigent the system becomes. Recognizing and leveraging the system of polarities is crucial over time.

Product quality and time to market. Taking care of the mission of the organization and taking care of staff. Institutionalizing best practices across an organization and also stimulating innovation. The absorption of solar energy into the planet and the radiation of that energy back into space. Inhaling and exhaling. Rest and activity.

> One **polarity,** initially invisible to Luz, was the tension between top-down change and faculty ownership. This was not a democratic process, and Luz had been brought in as a **disruptor.** At the same time, faculty ownership was key to success, and Luz's evident take-no-prisoners approach triggered faculty's deepest fears that they would have no voice. A sole reliance on Luz's authority would doom the initiative because of faculty mistrust and resistance. And left to their own devices, faculty would likely ride a sinking ship to the bitter end. Participation from both was essential.
>
> Another **polarity** was the tension between stability and change. Faculty needed some assurance that the things they valued most weren't being stripped away, and creating change as a collective was crucial. Organizing around either pole while ignoring the other would dramatically compromise hopes for progress.

Stillness

All systems have places of openness and uncertainty where things are not yet determined, and a system or decision can flip either way. *Stillness* is a pause. It is the immediacy of the felt realization that multiple possibilities simultaneously exist. When what will happen next is undetermined, there is a space for action outside of the ordinary and precedent.

The element of stillness can be a particularly strong leverage point in Complex systems because stillness is also a component of presence. As we will see in Chapter 7, stillness is our internal experience, in this immediate moment, of openness and possibility.

Holding our breath when everyone senses the elephant in the room, wondering if anyone will name it. The pause before proposing marriage, when we will either speak or not. The moment just before deciding to raise our hand in the meeting, casting our vote for president. The moment of deciding whether to launch a manned rocket or a death-dealing drone strike.

> A key moment came when Luz had the clear recognition that there were dynamics she simply couldn't see. At three o'clock one very early morning, sitting at her kitchen table, there came a palpable moment of clarity. Luz saw clearly that she

would have to learn to lead differently or she would fail. Her acceptance of this reality, though painful, was also strangely comforting. She didn't know what was next, just that something had shifted inside her. At the same time, she had no idea what to do differently, or even where to start.

*Luz's recognition was quickly followed by a deep **stillness**. She felt a pervasive sense of raw acceptance as she realized she was in a very different game than she thought. She saw both that failure was genuinely possible and that she could live with it. If she were really not the right person for this, she would still land on her feet. So would the institute. For now, it was time to rest, and then to begin afresh, learning how to approach her challenge in ways she could not yet see.*

Luz took a deep breath, felt her body relax, went to bed, and slept until ten o'clock the next morning.

This moment of stillness is simultaneously an element of complex systems and a direct experience.

In this moment of clarity and immediacy, Luz faced reality directly and without argument or rationalization. She deeply accepted that what she had been doing wasn't working, and it was time to get curious and be genuinely open to how she might approach her role differently. In that precise moment of acceptance, more became possible both for her and, though nobody could yet know, for the system.

While the realization of what is so can be painful, it is also liberating.

THE REALIZATION OF COMPLEXITY PRODUCES CLARITY

We can learn to recognize these system elements within the complex challenges that face us and our teams. Recognizing and naming these phenomena rapidly deepens our ability to freshly make sense of the world around us and then to act on our world in more informed and skillful ways.

Consider, for a moment, what might be possible if you actually had a more complete and inclusive view of the dynamics in which you are leading…

≈≋ PRESENCE PAUSE ≋≈

Let's be realistic, though. Having this new language and distinctions for observing Complexity doesn't actually tell us what to do! And we have urgent pressures, responsibilities, and goals to meet. We want solutions to immediate problems, and we need them right now!

I promised you stepping stones for navigating the territory of Complexity. Let's explore what this perspective, and the associated stepping stones, can do for us. And what they can't do.

Sensing the Context Doesn't Change It

First, the bad news. This way of Sensing the Context does not make the system around us either predictable or knowable. The realization that invisible but legitimate organizing principles are competing with what we have been trying to accomplish, or that our team has been systematically prioritizing their excitement about new innovations while ignoring a pattern of complaints from customers for some time, provides us neither a precise description of what is happening in the system nor a reliable prediction of what will happen next.

Sadly, our deepened understanding of our Context does not change it. The Context is still complex, and the future still unknowable.

Nor does recognizing and naming elements of Complexity tell us what to do. This perspective is not oriented towards immediate action and doesn't provide quick fixes. That said, our Sensing of the dynamism and the particular tendencies of the system around us may suggest high-leverage intervention points as we move forward.

Sensing the Context Changes Us

The good news, paradoxically, is that our realization changes *us.*

Recognizing and naming the elements of Complexity leads to a greater inner sense of clarity and acceptance. The realization and acceptance of what is true, of how reality is showing up, is not simply an intellectual understanding. Rather, it is the felt experience of clarity. Seeing the world as it is, even in its perversity and intractability, is reassuring to our psychobiology and to our meaning-making processes. We might not know what to do yet, but we can relax in the knowledge that nobody has faced this precise situation before. We can become more patient and compassionate with the lack of a clear and reliable strategy to solve the problem. It is a radically different experience to lack a strategy and assume it's our fault, and to lack a strategy while accepting that we are in a totally new game and there is really none to be had!

Seeing through new eyes opens new space. We have new language for describing the present-moment characteristics of the Context around us. Our world may still be unpredictable, but we begin to glimpse maps of the territory and new distinctions that scaffold observation and learning. We understand *why* things are unpredictable.

Sensing our Context, normalizing it, and accepting what is actually true paradoxically invites new learning out of which, ultimately, new leadership strategies can emerge. A more informed view of our Context, and a relaxed inner state, are far more helpful in Complexity than simply working harder at what has always worked before but is now failing us. While doubling down is a natural default strategy for many of us, it's actually anti-helpful in Complexity!

Having new language can open up different kinds of conversations with other stakeholders in the system. Normalizing and exploring, together, the challenges that face our organization through the lens and language of Complexity, polarities, disruptions or feedback loops can lead to a greater shared understanding and realization of the dynamics that are already affecting everyone. This can provide a huge collective relief.

Last, your *realization provides both permission and logic for slowing down the train and NOT taking immediate action*. You likely tend towards being action-oriented, since you self-identify as a leader. You might, at this point, be thinking, "So, what do I do with this? This is all a bit heady and theoretical, and while it might be interesting, it sheds no light on what I should do differently."

Fair enough. Hold on, though. My claim was never that this approach offers quick prescriptions and solutions. Rather, this perspective leads to a deeper appreciation for how the system around you is *actually* working in reality (as distinct from your mental models of how it *should* work).

Let's get off the action/reaction/action train (often a feedback loop of some sort!) and take a deeper dive into Complexity, towards the end of a fundamentally different internal stance from which to ultimately act. This work is about changing yourself first; only then can you change the world.

This is stillness: the moment in which you recognize that something new is needed, and you don't know what it is. And, yet, here you are…

≈⊙ PRESENCE PAUSE ⊙≈

Experiment 5.1:
Exploring Dynamism in Your Complexity Challenge

Please spend some time exploring your responses to the following questions. Grounding this material in your own situation will make it less theoretical and will support your own realizations about what is at play.

There are many questions here. They will likely not be easy to answer—if they were, they wouldn't actually be useful!

Please be curious as you try on this new Sensing. These are intended to be guiding questions, so feel free to take the questions anywhere that is useful to you.

And don't worry if you don't find responses to everything. Take it lightly, and do what you can with it. Please be realistic that we are simply tilling the soil here. There's no intention to derive actions from this experiment. We are simply inviting a new sense of curiosity, clarity and acceptance about your situation.

- Restate your Complexity Challenge. What are you facing that seems to be unpredictable? Where are the sensible actions on your part producing perverse results?
- *Stasis*: What historical assumptions have you and your colleagues made about stasis that have now been upended by emerging events? What do you suspect you might be seeing as relatively stable and predictable that might actually be more precarious or subject to major change than you thought?
- *Emergence*: What phenomena seem to be appearing out of nowhere that are mysterious and unexpected but that also might reveal underlying conditions and causalities? How is the system behaving in surprising ways?
- *Feedback loops*: What balancing feedback loops do you see which tend to limit change, growth, or instability? What reinforcing feedback loops do you see where one factor exacerbates another, which exacerbates the first, in an accelerating cycle?
- *Disruptors*: What outside environmental factors are disturbing your illusions of stasis? What internal persons or forces are forcing change? How are you a disruptor? Or, what are you tolerating that perhaps you should disrupt?
- *Organizing principles*: What are the forces, people, and cultural norms that seem to have an outsized influence within your Context, either for better or for worse?
- *Polarities*: Where are there entrenched tensions between seemingly opposing interests, both poles of which have positive attributes? What is good about each? What would happen if each were privileged to the complete exclusion of the other?
- *Stillness*: What is unknown? Where is there mobility and radical possibility in the system? What decision is imminent that could really go any direction?

Now, stepping back, where is there new clarity?

What is the internal feeling of whatever realization has resulted from these questions?

CHAPTER SUMMARY

The central realization of this chapter is that while Complexity is dynamic, unknowable, and unpredictable, observing the elements of this dynamism and making them visible is fundamentally reassuring and clarifying. Paradoxically, Sensing the outside Context in new ways doesn't change the Context, but it changes you in ways both subtle and important.

To observe your situation differently, it is helpful to have the stepping stones for differentiating system elements in Complexity. Some useful distinctions include:

- Stasis
- Emergence
- Feedback loops
- Disruptors
- Organizing principles
- Polarities
- Stillness

Naming and describing the elements of Complexity provides a new way to objectify what you were perhaps previously unable to see. While Sensing by itself doesn't automatically change anything, it does reveal potential opportunities for eventual intervention: nudge points where the system might be more open to shifting.

For now, you can relax and accept that things truly are unpredictable and uncontrollable. At core, you realize and accept that it is not a failure of your leadership to not know how to navigate an entirely new territory. What a relief! When you face reality as it is, and accept that your leadership actually requires something new and different, you can take a deep breath and welcome the invitation that your perverse challenge offers. You can experience clarity at seeing things as they are.

Presence, and stillness, enable this more neutral acceptance of reality as it is. Complexity becomes an observable phenomenon, not a mysterious threat. You can get curious.

You are, I trust, facing the dawning realization that leading in Complexity is not simply a matter of "figuring out" what to do. Leading in Complexity is a deeply human endeavor. Your relationship with Complexity, and with yourself in Complexity, is at the core.

Take some time to reflect on what you now realize as a result of this Pane.

- What do you understand differently?
- What are you now curious about?
- What experiments might you try?

～ PRESENCE PAUSE ～

	CONTEXT	IDENTITY	SOMA
SENSING	Observe The System	RECOGNIZE IDENTITY AT STAKE	
BEING			
ACTING			

Sensing Identity:
Recognize Identity at Stake

*The most fundamental assumption of the underground
managerial world is that truth is a good idea when it is
not embarrassing or threatening—the very conditions
under which truth is especially needed.*

– Chris Argyris

*Theories should not begin with assumptions about the
subject under inquiry; they should begin with a close look
at the tool—the mind—that creates these assumptions.*

– Robert Burton

I N THE PREVIOUS CHAPTER, YOU BECAME MORE PRESENT TO YOUR CONTEXT,
viewing the Complexity around you through the lens of new distinctions. You
lifted your own Bell Jar to see Complexity itself with new perspectives and
more clarity. You realized that these new views change you.

This new chapter shifts perspective to look at the self, the next most intimate
level of scale down from Context. Here, you'll experiment with lifting the Bell Jar
on your own *Identity*. This new perspective will support your realization about

how your Identity is constantly and pervasively challenged by the complexity of your Context. And how, at the same time, your Identity is constantly and pervasively shaping that Context.

Sensing your Identity as an integral element of the system of which you are a part will help you make new sense of the ways in which you have been reacting, automatically, to system dynamics. You will begin to Sense the interconnectedness of Context and Identity. As you will see, your Context and your Identity actively create each other. Every level of the Complexity system is dynamically interdependent with the rest.

However tempting it might be to focus outside yourself in the effort to solve problems, any perspective that excludes your own Identity is partial and myopic.

Luz's Identity on the line

Before the liberating breakdown described in the previous chapter, Luz had come to a crisis of confidence. Her first four months on the job had been characterized by setback after setback. Continual questioning of her motives, methods and integrity had eroded the strong self-confidence with which she entered the picture, and the clear mandate from the administration had made little progress.

Clearly, it was up to her to establish direction. Over and over, Luz made the arguments for the needed changes in structure, performance evaluation and accountability, recruitment of strong green design thought leaders, and re-branding efforts. To her, the changes were common sense. Her case in public was that the future of the institute depended on these changes. In private, she felt her career path and reputation as a strong leader were on the line.

When otherwise brilliant faculty kept putting their heads in the sand, acting as if everything were fine and stubbornly resisting her efforts to coalesce a consensus for change, it was infuriating to Luz. The more they resisted, the more urgent her efforts became, and the more fierce and personal the resistance became.

After months of personal attacks in faculty meetings, passive-aggressive ignoring of dean's office directives, and dysfunctional committee meetings, Luz was working longer and harder than ever. She was anxious, sleepless and frustrated. Trying to shift this organization was like one of those Whack-a-Mole games: Every time she solved a problem, another would creep up.

Each of us has a core social Identity[30] that we, mostly unconsciously, construct and defend throughout our lifetime—and that, to a large extent, developed from the conditioning of early childhood and countless other historical influences.

We are, in essence, three-year-olds in the bodies of CEOs, coaches, activists, executive directors, and engineers!

Our Identity is who we hold ourselves to be. "I am a kind person." "I am a strong leader of change." "I am a creative innovator, a pioneer, a caring mom, a committed activist, etc., etc." Identity provides us with a reassuring sense of orientation, worth, meaning and value. It's our self-representation and our felt experience of who we are.

While these self-descriptors may be largely true, they also are constructions of our psychobiology. Identities are the organism's way of meaning-making about who we are in the world. They are simplifications that equip us to navigate a complex world.

Identities also restrict our possibilities. Our Identities are Bell Jars through which we filter the complexity of reality, attuning to what is important and relevant to the preservation of our Identity, and ignoring what our psychobiology filters out, below the level of awareness, as not relevant. The tremendous cost of this oversimplification is that we mistake this filtered reality for actual reality.

As leaders, we must access perspectives sufficiently outside of ourselves to realize how the Complexity in our Context both evokes and challenges our precious Identity. This is the first step towards observing our unconscious reactions and tendencies. Only then can we hope to intervene in ourselves in new ways that can potentially be dramatically more effective at evoking the results that we care about most.

Identity Has a Mind of Its Own

It can be helpful to think of our Identity as a willful intelligence unto itself. Although we usually are blind to this, as we become more present to ourselves, we also become more able to see how our Identity is impacted by the human systems around us, and how it constantly and skillfully self-organizes in order to preserve itself.

Recognizing Identity

As we discussed in Chapter 2, our Identity develops in a set of conditions to which we adapted through an accumulating set of strengths, behaviors and meaning-making that eventually became ossified as a personality. In fact, because Identity is just "the way we are," we tend to be blind to it, just as the fish can't recognize the water it swims in. Identity is our Bell Jar. It has an internal stability, a *stasis*, that is astoundingly impervious to new information, to self-reflection, and to change.

I offer this brief background on myself as an example both of how Identity develops—and how crucial it is to recognize it as a key driver of our behavior and our meaning-making.

A personal story of Identity formation

I grew up in a family of achievers. PhDs run in my family. I grew up assuming I could do what I wanted in life, and while I often made things considerably harder for myself than they needed to be, I had an underlying basic trust in my capabilities, which got reinforced by putting myself into situations that would be challenging and would require me to figure things out.

Invisibly to me, this sense of capability was reinforced by a world that privileged being white, male, tall, American, heterosexual and educated. As an adult, people assumed I knew what I was talking about (even when I didn't) and extended to me a certain respect that I took for granted. From inside my Bell Jar I was unable to recognize this privilege, even though it shaped me from an early age.

As a skinny, nerdy kid, I was also an easy mark for physical and emotional bullying at school. Several years were excruciating. I learned painfully about being excluded, gave myself nosebleeds to escape the torture of gym class, and practiced being small and inoffensive in order to not be a target.

At the same time, I liked intense experiences. High-risk adolescent behaviors evolved into a core Identity of adventure and experimentation that demanded constant new experiences that required new skills and capabilities.

It's also true that this Identity (even now) seems to need constant reinforcement. As an intensity junkie, I don't quite know how to orient myself in life without some kind of challenge. One perspective is that I am adventurous; another is that I need continual affirmation of this fundamental sense of self through deeds and the appreciation of others.

I am aware of a strong internal voice that criticizes what I have done or finds it wanting compared to the braver, more noble, or greater accomplishments of others. This voice implores me to do more, to stay busy, to create new things, to write books, to do works in the world. This voice does everything possible to prop up this Identity of mine in ways that have worked acceptably well for over sixty years.

Talking about my Identity also feels a bit self-conscious: like exposing some dirty little secret that is best left in a dark closet in the corner!

I suspect that you, writing or speaking publicly about your own Identity, would also feel some self-consciousness. For the most part, I want to reassure you, our Identities are a useful and worthy phenomenon. It is psychologically necessary to think of ourselves as good people who are well-intentioned, competent and doing the best we can.

Yet it is important to both describe and own our Identity, including the shadow aspects that drive our incessant and urgent efforts to underpin and perpetuate it. These are particularly difficult to recognize, precisely because they are contrary to the self-image we are working so hard to maintain. I like my adventuresome, experimental self. And I'm not so proud of the insecure, defended aspects of me that self-organize to validate my Identity through the acceptance and appreciation of others.

Recognizing and Sensing our own Identity at work is a fundamental part of making the Complexity system visible. As a leader in Complexity, it is convenient to leave out this piece of the puzzle. However, this is perilous indeed: Even when we don't see it, others already have. And, it affects everything.

So, please take a look.

Experiment 6.1:
Describe Your Identity

Take a few minutes to write out a statement of who you are. This should include the things you are proud of, the ways you hope to be seen, your sense of who you are at core. And what are you not so sure about? What do you doubt? How do you organize yourself to perpetuate and validate this Identity?

"I am…."

Identity Drives the Train

It is also hard to see how our Identity is foundational for everything we think and do. Identity serves as a working construction of a self, and so we actively enhance and defend it every moment of every day. The realization of the pervasiveness and invisibility of the *organizing principle* of Identity explains much about why we react as we do. While

Identity motivates us and propels us through life, it simultaneously and drastically limits our range of possibilities, especially in conditions that require creativity and resilience.

Luz's Identity as a strong leader of change was deeply threatened by the natural behaviors of the system around her, and this was existentially difficult for her to see. From inside her Bell Jar, it looked like the faculty and leadership team of the institute were myopic and self-serving. Luz was completely unable to see how her own Identity was at stake. Nor could she see how her psychobiology continually generated behaviors in the system that were anti-helpful and that actually reinforced very destructive feedback loops.

Identity is always a driver

I will share a bit more of my own journey before moving into an approach that can help us realize how our Identity contributes to what we don't want to have happen.

In the late 1980s, I cofounded a boutique consulting company integrating outdoor experiential-training methodologies with more traditional organization development. Work frequently took me across the U.S. and overseas. It was heady and exciting and challenging. I loved having my own business, and the feedback from clients continually reinforced my Identity as smart, resourceful, caring and authentic. I was producing income for my family, which is a core component of my male Identity, engrained from an early age.

At the same time, my home life felt complex: a challenging relationship, young children, and all the messiness of a growing family. I was in the midst of the classic tension that so many leaders experience: seeking to balance professional commitments with home and family.

I'm not proud of how the dynamics of Identity preservation drove me at that time. With 20/20 hindsight, it is easy to see how compulsive my professional drive became. My worklife was inherently interesting. It also strongly reinforced my sense of self-worth. Disappearing into my professional world sometimes selfishly contributed to avoiding the difficulties and messiness of home, which reliably revealed my limits and flaws!

We had young children. Walker, my wife, pushed back, telling me I was gone too much. I resented this, justifying my own behavior as being what my nascent business needed and as being good for our family economics. While this was true, it also conveniently masked the shadow side of my Identity and allowed me to avoid addressing the marital polarization that my behavior was producing. In my Complex Identity system, business was trumping family.

Eventually, we negotiated a reasonable agreement that limited my work travel and provided more balanced roles at home. However, it wasn't until my

*Identity **included and transcended** my professional life to find fulfillment in the messiness of home that Walker and I emerged from being adversarial into seeing our interests as being fundamentally aligned.*

This example is different from the Bend of Ivy example in Chapter 2. Yet with what I have shared here about my Identity, it is probably not hard for you to imagine how my personal and myopic drive for accomplishment later ended up sabotaging Walker's authority on the construction site. In both situations, my Identity, unbeknownst to me, was driving the train.

Yours is too.

～ PRESENCE PAUSE ～

Triggers, Attachments and Aversions: Identity Preserving Itself

The organizing principle of our Identity system is to produce a moment-by-moment stabilization of our sense of self, one that is stable, positive and assured. It is also relentless, unconscious, and automatic.

This relentless, automatic drive toward a reliable sense of self is mostly invisible to us, though often blatantly obvious to others. For example, Walker could easily spot my work addiction, while in my mind I was "earning a living."

Scaffolding this sense of Identity is the very ground of our Being. It guides our meaning-making and our resultant actions throughout our entire lives. Like heat-seeking missiles, we pursue experiences and opportunities that nourish our Identity and our sense of self; we avoid experiences that challenge our Identity too much.

Yet, stuff happens. We advocate for an idea in a meeting and someone questions our integrity. We get an unexpected request that derails our priorities. Our funding is cut off. A competitor introduces a disruptive new service. These events are ***triggers***: external inputs that ***disrupt*** our well-laid vision of how things will happen and, with it, our internal experience of ***stasis***. Triggers typically elicit unhelpful reactions that arise from our psychobiology's embodied Identity-preservation mechanisms.

The realization of this, in the present moment, is fundamental to behavior change and to development.

～ PRESENCE PAUSE ～

EXPERIENCING IDENTITY PRESERVATION

Our psychobiologies are marvelously designed to produce and defend our identities. We experience evidence of our own self-organization in:

- *Triggers*: events or stimuli that our nervous system interprets as a threat or an opportunity.

- *Attachments*: the internal drives for "positive" experiences that will enhance Identity.

- *Aversions*: the internal drives to avoid "negative" experiences that threaten identity.

Before every action is an **action impulse**. These action impulses are somatic, conditioned urges. They are design features of our nervous system that we can Sense, recognize, and intervene into. While they originally served our physical survival, for most of us, they serve the purpose of perpetuating Identity. To our psychobiology, physical and Identity survival are one and the same.

Our action impulses have two directions, depending on whether they are driven by **attachments** or by **aversions**. My two previous books,[31] and extensive references throughout Buddhist literature,[32] offer thorough explorations of attachments and aversions.

We experience **attachment** as a pull or an urge towards an organizing principle of some sort. That organizing principle might be another person, power, a substance like wine or chocolate, or a particular quality of experience. The attachment itself is internal, even if the object of the attachment is something outside our self.

We respond to attachments with increased energy and excitement. We are deeply conditioned towards sex, towards eating and drinking things that lead to feeling good, toward achievement and recognition and power and comfort and money. Attachments by themselves are value-neutral and biological, although Identity-preserving attachments naturally lead to actions that might be either life-affirming or destructive. The attachment to the rush and excitement of creative problem-solving can lead to socially conscious business ventures or to robbing a bank. The attachment to achievement can lead to new innovations or to damaging others to climb faster up the corporate ladder. The attachment to being a provider led me to a successful business as a consultant and author, but it deprived me and my family of precious time together when our kids were babies.

Aversions are the opposite. Again, aversions have an object: an organizing principle outside ourselves that we resist or avoid because we don't want to experience unpleasantness, pain or injury. The original reasons for aversions are obvious: Avoiding deadly snakebites, moving away from someone intending violence, or stepping back from the edge of a high cliff are sensible self-protective urges designed for survival. And this same felt experience of aversion now drives us to avoid holding delicate conversations, delegating tasks that feed our Identities, speaking truth to power or questioning widely held assumptions in our own organization.

Our Identity-based attachments and aversions distort our responses to our worlds, privileging our Identity's need for reassurance and validation over what might actually be helpful. In fact, attachments and aversions are the unconscious means by which our psychobiology self-organizes in order to maintain stasis.

Often the needs of our Context for creative new responses are not aligned with our Identity's needs for stasis. Something new is being asked of us, but our historically conditioned attachments and aversions are dedicated to preserving Identity, not necessarily to responding optimally to what the world is asking of us. In fact, our Identity Bell Jar filters out relevant information and blinds us to the potentialities of a bigger perspective.

Attachments and aversions precede and drive every action we take. They are triggered by what happens in our Context, and they drive actions that in turn impact that Context. In this co-arising and dynamic interaction of Identity and Context, you might recognize the shape of a feedback loop.

The moment-by-moment realization of how we are unconsciously preserving our Identity is a crucial step towards a more nuanced understanding of how our Identity and our Context interact and influence each other.

Experiment 6.2:
Attachments and Aversions

Please note a couple of places in which you experience Identity-based attachments and aversions within your Complexity Challenge.

1. What attachments do you recognize? What are you drawn towards? (Attachments are often experienced as a drive, an urge, a surge of energy.)
    *   I am attached to:
    *   I want to be seen as:

2. What aversions do you recognize? What are you avoiding? (Aversions are often experienced as a contraction, revulsion, or a move away.)
    *   I am averse to:
    *   I don't want to be seen as:

COMPLEXITY INHERENTLY CHALLENGES IDENTITY

Realizing that our experience within Complexity is always and perpetually Identity-based is a crucial stepping stone in accessing our capacity to respond to it differently. The inherent unpredictability of Complexity means that stasis is precarious; Identity finds itself threatened, sometimes existentially.

Our Identity is linked to success, and therefore to predicting and controlling and solving. We are attached to solving a problem or making progress or achieving results. (Our definition of success.) We have an aversion to looking inadequate, feeling stuck, not getting a good performance review or a promotion, or failing. (Experiences inconsistent with our Identity.)

We can count on Complexity's threats and disruptions to trigger our psychobiological attachments and aversions. While these Identity-preservation mechanisms intend to be our friends, they also generate a constant stream of self-justifying internal chatter. And they produce behavioral responses that are automatic, reactive and sometimes tragically maladapted to our own aspirations.

These phenomena are simply the result of our historical conditioning. They are secondary to the natural and pervasive processes of constructing and maintaining intact our sense of who we are.

Luz responded to organizational resistance to her change initiative by selling the vision and driving new institutional processes. Tightening down and pushing harder were natural expressions of Luz's instinctual attachments to power and success. She experienced a strong aversion to resistance that clearly posed a threat to her success and therefore to her Identity. The stronger the resistance, the more threatened her Identity became, and the more she tightened down in ways that were anti-helpful: a classic reinforcing feedback loop.

As with Luz, few leaders are trained to Sense the Complexity dynamics of the systems around us. Rather, we Sense, and react to, the particular symptoms of those dynamics that our psychobiology interprets as Identity threats or opportunities. Attachments and aversions arise, and we then act to advance success as our Identity has defined it.

But, like Luz, we don't even see how Identity functions as an organizing principle that values some possibilities at the expense of others. As a result, we simply don't see other possibilities that might be far more generative and useful. They are simply unavailable.

Identification

We are starting to see how intimately the Identities of leaders become entangled with the dynamics of the Context. These two levels of system—Context and Identity—are continuously influencing, and are influenced by, the other.

Identification is when our Identity fuses with the Context to the point that our sense of self "in here" is predicated on the results we obtain "out there." This lack of boundaries makes it exponentially harder to know how and where to act as a leader in Complexity. Everything has become personal, and thus a reflection on ourselves.

Are we intervening in the Context because that's what the Context needs, or because that's what our Identity needs? When we are identified in this way, it is literally impossible to tell. Context and Identity are connected, but not differentiated. Luz's sense of herself became so personally entangled with her role and the changes she intended that she lost her perspective and became overidentified with the role.

Luz gorgeously illustrates the costs of identification and of its invisibility. Focused externally, she experienced the systems she was leading as intractable and perverse. It seemed impossible to find a way to intervene that made a difference.

For Luz, it was both difficult and liberating to realize how her Identity had become "hooked" and how her Identity-defending attachments and aversions were actually contributing to the dynamics she experienced as perverse and intractable. Only by differentiating her Identity from the Context could Luz begin to find new leverage points that eventually produced something very different.

Dis-Identification: Differentiating Identity from Context

Four key differentiation questions provide useful entry points for this essential dis-identification process. By realizing the nature of our interconnections between our Identity and the Context within which we are leading, we come to see that the very relatedness requires differentiation as well.

What aspects of the Context trigger our attachments? Some elements of our challenges nourish and feed our Identity. There are aspects that inspire us to do our best, and the very taking on of a challenge is a reflection of our Identity as we sense an opportunity. We are energized by the sense that our work matters, that we have an opportunity to develop people, to solve problems and to bring new possibilities into being. Our Identity is fed and enhanced by these "good things."

What aspects trigger our aversions? There are also elements in any challenge that we resist. We have aversions to specific people, to policies, to failure, to authority, to unpredictability, to interpersonal tension, etc. These difficulties tend to trigger self-doubt or reactivity as our Identity senses a threat of some sort and responds accordingly. Recognizing the sources of these threats is the first step towards building the resilience to face difficulties with less reactivity and more creativity.

For what aspirations do we serve as an organizing principle? Our Identity, and the resulting ways we show up in our Context, can be a powerful organizing force in the system. Our existence in our team or organization is a blank screen onto which others project their own Identity-based aspirations and fears. Knowing what we represent in our Context, and what we trigger in others that is helpful, is profoundly revealing.

What do we trigger in the system that is unhelpful? There are also ways that our Identity serves as a trigger in the system for dynamics that are unhelpful. Of course, that's not our intention; most of us are consistently doing our absolute best to construct and maintain a sense of self in a complex world. But, good intentions aside, our behaviors also reliably trigger the attachments and aversions of others.

With the benefit of hindsight, or through outside perspective, these dynamics are sometimes easier to see. It's likely you could see some of the entanglements playing out in the story of Luz we have been unfolding over the past couple of chapters. However, it's very unlikely that from within your own Bell Jar, you could possibly recognize all of the many ways in which you have become identified with your Context. (By the way, though this is not the topic of this book, a marriage or intimate relationship is most certainly a Context in which these dynamics play a big part and are

---

FOUR DIS-IDENTIFICATION QUESTIONS FOR CLARITY

Our Identities are entangled with our Context. We increase clarity by Sensing the dynamic interdependence of these two levels of system. These questions help:

- What aspects of the Context trigger our attachments?
- What aspects trigger our aversions?
- For what aspirations do we serve as an organizing principle?
- What do we trigger in the system that is unhelpful?

particularly difficult to see because of the emotional intensity and the many ways our Identity is at stake.)

Let's revisit Luz to see how she became able to realize her own contributions to her difficulties.

Luz recognizes her overidentification

Luz, at the end of Chapter 5, had a realization, paradoxically finding peace in the acceptance that what she had been doing was actually not working. She reframed her challenge from that of driving this change process to that of seizing a remarkable and unique opportunity to develop as a leader. This started with looking in the mirror.

Luz had come into her role with a remarkable track record as an academic. She was great at raising grant money and running research programs. She had led departments at other universities but never a difficult turnaround in a big, complex organization. Luz's realization revealed the fundamental inadequacy of her go-to strengths for a significantly new Context.

Luz reached out for coaching support. Stepping back from her situation, which was getting more intractable and hostile every week, she began to tease apart the system dynamics, including how she was affected by, and contributed to, them.

*Luz began to see the many ways her Identity had become entangled with the change process. Significant change had been advocated by the university administration during hiring. **Attachments to her Identity had been triggered by the hiring committee**, who had complimented her as a strong and fiercely committed change leader. This attachment amplified Luz's natural driving energy, which was immediately visible to faculty during her hasty onboarding process. Her personal aspirations were all over vision for change.*

*Faculty in the system were mostly attached to **stasis**; Luz was obviously a **disruptor**. The organizing principle for Luz's Identity was visionary and rapid change, and she intended to inspire others by communicating this direction clearly and frequently. However, **her leadership Identity actually served as an organizing principle for others' aversions.** Luz's passion and energy threatened many faculty with the potential loss of a tacit arrangement with the institute that benefited them, even at an unsustainable cost to the organization. This made Luz a lightning rod for concerns and fears.*

She cared deeply about and was committed to success. However, she automatically interpreted resistance as a threat to her Identity. The resistance, of course, was a natural and inevitable expression of underlying system dynamics of polarities, feedback loops, stasis and her arrival as a disruptor. Lacking this *perspective, **Luz was triggered by her aversions to behaviors that, from within her Bell Jar, she saw as regressive and childish.***

*Luz began to recognize the perversity of the reinforcing feedback loop she was unintentionally contributing to. Her reactivity led to doubling down on the very actions that evoked the resistance in the first place. Through Luz's overidentification, her **Identity became a trigger for the organizing principles of stasis and resistance**, rather than for the aspirational vision she cared so much about!*

*It became imperative for Luz to slow down, to cultivate a better understanding of how the system was really working, and to enroll as many faculty as possible as partners in the process. She needed to **become an organizing principle that could coalesce energy for change**, rather than driving it through will, effort and persuasion.*

Luz was astute enough to recognize, after a very rough start, that she now faced a major developmental opportunity. Clearly, her Identity was a key element in this Complex system.

More generally, it is a given that leader Identity dynamics will have an important influence on systems. Our personalities, and the behaviors and interpretations that arise from them, are crucial components of the conditions from which a system self-organizes to produce precisely the results it gets. Yet, paradoxically, our Bell Jars, and the self-justifying narratives they produce, mean that we often don't recognize the Complexity dynamics of how we and our Context influence each other. As leaders, we must become skillful at recognizing and negotiating more skillfully with our own Identity, about which we tend to be rather blind.

A crucial stepping stone towards this foundational capacity is ***self-observation***. In self-observation, we take on a structured practice of witnessing ourselves in action. We begin to develop a new perspective. We witness how we are hooked by the system, how we act habitually in ways that might not be so helpful. And we begin to recognize the narratives that we have held as truth but that might actually be either partial or wrong.

Experiment 6.3:
Differentiating Identity from Context

Explore the interactions between your Identity and your Context. Use the four questions to discover how aspects of the Context might be triggering you. And how your Identity, for better or for worse, might be acting as an organizing principle for others.

Questions:
- What aspects of the Context trigger your attachments?
- What aspects trigger your aversions?
- What aspirational organizing principles do you represent?
- What are you actually triggering in the system that is unhelpful?

In summary, what is at stake for your Identity? What reframing of your Identity might be possible here?

Core Practice 6.4:
Self-Observation: Identity in Action

Self-observation is a powerful practice for observing yourself in action. Over time, it can produce significant improvements in your capacity for awareness and choice in the moment. Self-observation is a way to bring presence and awareness to a particular aspect of Complexity that has been previously invisible, but about which you will benefit by being more aware.

Self-observation rests on doing it with rigor over some period of time. It doesn't have to take long. (Say, ten minutes a day.) But it does have to be done consistently. (Like, every day!)

- For this particular practice, select your response to one of the four questions in the previous experiment. Choose the one that is interesting to you and where you suspect the dynamic might be significant.
- At the end of each day (before leaving work, at bedtime, or at a consistently maintained time convenient to you) simply jot down a few notes on paper about when this particular triggering event was occurring. Who were you with? What happened? How did you feel? What did you do or say? What was the effect?

Do this daily for at least three weeks.

Then, jot notes about what you noticed as you look across several weeks of self-observations. What patterns do you see? What significance might this have? What new possibilities are being revealed?

CHAPTER SUMMARY

You took a new perspective on your Identity itself, stepping out of your Bell Jar to see its centrality and to recognize the embodied mechanisms that defend and preserve its stasis.

It is the very nature of Complexity to trigger your Identity in ways extremely difficult to recognize because of your identification with your Context. This is the core realization of the chapter. Differentiating your Identity from the Complexity around you, and recognizing your triggering as it arises, are fundamental to skillful leadership.

As stepping stones for this exploration of Identity, you worked with new distinctions that help you observe and make sense of how your Identity is challenged by your Context, as well as how you likely trigger others. You saw how these two interdependent levels of system (Context and Identity) are continually influencing each other.

Towards the present-moment realization of these dynamics, and your ability to make choices in the moment, you now have new stepping stones and distinctions that can support your observation of yourself in your leadership Context:

- **Triggers:** external inputs that your psychobiology instantly interprets as opportunities or as threats
- **Attachments and aversions:** the automatic internal urges that are rooted in your psychobiology and that support and protect your Identity
- **Identification:** the fusing of your Identity with the Context
- **Dis-identification:** the differentiation of your Identity from the Context
- Four questions that can help you dis-identify from the Context by realizing the nature of their interactions.

With these distinctions, you can observe the intricate dance of entanglement between your Identity and the Complex system in which you lead.

You might take a moment to appreciate the perverse irony here. The very unpredictability of your Context, which requires clarity and creative new thinking and actions, triggers exactly the opposite in you, a central component of this Context. Dis-identifying from this Context enough to get clarity about how you are truly being affected is the first step to returning to resourcefulness.

Presence supports this more detached and accepting perspective on yourself. New practices now available to you include recognizing in the moment how you are triggered, using the four questions to disentangle your Identity from the system, and doing self-observation of your Identity reactions over time.

Applying these practices to your own Complexity Challenge will begin to invite more daylight on the connectedness between your Identity and what's happening in your Context. This realization of the interaction of these two levels of system can be quite liberating!

Take some time to reflect on what you now realize as a result of this Pane.

- What do you understand differently?
- What are you now curious about?
- What experiments might you try?

⋙ PRESENCE PAUSE ⋘

	CONTEXT	IDENTITY	SOMA
SENSING	Observe The System	Recognize Identity At Stake	ATTEND TO EXPERIENCE
BEING			
ACTING			

CHAPTER 7

Sensing Soma: Attend to Experience

*There is deep wisdom within our very flesh, if we can
only come to our senses and feel it.*

— Elizabeth A. Behnke

*Somewhere in this process, you will come face to face
with the sudden and shocking realization that you are
completely crazy. Your mind is a shrieking, gibbering
madhouse on wheels barreling pell-mell down the hill,
utterly out of control and hopeless.*

*No problem. You are not crazier than you were yesterday.
It has always been this way and you never noticed.*

— Henepola Gunaratana

*If the brain were so simple we could understand it, we
would be so simple we couldn't.*

— Lyall Watson

Luz's body tells the truth

*When I met Luz, she was pretty stressed. Although she had already experienced
the moment of epiphany and stillness described in Chapter 5, it came after
months of real struggle. Her deep realization led to acceptance that she was*

suffering and very likely to fail unless she made some significant but as-yet unfathomable changes. Recognition of the need to change was not a solution. It was simply an opening.

Luz had not been sleeping. She had been spending long hours in meetings, making the case for change, trying to align prima-donna faculty and department heads, and responding to accusations and rather personal attacks. Some of these attacks were ungrounded, and some had enough basis that they stung. Her neck was tight, her back hurt, her blood pressure was up again, and she was exhausted.

Luz's was a body revealing in every possible way that her struggles were to no avail. Her profound moment of stillness, and the deep relaxation of her body, can be seen as a dramatic collapse of her Identity-preservation strategies.

Paradoxically, this tacit admission of failure is both dramatically vulnerable and liberating. In that moment, the likely trajectory of her deanship (and her health) had finally become undeniable and she was able to face the truth of this for the first time.

In this shift to accepting reality as it was, Luz's reset began.

In the previous chapters, you double-clicked the Pane of **Sensing Context** to begin to realize some of the ways in which Complexity produces the experience of unpredictability and even overwhelms.

You double-clicked on **Sensing Identity** to realize how your psychobiology defends your sense of who you are. You began to experience how your Identity works overtime to preserve itself, reacting strongly and unconsciously to perceived threats, constantly interacting with the Context. You are realizing that this has implications for your Complexity Challenge.

Still, Identity clearly has its own volition, and your best intentions are sometimes hijacked by automatic reactions to triggering events. A key to building increased mastery as a leader is to include your interior experience in your deepening understanding of the dynamics of Complexity. It is time to turn your attention to **Sensing Soma**: the most intimate and interior of our three nested levels of system.

By directing your attention to these nuanced internal phenomena, you will begin to sense the psychobiological underpinnings of your Identity. This next smaller level of the system contains the deeply human but previously hidden internal processes of thinking, feeling and sensing. This perspective is a profound window into your psychobiology as it metabolizes energy and information, self-organizing moment by moment.

You will realize that your Soma system is something that you can both intervene in and leverage. You will double-click on Sensing your Soma, which of course is in dynamic interaction with Identity and Context. Including this more intimate level will reveal pragmatic and nonconventional opportunities for shifting the whole Complex system.

SOMA, IDENTITY AND ATTENTION

What does the body have to do with things? Well, everything. Or, nearly everything.

Every idea, action, behavior, or project begins in the body. Recall that our *Soma* is the conditioned physiological structure (psychobiology) that holds our Identity in place. Soma is the source of our entire experience, ranging from anger, irritation, frustration and fear to our sense of connection, awe and gratitude. Soma is the source of the behaviors and actions that arise from within to express our leadership.

To reiterate, ***attachments and aversions*** are underlying predispositions of the Soma. They are organizing principles for the construction and preservation of Identity. We instinctively seek rewards (chocolate, a slot machine payoff, sexual intimacy, the feeling of power, success and accomplishment). We avoid unpleasantness (things that taste bad or that we have been conditioned to avoid: emotional and physical pain, interpersonal tension, a challenge to our Identity, the loss of wealth, power or privilege, etc.).

Together, these attachments and aversions underpin every action. The bad news is that these largely unconscious but omnipresent attachments and aversions drive us to a degree we cannot begin to imagine.

The good news is that awareness of our ***inner states***—the internal constellations of experience that reveal our attachments and aversions at any moment in time—is the key to choice. Through awareness of our states, we can navigate Complexity more wisely. We can lead in ways that are less driven by our Identity and more supportive of the results we actually seek to evoke.

Our Soma Is Committed to Protecting Our Identity, Not to Being Reasonable

When I have made mistakes, especially the innocent ones that become hard-earned learning moments, 20/20 hindsight often reveals where I overrode some gut feel at the time. I am remarkably capable of dismissing my *felt sense*[33]—

this gut feel, or inner knowing—in favor of a ready-at-hand narrative that conveniently supports my Identity in some way.

For example, during the Bend of Ivy Lodge construction, I recall the precise internal feeling that preceded my intervening with the carpenters. As described in Chapter 2, my interventions undermined my wife's authority on the job site, creating easily preventable project and marital messes.

I'm not proud of this, but hindsight provides a clear picture of what happened. I would visit the job site after returning from travel. I'd see a problem that wasn't being attended to, or something that wasn't being done right. I felt a rising energy in my chest, an emotion of impatience and frustration, and an internal commentary that the problem would mean costly delay or rework. I told myself that Walker might not see this problem, that fixing it without involving her would be helpful. If there was a queasiness in my belly, or a sense of unease about jumping in, my psychobiology rescued me from this fleeting discomfort by instantly producing the stronger urge to jump in to intervene in the carpenters, immediately followed by the quick and reassuring narrative that she'd be okay because of my good intentions. "After all, it was for the good of the project."

I was hijacked, unconsciously but certainly, by my attachment to my Identity as a knowledgeable builder and a supportive husband. I took care of this Identity by overriding my *felt sense*: this subtle inner knowledge that was available to me but that, surfing the wave of my attachment, I blew right past. Of course, I knew that something was off. But justifying my action with a convenient narrative, I sabotaged my wife's authority in the delusion that I was helping her, rather than just indulging my own attachment.

With hindsight, I can see clearly how processes in my inner state justified destructive behavior. Propping up my own Identity was incurring big costs in the project and my marriage. What might have been different if I'd had that awareness in the moment? What different choices might I have made?

Somatic Literacy and the Sensing System

Present-moment awareness of our somatic experience in Complexity is available to us in every moment. It opens access to valuable information about the underlying drivers of our behaviors as we become more present to ourselves. However, it requires slowing down enough to pay attention to our inner experience. It requires developing *somatic literacy*—a sensitivity to, and awareness of, our own internal thoughts, feelings, sensations and urges.

In our work together in this book, this present-moment awareness is not for the sake of feeling good. Full disclosure: It's not remotely our goal to be blissed out in the midst of difficulties!

On the contrary, we seek skillful means that lead to results that matter. Since our actions arise from internal conditions, becoming more present to ourselves allows fuller understanding. This understanding of the whole Complex system directly and pragmatically shapes the choices we make about how to lead.

Sensing the Context itself is important, of course. So is recognizing how our Identity is at stake in this Context, and how it serves as an organizing principle for everything that we think and do. However, *Sensing our Soma—the third of our three nested levels of system—leads to the present-moment realization of our Identity-preserving processes themselves.* Directing our attention into our inner experience, we access early signals about how our psychobiology is responding to the world. We recognize our Identity-preservation reactions *before* they manifest in behaviors. Somatic literacy provides an early warning system that allows different leadership moves than might otherwise be available to us.

Awareness as an Iceberg

I have several times had the rare privilege of sea-kayaking in the presence of giant icebergs. White and sublime, they are one of the most beautiful and moving sights I have experienced in a lifetime of seeking awe.

Its elegant and graceful form seeming to float above the water, the iceberg hides its vastness beneath the surface. What is visible is actually determined and supported by the great invisible mass of ice submerged.

In our metaphor, the ice that is visible represents the contents of our consciousness at any point in time. The psychobiological origins of this consciousness, however, exist below the surface. They are invisible, yet absolutely determine what is visible.

Hundreds of billions of neurons in a seething intricate dance of electrochemical processes give rise to everything in our awareness. Every experience we have or ever will have is given to us by this miracle. Your experience in this very moment, reading these words, is the result of automatic sensory and meaning-making processes taking place far below the level of your awareness.

Take a moment to pause and to Sense into this marvelous consciousness.

≈⊚ PRESENCE PAUSE ⊘≈

Science is only beginning to understand how consciousness arises from the meat that we are. And, for our purposes, it's actually not that important. For us, the important realization is that *anything that arises to awareness, above the waterline, was previously determined below the waterline.* "Competing coalitions of neurons"[34] vie for our attention based on the conditioning we have embodied. Our embodied habits, below the level of awareness, decide what is important enough to run up the flagpole of our awareness.

Originally designed for our physical survival, these automatic processes now work equally well to construct and defend our Identity. In fact, to our nervous system, this is pretty much the same deal. "Hey! There's a lion! Run!" "Hey! Your boss left a message! High alert!" "Hey! Finish this email before you go home or the world will fall apart." All of these alarms arise from the same components of our psychobiology.

For most of us, most of the time, our moods, sensations, and thoughts just happen in the background as we are paying attention to what's happening outside ourselves. Even as they are pervasively shaping our experience and driving our behaviors, we don't recognize them.

Sensing the subtleties of our internal experience gives us a radical new stepping stone for mastery. The key is attention.

Executive Control of Attention

Our built-in capacity to choose what we pay attention to is the big enchilada of presence. Our *executive control of attention* is a built-in functionality of our nervous system. Having this means we can focus our attention wherever we wish. This is the ultimate source of agency.

Our executive control of attention allows us to:

- Access information and wisdom available internally and externally

- Increase sensitivity to the subtle internal urges that precede every action

- Exercise inhibitory control to stop ourselves from unhelpful reflexive behaviors

- Regulate our state to access resilience and creativity

- Choose deliberate new actions

- Embody new learning by propagating inner states across our entire nervous system

- Maintain internal stability in a complex world

- Cultivate leadership presence palpable to others

Yes. These are big claims.

Executive control of attention is central to everything that follows in this book. It is the connective tissue that cuts across the Nine Panes, allowing us to shift fluidly across nine unique and complementary perspectives, to double-click on any one of them, or to see them as an interdependent dynamic whole that gives us aliveness, depth, and meaning. It is the key to leadership mastery, and to developing the capacities for clarity and resilience that are the core promise of this book.

Training your attention is the foundation. Witness that you are, in this moment, actively choosing what you do with your attention. Relish your executive control of attention. It provides the keys to the kingdom.

⁓ PRESENCE PAUSE ⁓

In the next section, you will begin to practice with your executive control of attention. Your development of this capacity will provide a reliable foundation for nearly everything that follows.

THE AWARENESS MAP

Your awareness is like a radio that can be attuned to any of many stations with different content. Your executive control of attention is like the manual dial with which you can selectively attune to any portion of your experience. The more refined your executive control of attention, the more focused and selective and strong becomes the signal you are attuned to.

In our own *inner state*, we can easily differentiate between four distinct *channels of awareness*.[35] Each is a category of experience, representing ways of labeling, with language, different aspects of Soma. Together they create an Awareness Map: a visual representation of this inner state at any moment of time. (See Figure 7.1.) This map helps us differentiate, and therefore bring attention to and observe, the nuances of experience that are present in our inner state at any moment.

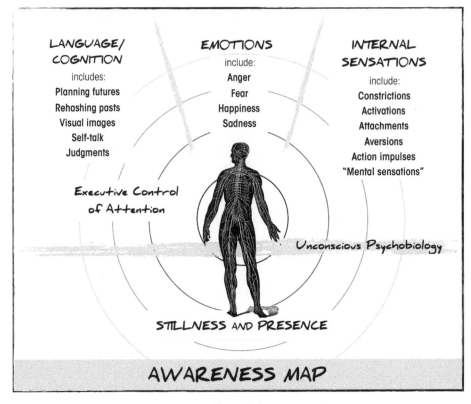

Figure 7.1

These channels are:

- *Language and cognition* (images, words, thoughts, narratives, mental models, etc.): This is content of the monkey mind—the chattering content that most often characterizes our mental processing. *Awareness of our cognition, by making the contents of our minds explicit, allows intervention and shaping of how our mind is processing information.*

- *Emotions* (joy, anxiety, anger, fear, happiness, contentment, etc.): Emotions are qualities of our internal state. They are our body's preparations for certain kinds of actions. *Awareness of our emotional states informs us of how we are primed to receive and respond to information in particular ways.*[36]

- *Internal sensations* (sensory experience of ourselves... breath, energy, constriction, pulsing, tension, numbness, hunger, attachments, aversions, action impulses, etc.): These are the indicator lights on the Soma's instrument panel. ***Awareness of sensations*** *provides the most immediate, direct and complete information about the state of the organism and how our psychobiology is responding to the world around us.*

- ***Stillness*** (spaciousness, possibility, emptiness): Recall that stillness is one of the system elements from Chapter 5. Stillness is also a quality that we can experience directly; it is the ground out of which other experiences arise. ***Awareness of stillness*** *reveals our freedom and the possibility of real choice in every moment.*

These four channels, or categories, of awareness all arise from the automatic processes of your unconscious psychobiology. Your executive control makes available the realization of each at will. Such is the power of your attention.

A word of caution about trauma. A significant driver of our incessant mental and physical activity is our avoidance of difficult-to-tolerate sensations and emotions. Becoming more present to our inner experience on the channels of awareness means accessing information that was previously below the surface.

This, of course, is precisely the point. The vast majority of the time this enhanced awareness is enormously liberating and clarifying. And, sometimes, for people with difficult experiences that have been overridden sometimes for decades, becoming present to ourselves can reveal forgotten memories or deep and even overwhelming sadness, fear and anxiety. I am saying this in part to normalize these experiences if they arise through this or any of the practices in this book. And, also to say that if your experience in any way feels overwhelming or more intense than you know how to work with, then seek guidance and support from a professional.[37]

With that caveat, let's use your attention as a vehicle for a guided tour of the contents of your awareness.

Cognition

Cognition is the arena of the Awareness Map often most familiar to us, the modern-day "center of gravity" in consciousness where we spend most of our energy. Cognition arises through language, images, concepts, narratives, mental models of reality, memories and dreams.

Our world, and in particular Western civilization, with its Cartesian separation of body and mind and the supremacy of rationality, has placed little value on sensations, emotions and subtler modes of consciousness. In most professional Contexts, the operating assumption is that emotions and sensations are background noise that distract us from the fundamental activity of thinking.

This assumption, of course, is itself a Bell Jar. It is a belief generated by our psychobiology for Identity-preservation purposes. The belief keeps some ways of knowing dominant while precluding others.

Recognizing, in this moment, that this itself is a thought and that other kinds of experience are available—such as emotions and internal sensations—is an example of witnessing your cognition!

∼≋∽ PRESENCE PAUSE ≈✑∼

Here are a few examples of the expression of our psychobiology through cognition. I believe these may seem familiar to you! Note, on reflection, how intimately these automatic thought forms are related to Identity.

- *Planning the future:* We spend a good portion of our time anticipating and planning for the future. We anticipate what will be exciting and rewarding and produce success; we plan to avoid difficulties and unpleasantness.

- *Rehashing the past:* We review, over and over, events that have happened, especially when they didn't go as we wished or resulted in difficulty. Theoretically, this review of the past could help us learn, but we can also obsess about what didn't go well, fueling regret or self-judgment.

- *Visual images:* Mental pictures of ourselves or others, including of ourselves in action, can be a way to process the past or prepare for the future.

- *Self-talk:* Judgments about ourselves are often revealed as "I should have…" or "I'm so…" This constant narrative about self, and the comparison of oneself to others or to internally generated standards, is perhaps designed to motivate and guide us, but it also can be debilitating when a constant stream.

- *Judgments about others:* We position our Identity by mentally making others "less than" or "better than" ourselves. These comparative judgments serve the psychological function of making more knowable our status and location in the web of relationships, thus shaping how we should behave.

When we begin to look, we see that our mind is generating thoughts incessantly, virtually nonstop, in service to our Identity.

Experiment 7.1:
Witnessing Stream of Thought

Set a timer for five minutes, and have a pen and a piece of paper ready. Or, speak into a smartphone voice memo app; talking is more personal and provides better access to the subtle and intuitive workings of our cognition.

Begin with the words "I am thinking about..." Then, write down or speak words as they arise. Anything. Suspend all standards. It doesn't need to make any sense whatsoever, nor follow any sequence. Content and handwriting don't count. The sole purpose is to capture as much of your cognitive stream as possible, and to be curious as you see it arise. Feel free to sketch images or simply scribble if you wish. Just watch what emerges.

This can be challenging to do, because we do have standards, and we organize our thinking often around particular purposes. However, left to its own devices, the mind will generate content ad infinitum.[38]

Emotions

Our emotional experience is one of the most important determinants of what we would call quality of life, fulfillment and satisfaction. Some lists of human emotions differentiate hundreds of different emotions. Others reduce them to as few as four basic building blocks (anger, fear, happiness and sadness[39]). Most lists have six to eight basic emotions.

Our attachment to happiness and aversion to unpleasant emotions can steer us into unhelpful action or avoidant inaction. For example, we may unconsciously shape a conversation in order to receive a compliment because it feels good, or we work ourselves until sick in order to earn the appreciation of others. We avoid giving difficult feedback because we don't want to feel the tension, or we postpone letting someone go who is damaging the organization because we don't want to feel the unpleasant feelings that come with firing someone we've known for a long time.

We don't get to choose just the pleasant ones; nor will we be effective if our actions are primarily driven by the unrecognized need to produce, or avoid, particular emotions. Andrew Weil talks about the "toxic cultural assumption that we should all be happy."[40] It's understandable that we are attached to, and seek, experiences of joy, pleasure, gratitude, and happiness.

However, the countless nuances of these four basic emotions, both pleasant and unpleasant, are all part of life. What we experience as emotions are simply fleeting states of physiological and psychological arousal that reflect an underlying mobilization of the organism to respond to a current set of conditions, of which we may or may not even be conscious. As such, emotions are simply well-intentioned, if sometimes problematic, adaptive responses.[41] And they predispose us towards particular kinds of actions, which may or may not be helpful.

Thanks to the work of Daniel Goleman[42] and others, emotional intelligence has gained stature as a core leadership attribute and as a predictor of leader effectiveness. It is in large part through a rich emotional life that we experience the fullness that human experience offers. When we can observe and feel our emotions, without either being overwhelmed by them or suppressing and denying them, we become much more able to respond to the world as it is.

Experiment 7.2:
Mood Check

Take a moment and name two or three emotions that you are experiencing right now. Hint: "good" is not an emotion, nor is "busy" or "tired" or "hungry" or "distracted," which are either ideas or physiological states.

"Anxious" or "happy" or "grateful" or "frustrated" or "impatient," on the other hand, are fabulous emotions to have. (All emotions are fabulous, even those we would rather not experience. We don't get to choose.)

Name two or three...

If you are stuck, you can make this multiple choice by Googling "list of emotions," finding a good list, and choosing several emotions that fit.

Mood checks are a valuable ongoing practice. Knowing what emotions we are feeling is important for recognizing our predispositions at any moment in time. Consistent self-observation and mood checks over time build the capacity to witness our emotions and to realize that they arise and pass on their own as we build presence.

Sensations

Turning our attention to the next channel, we explore information about the physiological condition of the body. To most folks, this is the most novel and least familiar channel, although there is profound richness available for the Sensing. As a simplification, we call this channel *internal sensation.*[43] Sensation includes pain and throbbing, itching, hunger, thirst, energy movements (such as pulsing, streaming, tingling), temperature, muscular sensations, the internal sense of breath and heartbeat, "air hunger," tightness, numbness, urges and action impulses, as well as many other sensations that comprise our unfolding internal experience.

Sensations have a location. We might notice, for example, tightness in the left side of our neck, a rising charged fullness in our chest, or an impatient itching in our right leg. This specificity of sensation is a powerful source of information for leaders, offering a continual stream of data about our inner state. Attuning to our sensation reveals much about how we are reacting to what is around us: Tension, stress and impatience are conditions of the body.

There are many kinds of sensations available to us, and the richness available to us through the life of the body is boundless. I want to highlight several here that are particularly relevant because they relate so directly to action and behavior.

- *Constriction* results from a tightening or holding in the body. This can be a defensive response to a difficult experience or simply the result of organizing ourselves tightly in one way over a period of time. We might notice a stiff sensation in our lower back, a hot tightness in our throat or an aching jaw from clenching it.

- *Activation* is a heightened sense of energy in a particular location in the body, often triggered by a thought or an external input. We can experience activation as a streaming or tingling sensation. Examples are the energy in the chest as we feel a challenge, the erectness of our spine as our attention is riveted or the energy in our arms and legs when we are impatient for action.

- *Attachments* are experienced as an urge or an attraction to the possibility of a positive experience. *Aversions* of course are the opposite: a revulsion or predisposition. Both can be sensed in the body as a generalized charge.

- *Action impulses* are precursors, in the body, to specific actions. They are our body's neural mobilization of energy towards actions that will dissipate the charged urges of underlying attachments and aversions. Focused and specific, uninhibited action impulses always lead to immediate actions. A rising sensation in our chest precedes interrupting someone. Or, we sense our shoulders shrinking as we shy away from speaking truth to power.

- *Mental sensations*[44] are experiences generated by our psychobiology as gateways to action. For example, the felt sense of certainty, of clarity or of having made a decision are biologically useful because they increase the probabilities of taking action, and therefore of survival. Yet, the experiences themselves are generated by automatic mechanisms beneath the level of awareness, and are not to be mistaken for empirical truth.

Experiment 7.3:
Attuning to Sensation

Play with your attention. Become curious about how many specific sensations you can discover. Read these directions, and then close your eyes and name sensations.

Each should have a *location* and a **sensation**. For example, in this particular moment sitting on a plane, the first five that arise for me are: "Belly... empty and rumbling. Tip of nose... coolness. Left side of neck... hot and tense. Heart... full and pulsing. Left leg... itchiness."

- Now you do it. Close your eyes and name at least five...

How was that? I'm guessing it was fairly easy. You could keep going, but I'm hoping that you are glimpsing the reality that directing attention and curiosity inwards reveals an unending stream of sensational experience delivered to you by your psychobiology.

- Now, anticipate a small snack or beverage that is actually available to you in this moment, and that you love. Imagine the taste, the texture, the feeling of this substance. Sense your anticipation of this.
- What is the location and sensation of this anticipation? Where and how do you feel the urge to get up and get this snack or beverage? See if you can sense specific located sensations associated with this urge.
- Now, make a conscious choice about whether to act on that urge or to let it go and continue reading.

Note that you can tune your attention to sensation at any time. Sensing the somatic precursor to a leadership action allows choice about whether to proceed or not. With practice, sensation will become a rich source of information for you as a leader.[45]

Stillness

Stillness doesn't mean that there's nothing going on. Stillness is simply the direct inner experience, however brief, of our psychobiology when thoughts and sensations and action impulses have not yet coalesced into particular structure of experience. It is the ground out of which other experiences arise. In stillness, we are without momentum towards something in particular. Anything is possible.

> ## CHANNELS OF AWARENESS
>
> Broadly, we can attune our attention to any of four channels of awareness. Within each, there are many subtleties:
>
> - Cognition
> - Emotions
> - Sensations
> - Stillness

On the level of Soma, stillness is a channel of awareness that is less about content and information to be listened to, and more about the space of possibility from which something can come forward. It is a doorway to presence: the experience of timelessness, spaciousness and possibility.

As you recall, stillness is a component of all three levels of system we are exploring. It is one of the elements of the complex Context system that we can observe around us—the pause in which something has not yet been determined, as illustrated in Chapter 5. It showed up in Chapter 6 as Luz realized the collapse of an old Identity and the emptiness of not knowing what would be next. And, we can directly experience stillness in our own Soma.

As we will discover, stillness is a key component in the state-shifting practices we will explore in the next chapter.

Experiment 7.4:
Sensing Stillness

Read these instructions. In a moment, I will ask you to stop reading. After this paragraph, *close your eyes* and attend to your own thought stream. Notice the words that are arising, unbidden, as your nervous system keeps generating language, all by itself! Then, take a pause. And, sense the space that is briefly there when you suspend the thought stream.

Now...

Stop now...

~~⊗~~ PRESENCE PAUSE ~~⊗~~

If you sensed a pause, however brief, in between words, you got a glimpse of stillness. Notice that, in this space, you couldn't actually know what's going to be next.

Of course, this rarely lasts long. Likely, your first thought that arose in this brief stillness was something like "Okay, I get this. Let's move on." And, you opened your eyes and jumped into this paragraph? Am I right?

Staying with stillness doesn't seem natural or easy at first. Our minds are impatient, and our nervous system quickly organizes itself to fill the vacuum. Yet in stillness lies real possibility. It is always present, underneath the more dominant streams of experience. It is the ground out of which thoughts, emotions and sensations arise. And, at any level of system, in stillness lies possibility. Anything can happen next.

Strengthening Executive Control of Attention

Executive control of attention is the key to somatic literacy, which is the basis for observing, and eventually intervening in, our inner states.

Mindfulness is the practice of directing attention into our moment-by-moment experience. The benefits of mindfulness are too many to elaborate on here.[46] However, the core mindfulness practice of attention training will, over time, produce significant changes in physical health, equanimity under pressure, focus, and resilience.

If you are already a meditator, of course, please continue your regular practice. If you are new to this and want a deeper dive than I am offering here, I recommend working with a meditation teacher, taking a Mindfulness-Based Stress Reduction course at a nearby university or progressive medical center, or using a book-based self-study course.[47]

Core Practice 7.5:
Attention Training Through Sitting

Daily attention training is a crucial and foundational practice. Doing this for as little as ten minutes a day can produce remarkable physiological benefits, as well as increasing your capacity for maintaining focus, attention, and equanimity.[48]

I recommend that you make a strong commitment to this practice. Begin today and continue until you complete this book or for the rest of your life, whichever is longer.

Of course, if the "rest of your life" feels like too big a commitment, then commit to thirty days, or until you finish the book, and then honestly assess the benefits and make a grounded decision on continuing. But begin.

For those with a history of trauma, working with a skilled practitioner informed about trauma and the body will be most important.[49]

Doing this practice consistently will support everything that follows in this book. I recommend doing this at the same time every day so that you embed it in your routine and it becomes a habit.

- Dedicate a quiet space to this activity. Set a timer for ten minutes.
- Sit up straight in a chair with your feet flat on the floor. Close your eyes, or gaze at a spot on the floor six to eight feet in front of you.
- Bring your awareness to your breath—either the sensations in your abdomen, which rises and falls as you breathe, or at the tip of your nostrils where the air enters and leaves your nose. Select the one you can feel most easily. Do not change your breathing; simply begin to observe it. Do not change your object of attention.
- Say quietly to yourself "in" when you inhale, and "out" when you exhale. Focus all of your attention on your breath. When you notice your attention wandering, and you will, simply witness that you're distracted, and then bring your attention back to your breathing. When you begin to judge yourself as being a crappy meditator, simply notice that you're distracted, and return your attention to your breathing.
- Notice whatever arises. Sensations, thoughts, emotions, stillness. Just notice them, and let them go, coming back to the breath. Over and over. Just sit.
- There is no goal to still the mind. Most minds race, even in attention practice. Practice just makes your monkey mind more obvious. You're simply practicing the act of bringing your attention back to the present. You're not trying to be good at this. You're simply practicing. And with practice, you'll begin to notice a real difference in your ability to be present with others, with a task, and with yourself. Just sit.

Note to overachieving leaders: Do not expect to be "good" at this, to be entertained, or to achieve lasting bliss and peace! None of these is actually the point.

The goal is simply to practice. Most modern minds race, even in attention practice. In fact, attention practice just reveals the endless chatter that has always been there. Really, you're simply practicing the act of bringing your attention back to the present.

Staying with this will reliably produce a major difference in your equanimity and resourcefulness under stress and in your relationships with self and others.

AWARENESS OF INNER STATES IS PRAGMATIC

This might all seem soft and fuzzy. So what if we can feel and sense all this stuff? When we are under the gun with a presentation to get ready, a difficult meeting to facilitate or a bruising conflict with a colleague or a loved one, awareness seems like a luxury.

Awareness is eminently pragmatic. Yes, it is most easily cultivated with practices when nothing momentous is really happening. Sitting seems like doing nothing, and we all have too much to do. Yet, over time, as we build our somatic literacy and our capacity to bring ourselves into the present moment, we will become radically more resourceful and available for what we face.

The Cascading On-Ramp to Behavior

Leadership is, at first glance, mostly a set of behaviors. This is what others see in us and largely react to.

Yet behaviors are always simply the external expressions of a Soma doing its earnest best to perpetuate or defend an Identity. Recognizing how external behaviors arise from Soma helps us learn to intervene in the unconscious automaticity with which most of our behaviors happen.

Here's a useful perspective. Behaviors are the culmination of a well-traveled neuronal on-ramp with five elements. These include a *trigger, a constellation of internal responses that arise rapidly and sequentially through three levels of experience, and a resulting behavior.*

First, there is a *trigger*. Something happens around us that we sense. We receive energy and information from outside ourselves, whether or not we are aware of it.

Second, we have a *somatic response*. We, as biological organisms, automatically ingest and metabolize this sensory input. Our somatic reaction is observable as sensation (energy, tension, tightness, warmth, numbness, etc.). Attachments, aversions and action impulses are almost instantly present. The sensation-producing, reptilian portions of our nervous system are the oldest from an evolutionary standpoint. They are the most immediate, objective and impersonal elements of our experience.

Third, we have an **emotional response**. Emotions arise based on our own history and conditioning. These feel very personal and are observable as anger, anxiety, joy, excitement, etc. Emotions arise from the raw uninterpreted sensations that precede them. They contain an interpretive embellishment based on Identity and stimulate a Soma-wide mobilization towards action. Emotions arise from the limbic system, which is younger and slower than the reptilian brain that provides our experience of sensation.

> ## THE ON-RAMP TO BEHAVIOR
>
> The cascade of accelerating events that lead to action include a trigger, a constellation of internal responses that arise rapidly and sequentially through three levels of experience, and a resulting behavior:
>
> - Trigger
> - Somatic response
> - Emotional response
> - Cognitive response
> - Resulting behavior

Fourth, there is a **cognitive response**. Thoughts and narratives generate meaning from our experience, and justification for our response. Cognition is observable as language (stories, interpretation, justification, etc.). Cognition arises spontaneously from the sensational and emotional conditions that precede it and takes place in the later and more energy-intensive portions of the brain. Cognition is far slower than the previous two (although the entire constellation can arise in less than a second). Our cognition has the potential for reflection on our possible course of action. More often, it simply provides a justifying narrative for the course of action our body is hurtling towards (or has already taken!).

Fifth, there is a **resulting behavior**. Action flows out of the cascading constellation of phenomena that precedes it. Our action (physical movement, speech, etc.) dissipates the built-up activation of our attachments, aversions and action impulses and instantly changes our internal state. We likely have the "mental sensation" of agency, experienced in the body as the felt sense of having made and executed a decision.

Of course, as a result of our action, the Context has been altered. We can be highly confident that we will now receive some new energy and information from outside, and the cycle will then begin all over again! This is a rough sketch of the internal part of the dynamism that connects Soma with Context through the intermediary of Identity. It is not theoretical. This is what happens in any conversation, any meeting, any phone call with a daughter or a parent. It just happens so fast and automatically we don't normally see it.

We begin to realize that all action is the culmination of a cascading and largely automatic sequence of internal events. Significantly, we see that awareness means we can learn to witness the internal precursors of our behaviors. And, we can learn to recognize them in real time. We then have a precious opportunity to inject *stillness* as a pause, a profound interruption of the previous automatic cascades that generate behavior. From the spaciousness that this pause introduces, we can consciously choose whether to inhibit or green-light the behavior towards which our psychobiology has been hurtling.

Here's a super simple example of how this applies to a real decision.

One of a thousand daily choice points

Yesterday, as I sat writing, an urgent text arrived from a close friend and favorite collaborator, inviting me to join on a choice piece of work overseas, three weeks from now.

I could feel the attachment arising. My heartbeat quickened. My energy rose. I sat up straighter in my chair.

I felt a burst of optimism and excitement and happiness.

I watched my thoughts quicken and gather momentum around how to fit this into an already packed schedule. I felt the urge to open my calendar, simultaneously feeling the attachments swirling and noticing my narratives justifying taking the work. It will pay well, it's overseas in a cool place, it's with a high-profile client, it will be fun and gratifying to work with this colleague, etc. All true.

I paused, sensing stillness.

In this pause, I had a strong realization of the familiarity of this experience. I saw clearly how this work was triggering multiple attachments. I saw that these strong Identity-driven urges to say yes were pulling me towards a commitment that would feel good and be fun—and would also require abandoning several other promises that I had already made to my family, to myself and to this book project.

In the past, the yes would have been quick and automatic. I would have followed the urge, said yes, justified it to myself, and found a way to make it work. I would tell myself that I could manage any messes later. Now, I am able to Sense the multiple channels of awareness in this present moment and to recognize my Identity hijacking me into a course of action that might not be either necessary or wise.

I wrote a text to my colleague telling her that I appreciated the invitation but couldn't make it work. I then paused to relish another moment of stillness. I felt both divergent possibilities existing simultaneously in the present; I felt the moment of choice. Until I pressed Send, the future was open. And the choice was clear.

I clicked Send. Then turned back to my book, sitting on a rainy morning next to my wife and my dogs, writing what is mine to write.

Awareness Reveals Inner State

As in my simple example, when we slow ourselves down and become aware of our internal experience, we get tons of information that we miss when operating flat out (like most of us do, most of the time). Without awareness, we tend to prop up our Identity at the cost of surrendering the precious control of our attention to an embodied urgency we don't even recognize.

This particular example included the luxury of not having someone in my face expecting an answer. There was time. That said, somatic awareness always increases choice; moments of stillness are always available, and if we are present enough to recognize we need time to process, it's nearly always possible to find it.

Awareness includes the Sensing of our inner state. Awareness then enables recognition of when our inner state is automatically predisposed to a certain course of action. By staying present, we can recognize any default momentum.

Unless and until we bring awareness to illuminating the cascading drivers of our behaviors, they will absolutely run us. We must learn to recognize when our Identity is evoked or challenged by unpredictable circumstances not within our control, and how our Soma mobilizes around threats or opportunities. Sensing these phenomena through the fundamental practice of **self-observation** gives us access to information that has always been available. We just have to learn how to look.

Once again, we are finding the stepping stones of new distinctions. That said, awareness is not ultimately about parsing components of experience.

Rather, we are building the very foundation of somatic literacy. Our mastery, enabled by presence, allows us to recognize our reactive Identity-defending inner states before they get us in trouble. And to intervene in our inner conditions in order to cultivate more resilient states as leaders in Complexity.

Luz reboots herself

Luz's felt experience of realization was an acknowledgment. Her deanship was failing. She began to retool her approach to the change process by retooling herself.

It was startling to Luz that the undeniable tensions in her body ultimately led her to this realization. She had plenty of passion and energy, was in decent shape, and was accustomed to powering through. However, in this situation, the toll on her body had become inarguable.

Among other things, her coach offered her self-observation practices that developed a beginning somatic literacy. While body-mind practices would later become a central strategy in her reinvention of herself as a leader, they were initially simply a tactic to reduce her reactivity to triggers at the institute.

Luz's self-observation increased her capacity to recognize the feeling of tightness in her belly when certain people walked into the room. She felt her energy rising during meetings, sensed her jaw clenching, her shoulders rising. She felt her anger and irritation, which previously she had been aware of in hindsight but had never fully named. And she saw how she manufactured a story that faculty members' selfish egos were obstacles blocking her way.

*This awareness, while it might seem small, was actually a revelation for Luz. She began to recognize the early signals that **preceded** the sarcastic reactions that dramatically amplified the tension and polarization in the system.*

Luz began to hold back more. She was more relaxed. She made decisions, in the moment, to not respond to provocations. Luz saw that present-moment awareness was leading to actual subtle but real changes in outward behavior.

Her new awareness was the first step towards a more presence-based approach to leadership, and to de-escalating the polarization that was keeping the system stuck and incapable of changing.

Experiment 7.6:
Create an Awareness Map of a Triggered Reaction

Consider some significant recurring situation in your Complexity Challenge that you experience as triggering and to which you react in ways that aren't helpful. It might be a problematic relationship or a difficult dynamic with a team or stakeholder. Likely you can see in hindsight that the way you react is not helpful, but in the moment you seem to be gripped by some habit you can't quite intervene in.

Take a piece of paper and sketch the rough shape of the Awareness Map in Figure 7.1, including the lines that separate the channels of awareness. Then, write down the components of your experience of this triggering situation.

- What are the sensations in your body right **before** you respond? Get detailed and specific: Name five sensations and the location in which you feel them.
- What are the emotions in that moment after being triggered and **before** you act?
- What story are you telling yourself about the other person or the situation that justifies the action you are **about to** take?
- Where is there **stillness** in this situation? How and where might you introduce a pause?

You have just created a simple Awareness Map of a triggered state for a particular situation. This provides much more information about how your psychobiology is triggered and more familiarity with the state that is the immediate precursor to a problematic reaction.

Core Practice 7.7:
Self-Observe a Triggered Reaction

Following the previous experiment, you can take this self-observation out into your Context and begin to build awareness in action. This is a powerful practice, and central to the Presence-Based Coaching methodology.[50]

Self-observation is best done on a daily basis. Frequency and consistency count.

Create a template for yourself. This is best done on paper (use your journal or create multiple printed copies) rather than a device, but choose what will enable the practice. Keep it simple.

Use the following questions:

- When, today, was I triggered in this way? With whom? What was happening?
- What were the sensations in my body? Name specifics and locations.
- What were my emotions in the moment?
- What story was I telling yourself?
- What action did I take? What were the results?

At the end of each day, or twice a day as appropriate, use the template to write out quick notes. This doesn't need to be elaborate prose. However, writing something down is important and gives your self-observation physical substance and rigor. Five minutes is all that's needed.

Self-observation is a structured practice for reflecting on specific triggering incidents and taking a balcony perspective. **NOTE: You are not seeking to change your behavior.** (While that is important, it will come later.) Rather, you are simply exercising the muscle of awareness and building somatic literacy around a specific reaction.

As you will see, awareness and presence lead inexorably towards self-correction and resilience.

CHAPTER SUMMARY

This chapter's perspective invites you to access the intelligence of your entire nervous system. Through the deeply human process of directing your attention inward through Sensing Soma, you recontact your innate wisdom and intelligence.

The core realization of this chapter is that you actually can observe your psychobiology in the process of metabolizing energy and information. Doing so brings you into the present and reveals ever-greater choice over previously automatic behaviors.

The following stepping stones are particularly useful as you develop access to this perspective:

- Recognizing your inherent *executive control of attention*: the capacity to direct your attention at anything of your choosing
- The Awareness Map, and the parallel channels that include these aspects of your moment-by-moment experience:
  - ▶ Cognition
  - ▶ Emotions
  - ▶ Sensations
  - ▶ Stillness
- *Somatic literacy:* the developable sensitivity and awareness of your internal experience on all channels
- *Inner states:* the constellation of experiences at any given time that reveal your condition
- The recognition of how the cascading on-ramp, unless witnessed and inhibited, leads to automatic and sometimes suboptimal behaviors
- Core practices of attention training and self-observation

These stepping stones support the realization that your Soma allows you to access valuable information, internally and in the present moment, about how your psychobiology is reacting to the complexity in your environment. With awareness, you can intervene in automaticity. You can stay within this moment, right now, with exquisite and unshakable clarity, regardless of what else is going on.

Your Soma is a vitally important component of the dynamic Complex system in which you are a leader. Your Soma actively and vigilantly maintains the very Identity through which you influence your Context. Sensing the interdependence of these three co-arising levels of system provides a more inclusive clarity about how reality is organizing itself towards, or against, what you intend.

Take some time to reflect on what you now realize as a result of this Pane.

- What do you understand differently?
- What are you now curious about?
- What experiments might you try?

≈∾ PRESENCE PAUSE ∾≈

PART

THREE

Being

Would you like to save the world from the degradation and destruction it seems destined for? Then step away from shallow mass movements and quietly go to work on your own self-awareness. If you want to awaken all of humanity, then awaken all of yourself. If you want to eliminate the suffering in the world, then eliminate all that is dark and negative in yourself. Truly, the greatest gift you have to give is that of your own self-transformation.

– Wang Fou

BEING IS YOUR INNER STATE AT A PARTICULAR MOMENT. The foundation of Part Two is the **realization that you have an inner state that you can both observe and intervene in**. It is from this realization that you lead with presence and authenticity.

Sensing changes your inner state; Acting arises from it. While all three co-arise in dynamic interdependence, it's fair to say that **Being is the leverage**; it is the internal intermediary between inputs and outputs. **Out of Being arise the actions that are the external expressions of your leadership.**

Being is the opening for you to introduce more spaciousness, intervene in cycles of reactivity and stop getting in your own way. It is you, bringing attention and choice to how you metabolize the energy and information you take in from the world.

It is the second of our three meta-competencies, and it is most effectively accessed through the system element of *stillness*, that previously discussed doorway into *presence*.

In Part Three, you will explore Being on three levels of scale: Soma, Context and Identity. One chapter for each, in that specific sequence. Yes, this sequence is a bit different from our exploration of Sensing: Being and Sensing are different processes. The framework of the Nine Panes remains illuminating and useful—just our entry point changes.

In the previous chapter, you paid attention to the channels of awareness, witnessing the nuances of your inner state. In Chapter 8, beginning your work with Being, you make the potent discovery that *attention not only provides information but also instantly changes and regulates your inner state*. This realization reveals specific practices that will increase your access to helpful, creative and resilient inner states from which to lead.

Experimenting with your inner state in relation to your Context, the work of Chapter 9, reveals that *you can decouple your internal state from what's going on around you*. Being stressed out in a stressed-out system takes little self-mastery. But *self-regulation*—the process of intervening in the workings of your own nervous system to change your inner state—leads inexorably to the liberating realization that your internal state, your Being, is influenced but not determined by the conditions around you. In fact, you can be relaxed and focused when others are stressed and distractible. This seminal insight is the key to *resilience*. Being calm in the midst of frenzy makes you a potent resource for yourself and for the entire system.

Liberated through self-regulating and by decoupling your inner state from the Context, you can now begin to *cultivate an Identity of your own choosing*. This is the topic of Chapter 10. Rather than unconsciously defending the Identity produced by your history, you can begin to nourish a chosen leadership Identity congruent with the future you intend. You embody a future that you care about, such that you act consistently with that future now.

This is the essential practice of presence.

	CONTEXT	IDENTITY	SOMA
SENSING	Observe The System	Recognize Identity At Stake	Attend To Experience
BEING			REGULATE INNER STATE
ACTING			

152

CHAPTER 8

Being as Soma: Regulate Inner State

*The emotional brain responds to an event more quickly
than the thinking brain.*

– Daniel Goleman

*My experience is what I agree to attend to.
Only those items which I notice shape my mind.*

– William James

*The body is a multilingual being. It speaks through
its color and its temperature, the flush of recognition,
the glow of love, the ash of pain, the heat of arousal,
the coldness of nonconviction… It speaks through the
leaping of the heart, the falling of the spirit, the pit at
the center, and rising hope.*

– Clarissa Pinkola Estés

W E ALL KNOW LEADERS WHOSE PERSONALITIES SEEM TO REAR UP IN UNHELPFUL WAYS. Our dawning understanding is that their psychobiologies generate these behaviors for their own Identity-preservation purposes. The preceding chapters have provided what could be seen as a neat, no-fault explanation: We are all simply the only persons we could be, doing the best we can with very little actual control over what our psychobiology produces.

This might be philosophically true and convenient. It's also neither satisfying nor pragmatic to fully cede our agency to biology. We turn, in this chapter, to how we can turn the power of attention and presence to creating real-time shifts in the biological substrate of behavior.

Rajeev changes the world

Rajeev was a very successful fundraiser from a humble background in rural India. His director and board had publicly committed their international development nonprofit to an ambitious pivot to a micro-lending strategy. Rajeev's team was accountable for capitalizing the project through partnerships with wealthy donors and progressive lending institutions.

Rajeev was physically small but firecracker smart, charismatic and visionary. His personal story was compelling. He had grown up poor and, through relentless tenacity and some lucky breaks, became the first in his family to leave his village and attend college. Decades later, his rarefied professional world was populated with bankers, social entrepreneurs and the wealthy. His story, deep passion and a reputation for getting results at any cost to himself had led to a meteoric career.

This new initiative being deeply personal for him, Rajeev felt a sense of ultimate responsibility for the thousands of rural poor across several continents that this project would lift out of poverty. As such, he became increasingly concerned about his team's lack of initiative and passion. Privately he feared that others would discover he had somehow faked his way to the top of his field but actually didn't fit. He could keep the illusion going only through hypervigilance, extraordinary personal effort, and lightning-fast involvement in every detail.

Rajeev's relentless drive and passion for the work instead produced well-intentioned behaviors that disenfranchised the very team members that he relied upon. Every conversation became a chance to inspire. In meetings, when someone would offer an idea, Rajeev would grab it and imbue it with his personal twist. But the originator would often sit back in her chair, fold her arms, and say no more. Rajeev's hypervigilance had an addictive quality to it. His people, essential to the vision, were exhausted and frustrated by his way of Being.

Rajeev understood, in principle, that his leadership style actually undermined ownership by others. However, it felt nearly impossible to change. After all, his tenacity had brought him further than anyone around him could begin to understand!

Rajeev's embodied habits had served him well, but they were now real threats to the success of his most important project yet. He was up against a developmental edge, but could not clearly see what he was doing nor how to change it.

We all have habits. Like you and me, Rajeev had embodied a way of being that had worked well enough up to now. Like you and me, he sometimes became hijacked by his attachments and aversions into inner states that produced behaviors that were not the best. And, we all have a capacity to shift and regulate this inner state.

In Rajeev's example, we can see echoes of the Awareness Map: his self-talk about his responsibility, fears about what might happen if he let down his guard, constant anxiety and hypervigilance, passion. All of this shaped the way he came across to others. Yet, Rajeev was largely blind to how his inner state affected those around him.

The previous chapter explored how you can use the Awareness Map to focus your attention and cultivate awareness, making available more of the information that has always been available in the subconscious landscapes of your psychobiology.

The pivot you make now is from *observing* your inner state to *actively shifting* your inner state. Your capacity to align your inner state with what is important to you, rather than accept it as an automatic reaction to what is happening around you based on your history, is what you will unfold in this chapter and those that follow. *Your inner state is the foundation for resilience: the capacity for creativity, resourcefulness and skillful action, no matter what's going on around you.*[51]

You will, through practice, learn to regulate and refine your inner state. This builds resilience—and this is the big idea—because the more you can regulate your inner reactions to the complexities of the world, the more you can respond in fresh and original ways in order to evoke what matters.

ATTENTION AND INNER STATE

With new practices, we realize more about our constant, intricate and dynamic interaction with the world around us. We learn to *differentiate* and to Sense our responses, as they arise, in our Soma. We learn to direct our attention to *connect* to the experience of our thoughts, emotions, and sensations, along with precious moments of stillness.

And, we discover the profound and startling realization that the act of ***directing attention itself changes the subconscious processes of our nervous system***. This has profound implications for leadership.

The Drivers of Our Behaviors Are Most Often Unconscious

How do we bring as much choice and awareness as possible into the momentary but critical decisions we make as leaders? Like deciding whether to interrupt someone in a meeting? Whether to hit *send* on an important email? Choosing to stay open to crucial information that might influence a decision, but which would be more convenient to ignore? Whether to issue the *fire* command to launch a drone-based missile strike that will end three lives twelve thousand miles away?

Each of these decisions come down to an instantaneous action driven by complex internal processes, the vast majority of which we cannot witness directly. Yet, the decision itself is irrevocable and changes the world in a moment, putting things in motion with unforeseeable consequences.

Much leadership development rests on providing leaders with feedback so that they can better see themselves as others do and adjust behaviors accordingly. However, this drive toward productive change rests on the capacity of the leader to recognize and take advantage of opportunities to make new choices.

This seems to me to omit the reality that the seething neuronal wilderness of our psychobiology decides what's important enough to place into the bright spotlight of our awareness. And, this choice is driven by deeply rooted Identity imperatives, not by what our brain thinks is a good idea.

Because they are the inevitable result of embodiment and habituation, these drivers tend to be invisible. We like to think that we are in charge, that we in fact choose what we do. While we do in fact have that potential, there's very strong evidence that we are choosing far less than we would like to believe.[52] As Emo Philips said, "I used to think that the brain was the most wonderful organ in my body. Then I realized who was telling me this."

Philosophers have debated forever if there is such a thing as free will, and intelligent people can still disagree about what is ultimately true here. The scientific evidence indicates that most of our thoughts and actions emanate from a psychobiological substrate, with the primary purpose of perpetuating a reliable sense of Identity, and without our conscious intervention. Behaviors arise from a set of conditions that are beneath the level of awareness, even though we think we are choosing them. ***Intervening to change these internal conditions is the most reliable way to shift the trajectory of our thoughts and actions***. This is where we are going.

Observing Executive Control of Attention Itself

I sometimes catch myself, in cold December woods with dogs, walking as an old man: hunched over, focusing on my tiredness or my sore knees or how far it seems to the top. When I notice myself doing this, I see it's a choice, one among several. I can also pay attention to the beauty of the forest and the strength in my legs. I can look up from the ground to where I'm going and sense the joy that is also within me. Awareness reveals a clear choice… pay attention to my aches and pains or to the beauty of the woods and the springiness in my step.

Time stops: There is a fleeting moment of stillness as I see the choice. And, then, I straighten my back and look up. I keep walking, and I feel different. I have used my executive control to make a choice and withdraw attention from one focus or awareness and direct it into another.

Doing so shifts my state, instantly and undeniably.

Now, you play. Look up from the book and out the window, then back again….

Do it again. Slow it <u>way</u> down. Take your time and see if you can find, and observe, the internal part of you that's choosing. It's fleeting, elusive, subtle. And it's real: You're watching yourself choose what to pay attention to.

≫ PRESENCE PAUSE ≪

In this brief experiment, you are making visible your executive control of attention, something of which you are generally completely unaware. You are witnessing your executive control of attention itself.[53]

Attention Shifts Inner State

In the Awareness Map, we differentiate four *channels of awareness*: groupings of the contents of our consciousness at any particular moment. Each of these is a source of information. By directing attention to any of them, we connect to rich information about what is going on internally. That is Sensing the Soma.

Now, in Being Soma, the precise act of directing attention (through executive control) to the contents of awareness brings us into the present. The realization of directed attention invites presence and shifts our state.

This is particularly true with the channel of internal sensations.

Let's do another brief experiment. Read this paragraph fully, twice. Then close your eyes and, using your executive control, direct your attention to your breath.

Specifically, when you close your eyes, take a deep breath, then stretch out your exhale, counting slowly all the way to six. Let your shoulders relax as you exhale. Feel your chest letting go as you exhale slowly. Feel the subtle movement of air through your mouth. Notice as much as you are able about the physical sensations of the exhalation.

Repeat this three times. Then, reopen your eyes and come back to the text. Do this now.

ᙍᗦ PRESENCE PAUSE ᗧᙎ

What did you notice? How do you feel different as a result of this brief experiment?

Now, I invite you into two realizations. One, there was information available. You could almost certainly feel the physical sensation of your exhalation, your shoulders relaxing, the warmth of air passing through your nose. This is Sensing your Soma (the previous Pane). This information is there all the time (after all, you breathe all day every day!). Usually, you simply don't notice.

The second realization is that directing attention into the body immediately affects the overall condition of your nervous system. This may have been subtle, but I'm hoping you noticed that there was some difference in how you felt before and after the attention practice. Most people would report feeling more settled, relaxed, alert... more aware... more present. This is a simple experience of state-shifting, the focus of this Pane.

As you continue through this chapter, you will expand on this second realization to cultivate reliable access to more creative and resilient states. These states will become increasingly embodied and therefore available. Practice builds capacity by shaping your psychobiology through your presence and attention.

More resourceful inner states can become an ever more reliable quality of your signature presence as a leader.

These two brief experiments—witnessing your executive control of attention and realizing that directing attention to your inner state shifts that inner state— lay the experiential foundation for the ideas and practices to come.

YOUR INTERNAL STATE IS A COMPLEX SYSTEM

Your Soma is a Complex emergent system. Your body is a continuous process of self-organization in service of the survival of your body and of your Identity. In fact, every system element that we explored in Chapter 5 (stasis, feedback loops, disruptors, organizing principles, polarities, stillness) can also be discovered within the complex system of your Soma.

Learning to recognize and shift between inner states at will is a powerful component of leadership mastery. In particular, learning to recognize when you are triggered and to use presence to access your innate resilience is essential for wise and conscious choices in difficult situations.

Internal Conditions: Stasis, Activation and Resilience

Specific states arise and pass momentarily. States are highly fluid, although we will learn to stabilize them at will through *somatic practices*: specific, ongoing practices that explicitly include awareness of the body.

It is also helpful to consider three broad *internal conditions*. Generally we are in one or another general condition: *stasis, activation* or *resilience*. These three conditions provide a general sense of our inner state; each can include countless variations of specific states, each comprising a constellation of sensations, emotions, thoughts, action urges, etc.

Stasis is where we hang out most of the time. We are just doing what we're doing, albeit mostly on autopilot. We experience stasis when our Identity feels secure, we are operating skillfully enough at the office or with our kids, and the world is behaving somewhat predictably. We experience this as normal, whatever normal is for us.

If we think of stasis as normalcy, we are likely to hang out there most of the time. These are internal conditions in which we are much less likely to do damage or make mischief, but we are also quite likely to miss opportunities. It is akin to not paying attention while driving and then spacing out and missing our freeway exit. The risks of being on autopilot seem obvious, but the comfort of stasis creates a stability remarkably impervious to change.

In *activation*, our attachments and aversions have been *triggered* by something that our psychobiology interprets as a threat or as an opportunity. Disruptions come in many forms: an angry phone call, bad or good news, an unexpected fabulous opportunity, a glass of our favorite beverage, or a challenge to our Identity. All bets are off when we get triggered; our internal conditions accelerate automatically towards states that are likely to produce a reactive and ill-considered action of some sort.

This is the place the most damage is likely to take place, because our discernment and our Sensing processes have been overwhelmed by our

THREE INTERNAL CONDITIONS

Your nervous system mostly hangs out in one of three general internal conditions:

- **Stasis**: "normal," status quo, autopilot

- **Activation**: acute reactive state, generally following some kind of a trigger

- **Resilience**: aware, liberated, creative states that allow resourceful responses

psychobiology's quixotic efforts to defend or nourish our Identity, regardless of cost. In stasis, we are asleep at the wheel. When activated, we are reacting to opportunities and threats that might be imaginary, might be very real, and might simply be phantom echoes of long-past events.

I propose that in Complexity, and at the pace with which most leaders are moving, we live in a state of nearly constant activation. Learning to recognize and work with our own activation in radically new ways is a tremendous opportunity for leaders to improve the conditions for success.

The third condition is *resilience*. This is the most resourceful, alive, creative and powerful of the three. It is enlivened by presence. When we are resilient, we are Sensing what is happening in the Context, how it is affecting our Identity, and what is arising in our Soma. We are acutely aware of our moment-by-moment experience and of whatever reaction is taking place within us. We might still be triggered, but we are aware of being triggered. We have a realization both of our reaction and of the opportunity to make real choices.

Obviously, this resilience condition is the one from which we want to be operating. Here, our maximum resourcefulness is fully available.

Experiment 8.1:
Three Conditions in Your Leadership

In your ongoing Complexity Challenge, I suspect that you can identify where each of these three kinds of states likely appears. Probably, all three will be there when you look, but it may be that resilience and stasis turn out to be in short supply!

Take a few minutes to respond to these questions:

- How do you experience an internal sense of **stasis**? Probably you can let go a bit, things seem normal, and you (and the system around you) are in some sense of stability and predictability. When is this state present for you? What conditions around you evoke this?
- How do you experience **activation**? Here, you find yourself reacting to events, trying to catch up. Your nervous system is on alert status, and you're maintaining a high energy level, perhaps over the long haul. What triggers you? When is this state present for you? What conditions evoke it?
- How do you experience **resilience**? This condition is characterized by creativity and re-sourcefulness. It might not be fun, but you're on your game. You're aware of yourself, and you're able to stay focused and effective even when others aren't. When is this state present for you? What conditions evoke this?
- Looking back across your responses, how much influence have you experienced over which condition you are in? When have you intentionally shifted into resilience? How did you do it?

In general terms, then, while stasis is manageable, it is crucial to recognize activation when it happens and shift our inner conditions towards resilience as much as possible.

State-shifting is how we do this.

State-Shifting

The Awareness Map is like the instrument panel in the front of the plane. What we are experiencing in any given moment—both our specific inner state and the more general conditions—are continually evidenced by the constellations of arising thoughts, emotions, and sensations revealed by the Awareness Map.

State-shifting requires a conscious fluidity of state, allowing the easy arising and passing of inner states, as well as the more intentional choosing of states. Both are crucial components of leading with stability and resilience within Complex situations.

State-shifting, of course, is enabled by awareness. The realization of our activation derives from sensing our Soma and from recognizing the now-familiar symptoms of triggering. We can then self-regulate by directing our attention to settle our activation.

State-shifting allows the cultivation and eventual embodiment of a more reliably resilient inner condition, allowing us access to stillness and presence so as to meet our triggers from a different foundation.

State-Shifting in Action

State-shifting is a foundational competency.

In the dynamism of leading, and of living, presence allows us to direct attention to our internal state. We can become skillful at realizing when we are triggered and reactive: The evidence is always there in our Soma.

Under pressure, state-shifting provides fluid access to the full range of capabilities and behaviors that would otherwise become less available when we are triggered into a more reactive state. We then self-regulate by directing our attention toward always available internal resources.

Rajeev is a leader for whom doing so was inextricably linked to his success.

Rajeev practices state-shifting

*Rajeev's development required learning to recognize and intervene in his fierce hypervigilance. Rajeev used the tools of the Awareness Map and self-observation to begin to sense and identify the complex emotions and sensations of nearly constant **activation**. He observed the tightening in his shoulders, the sense of urgency and impatience, the rising energy in his chest right before he interrupted others. He realized that he instantly interpreted every contribution in a meeting as being either "for me or against me." And he felt his impatience any time someone was suggesting something that he had already thought of.*

In response to what he was now recognizing, Rajeev experimented with simple self-regulation practices. Conscious breathing really helped when he felt wound up. This practice dramatically and quickly settled his state. He could do it undetected in a meeting. And the exhalation supported his impulse control, allowing him to choose to control his urge to interrupt others.

Another self-regulation move was to sit back in his chair and open his chest and arms wider. His default had been, he noticed, to lean forward, driving the meeting where he wanted it to go. When he leaned back, and coupled this new body posture with a genuine question, it stimulated his own curiosity and generated more lively exchanges across the table.

Last, he made a practice of inviting stillness and quiet in meetings. This was initially really hard for Rajeev; he would jump in to fill even a fleeting moment of silence. Soon, however, he began to really appreciate stillness. He allowed pauses to be longer. He even experimented with asking his team to consider a question in silence before responding. He found that this stimulated everyone's creativity on sticky issues. And, he discovered that previously quiet people often had more to say than he had thought!

Rajeev liked the inner practices of self-observation, settling himself through breathing and body posture, allowing stillness. Individually, they seemed like small things. But Rajeev's new, more relaxed affect began to have a dramatic effect on staff members and on the level of discussion and participation in meetings. This reinforced Rajeev's sense that he was on the right track.

CORE PRACTICES FOR SELF-REGULATION AND RESILIENCE

We can develop ready access to more useful states by practicing self-regulation consistently when the stakes are low. Then, when the stakes are high, our most resilient, creative, resourceful self is available.

The following four state-regulation practices will build a centered, grounded, stable, creative state that can increasingly be your default.

I don't ask you to take my word for it that these practices work. I recommend doing all four, several times a day, for one month. As with any practice, repetition is the pathway to embodiment.

Think of this as a scientific experiment that will take only a few minutes a day once you know what the internal attention moves feel like. Do the practices in good faith, with curiosity and full attention. See what happens.

After a month of this, I predict you will notice real differences in your way of Being. And, others will remark, unprompted, that you seem different in some way they can't quite pinpoint. More relaxed, more available, less reactive somehow. They might ask what you are doing differently.

> ### STATE-SHIFTING IOI
>
> These simple practices, with consistency and attention, will profoundly increase your resourcefulness and resilience in complexity:
>
> - Centering
> - Grounding
> - Stabilizing Breath
> - Stillness

Whether or not you choose to share your practices is, of course, up to you. Either way, you will validate for yourself that your practices are changing you.

Core Practice 8.2:
Centering[54]

Center is a neutral state. When centered, we are alert, relaxed, aware, ready. It is an inner state from which, regardless of what is going on around us, we can be at choice.

Work with the three dimensions common to any physical object, bringing your attention into each in turn.

- *Length*: Feel the weight of your body pressing down: into your seat, into your feet. Let your attention follow this downward press, finding a sense of ground, of support, of solidity. At the same time, extend yourself up. Draw yourself up into the full length of your torso, so that your head and neck are directly aligned with your spine. Relax your jaw. Look straight ahead, neither down at the floor, nor up. *Through the dimension of length, we access the felt experience of dignity.*
- *Width*: Now, breathe into your chest, feeling yourself taking up more space, more width. Let the right and left sides of your body sense the space to your right and left. *Through the dimension of width, we access the felt experience of belonging.*
- *Depth*: Sense the space behind you. Feel the history, knowledge, skills, and experience that live in you, that have made you the only person that you could be. Recognize that you have everything that you need. *Through the dimension of depth, we access the felt experience of fundamental sufficiency.*

With practice, centering yourself will feel like a quick and effortless "coming home." Centering becomes almost an instantaneous shift in awareness, just for the remembering.

Center yourself at least ten times a day. Initially do this on your own, using the directions above. Then practice in different circumstances, sitting down, in meetings, before conversations, and in preparation for stressful events. It doesn't take extra time; it simply becomes a practice in gathering our attention for whatever we are about to do.

Core Practice 8.3:
Grounding

This practice builds on centering.

Grounding is very helpful when there is a lot coming at us. When we need to take a stand for something of value. When we are experiencing strong emotions. And when we are in conflict situations or are with others who are having strong emotions.

- To begin, center yourself to gather your attention and bring yourself into the present.
- Feel your connection into the ground, into what you care about, into what you stand for. Let whatever energy is coming towards you pass through down into the ground. The more

intensity there is, the more you relax, breathe, bringing rigorous attention to your feet, your legs, the ground under you. Imagine growing roots deep into the earth.

- Allow what you care about, and the sense of foundation and ground, to stabilize and support you.

Core Practice 8.4:
Stabilizing Breath

This practice is super simple and easy and can be done anywhere. It will reliably settle activation and help you ground.

- Sit with your back straight and center yourself.
- Inhale through your mouth.
- Closing your mouth, exhale through your nose. Slow down this out breath; it can be helpful at first to count to seven as you exhale. While this may seem like a long exhale, extending your exhalation is the key to the practice. Exhalation stimulates the parasympathetic nervous system, which is precisely what relaxes you.
- As you exhale, press your breath down into your lower abdomen, about two inches below your navel. The image of a French coffee press can be helpful as you imagine the focusing and concentrating of energy in this important center in the lower belly.

Core Practice 8.5:
Stillness

Stillness is the direct experience of possibility. Stillness is quiet, a pause. Like a cat waiting, both alert and relaxed for the mouse that she knows will inevitably appear, stillness is being not in action, yet ready for action. Stillness is the *pause of presence* that leadership expert and author Kevin Cashman writes about[65] as essential for leading with intentionality and consciousness.

- Try this brief experiment. Stop reading. Notice yourself thinking. Then, close your eyes and notice the space at the end of one thought and before the next. See if you can prolong this space of no-thought slightly, focusing on the stillness itself. Be as still as the cat … expectant, waiting, ready for anything that might come.
- Or, notice your breathing. Sense the moment of stillness at the top and the bottom of your breath. You can prolong this moment as well. This is stillness: this brief and fleeting moment when you are neither inhaling nor exhaling.

This stillness, out of which all experience arises, can be cultivated. It is the moment of choice, the moment of awareness that we can do something new.

CHAPTER SUMMARY

The core realization of this chapter is that you can change your inner state—the subtle and usually unconscious functioning of your psychobiology—by directing attention inwards. Observing your Soma changes it, creating shifts in your Being, thus making new actions possible. Specific practices can enable you to shift your state in reliable and powerful ways.

In this chapter, you exercised agency and influence over your Being. You inevitably will be triggered, but now you can respond to this activation of your nervous system by directing your attention, bringing presence to your inner experience, and self-regulating your Being to invite more resilient inner states.

Important stepping stones include:

- Observing your executive control of attention itself, a factory-loaded functionality that allows you to direct attention where you choose
- Taking the perspective that your Soma is itself a complex emergent system and a key component of the overall Complexity system in which you are leading
- Recognizing when your Soma is in stasis, activation, or resilience
- Observing the dynamism of your Soma and shifting from activation to resilience
- Realizing that you can immediately affect your mood, inner state, and resourcefulness through directed attention and present-moment awareness

These insights and practices scaffold your growing personal mastery by engaging your Being through awareness and presence. Your conscious direction of attention is becoming a powerful tool for leadership. This realization becomes very pragmatic through four simple practices in state regulation and cultivation. These core practices are:

- Centering
- Grounding
- Stabilizing Breath
- Stillness

These practices, over time, support your resilience, key to engaging with Complexity in ways that you have the freedom to choose and that invite the results you care about most.

Take some time to reflect on what you now realize as a result of this Pane.

- What do you understand differently?
- What are you now curious about?
- What experiments might you try?

≈◎ PRESENCE PAUSE ◎≈

	CONTEXT	IDENTITY	SOMA
SENSING	Observe The System	Recognize Identity At Stake	Attend To Experience
BEING	DECOUPLE STATE FROM CONTEXT		Regulate Inner State
ACTING			

CHAPTER 9

Being in Context:
Decouple State from Context

*Between the stimulus and the response is a space, and in
that space lies our power and our freedom.*

– Viktor Frankl

*Grant me the serenity to accept the people I cannot change,
the courage to change the one I can,
and the wisdom to know it's me.*

– Modified "Serenity Prayer," after *Reinhold Niebuhr*

IN PREVIOUS CHAPTERS, you have learned how to Sense the Context and the
ways in which your Identity is entangled with it. You have spotted triggers and
the evidence of your reactivity. You have practiced self-regulating your inner
state. Taken together, these further your capacity to Sense the multiple levels of
the Complex system in which you lead, and to work with your inner state in
new ways through engaging your Soma.

The dynamics of your relationship with your Context are pivotal for
maintaining resilience, or regaining it when it is lost. In Chapter 6, you
worked with Sensing how you have likely become identified with aspects of
your Context, even overly so. While that realization is an important first step,

leadership requires you now to **decouple your inner state from your Context.** The resulting realization that your experience is **influenced but not determined by** what's going on around you is profoundly liberating.

Frankl's liberating insight

Viktor Frankl was a Jewish psychiatrist. Imprisoned for three years in Nazi concentration camps, including many months of slave labor in arduous conditions, he lost his mother, brother, and wife in the Holocaust. Immediately following World War II, he famously wrote the seminal book, Man's Search for Meaning, *in which he was able to take a balcony perspective on one of the most dehumanizing experiences a person could have.*

On an icy road, at night, the prisoner Frankl had an epiphany: "As we stumbled on for miles, slipping on icy spots, supporting each other time and again, dragging one another up and onward, nothing was said, but we both knew: Each of us was thinking of his wife... My mind clung to my wife's image, imagining it with an uncanny acuteness. I heard her answering me, saw her smile, her frank and encouraging look... A thought transfixed me: For the first time in my life I saw the truth that... a man who has nothing left in the world may still know bliss, be it only for a brief moment, in the contemplation of his beloved."[56]

This experienced realization, amidst the horrors of Auschwitz, was profoundly liberating. In our language, Frankl's realization decoupled his inner state from his Context. The Nazis could do whatever they wished to his body; they could take away life or inflict cruel pain. But, they had no control over his thoughts; he alone could choose where he directed his attention. With very little control over anything, Frankl could still focus his attention on his wife. And, could thereby sustain his body and soul in some of the most arduous circumstances imaginable.

This is **resilience**: the capacity for choice, resourcefulness, perspective and a range of actions no matter what's going on around us. Frankl, of course, sets a pretty high bar. Still, you can access tremendous resilience through decoupling your own state from that of the system around you at any given moment. This chapter will show you more about how to do this.

COMPLEXITY TAKES UP RESIDENCE

The cognitive portions of our nervous systems are working constantly to take in energy and information about the world, making meaning of events and then recognizing and acting on opportunities and threats to our Identity. We rehash prior experience in order to learn from it, and we plan for the future by anticipating problems and opportunities and then preparing for them.

The onslaught of energy and information from around us is intense and constant. It frequently contains triggers ranging from the mundane (a mildly irritating email, something urgent on our desk we suddenly remember we must attend to) to significant Identity challenges (a professional public failure, a conflict with someone who has more power) to the traumatic and overwhelming (a car accident, violence, strong experiences of racism or sexism). Obviously, these are radically different magnitudes, but the fundamental processes of disruption and triggering are similar. Our stress hormones go up, our heartbeat increases, our thoughts become rapid, we find ourselves reacting and constricted. Our inner condition is being determined by the outer Context.

In Complex Contexts this experience of disruption, reactivity and disorganization is pervasive and continuous. We get caught up in the mood, pace, and intensity of what is going on around us. We "take on" the state of the system. Unchecked, our inner state becomes fused with our environment as we react to unpredictable events unfolding around us over which we have little control. And the more responsibility we feel for what is happening around us, the easier it becomes to be in a continual state of reaction to what is going on around us.

When this happens, our leadership has been subverted by system dynamics that render us far less capable of accessing useful perspectives or leading change.

Kendra gets ambushed

Kendra was the new director of a nonprofit agency providing technical assistance for community-based land preservation projects. She was making her first strategy presentation to her board. It was an important opportunity to make an impression, and she had great new ideas for community partnerships to share.

She knew the board felt they taken a risk with her as the agency's first ever non-technical director. Additionally, Kendra was the only African American in the agency leadership. While she knew she was the right person and she didn't want race to be an issue, the entire board was white, and she felt pressure to prove herself, though also tired of having to prove herself.

At Kendra's first board meeting, Jim, a long-term member with an accounting background whose only involvement was annual meetings, interrupted Kendra midsentence. His voice was raised; he frowned. Jim asked a detailed and obscure tax question about how the costs for a new office expansion would be depreciated. Prepared to talk strategy, Kendra drew a blank.

The question caught her completely off guard; her throat felt tight, her heartbeat was racing, and her face flushed. She immediately thought, "I'm being ambushed." Two members of her leadership team, both of whom she believed were supporters, were in the room but provided no help. She couldn't be sure, but she thought another board member grinned at Jim. Kendra felt thrown to the wolves. Looking around the room and seeing only blank faces, Kendra immediately felt shame and flashed on childhood experiences of being scolded in front of class, and the pain of a lifetime of being treated differently because she was black.

Later, when we spoke about it, Kendra reported her strong emotional reaction. She knew the challenge wasn't about accounting; it was about her non-technical background and probably about being black. She resented this angry white man trying to undermine her in her first board meeting and the frustrating need to discern, yet again, whether this was about race or something else.

At the time, hurt and stunned, she looked around for support. When none was forthcoming, she responded with a stammered half answer. She felt near tears and off balance for the remainder of the meeting and saw the incident as significantly undermining her nascent credibility.

This brief example is a classic triggering situation. Kendra reacted to the ambush with irritation and lost face in the encounter. The question was irrelevant, and there were a number of ways Kendra could have responded more skillfully, but the damage was done.

Kendra's loss of resilience in the situation had nothing to do with her competence or her strength of character. It had to do, in part, with a soft spot in her Identity structure: the uncertainty of her worth after being hired for her community leadership experience when previous directors had technical backgrounds. And, it had to do with the pain of a lifetime of living as a racial minority, being treated differently, and feeling like she had to work twice as hard to overcome others' doubts and stereotypes. This Context was far bigger than the agency, or the meeting, or Jim… it was a whole historical Context that went back generations. Kendra was sick of having to prove herself and had looked forward to not having to do this in what she saw as a progressive agency.

This incident was unplanned and revealing of Complexity dynamics. The ingredients? A deep social Context of oppression, within which both Jim and Kendra had been enculturated. One board member with an Identity to prop up. One split decision that a couple of board members hadn't supported. One confrontational question.

Add up these elements, and Kendra was off to a rocky start.

DECOUPLING: THE KEY TO RESILIENCE

The good news is that we can learn to decouple our internal state from the Context. The function of "executive control" (discussed previously in Chapters 7 and 8) can be harnessed to direct our attention away from what is happening in the Context to something of our choosing: a value, a purpose, a goal, a state. Resilience, after all, is the capacity to access choice and resourcefulness no matter what's going on around us. Our intentional direction of attention is in itself a practice of this resilience.

Over the past four chapters, we have been building the capacities to sense our Context, to sense the threat to our Identity, and to sense and then self-regulate our own internal experience. Taken together, these capacities allow us to step outside ourselves and take on a new view that is tremendously freeing. Our inner state is not conditioned on what's going on around us; it is differentiated.

"The last of the human freedoms is to choose one's own attitude, regardless of the circumstances."[57] Frankl's profound realization is that we can always choose what we pay attention to; we can choose for ourselves an organizing principle regardless of situation. This is the transcendent realization of liberating attitude from circumstances, of decoupling internal state from Context, however difficult.

I don't claim that this is necessarily easy. Yet it is possible. Always. The decoupling of state from Context is crucial for leaders if we are not to be bound up in reactivity. When we become overwhelmed by or entangled with our Context, we essentially become incapable of intervening or changing much. Our internal state has become part of a feedback loop tying us up in our Context, and we have lost our differentiation. The collapse of healthy boundaries is a frequent condition in broken systems, and re-creating differentiation is an entry point.

It's up to you to recognize, and leverage, that entry point.

Differentiating between Context, Soma and Identity

Resilience is lost when we become entangled in the systems within which we seek to lead. The Nine Panes help us disentangle ourselves by differentiating the three levels of system at play in any situation. The meta-competency of Being is the territory for recovering our innate capacities within a system that seems to conspire to neutralize us.

The *decoupling* of our internal state—our differentiation of our Identity and Soma from the Context around us—is a fundamental shift. It introduces daylight between one level of the system—us—and the rest of the Context. We realize that the system can be in one condition, and we can be in another.

This is the cumulative realization of the previous four chapters. It follows a certain logic, but in practice happens spontaneously. Let's break down the components of this liberating realization.

First, we Sense and name what is happening in our Context (Chapter 5). We face the reality of the situation by lifting our Bell Jar to Sense more objectively. We can then see clearly what is triggering us or what feels overwhelming. ("There are people on this board that doubt my competence and will test me." Or, "This is a new phase for this agency; I'm the right person, but not everyone knows it yet.")

Then, we Sense and name our own reactions to this Context (Chapters 6 and 7). We recognize how our Identity is challenged and how this challenge shows up in us. ("I'm feeling challenged, and taking it personally by doubting myself." "Jim is poking me. Once again I have to think about whether this is race, and do I confront it or not?" Again, the Awareness Map is helpful: "I notice my thoughts are racing and my shoulders hunched." "I notice I'm trying to figure out why Jim is testing me.") We can take a balcony view, Sensing our Identity and Soma even in full-blown defense mode!

We stabilize our inner state (Chapter 8) in moments of reactivity precisely by staying fiercely present with our experience. The more intensely uncomfortable we are, the more rigor and commitment it takes to stay present, especially when every fiber in our Being wants to act. State-shifting practices—center, ground, relaxed breath, stillness—are good starting points. ("I am settling myself with breath. Slow down. Feel my ground. Breathe." "I am focusing back on what we have set out to do." "Don't fight. Just stay present. Pause. Stillness.")

In this moment, we have decoupled our inner state from the Context. This moment of realization, this stillness in which the next move has not yet been revealed, is now present in us. We can now actively direct the full power of our attention to a chosen organizing principle within ourselves: a sensation, an experience, a state or a value that is internal to us and thus readily accessible. We have recovered agency through self-regulation, even as Frankl did on that lonely icy road.

Now, we have taken responsibility for the inner condition from which any response will arise. The meeting is still going, the question still requires an answer, but we are addressing the situation on our own terms, from an inner state of our choosing. Once we are centered and resourced again, we can choose what to do.

This is liberation: the experienced realization, in the moment, of freedom and choice.

~⊷ PRESENCE PAUSE ⊶~

Access an Internal Organizing Principle

When leaders can decouple our state from the Context, we can embody optimism and creativity and settledness and kindness. We do this even when, especially when, the system around us is overwhelmed and reactive and chaotic and mean-spirited. Only after decoupling our state from the Context can we lead in a way that is transformative and something new can emerge.

I am not putting the burden of changing the system on those who have been oppressed. Kendra, our new director of a not-for-profit organization from the last chapter, was simply wanting to do a job she cared about deeply. Yet, there she was again, even in her exciting new role with a notably progressive agency, triggered and having to sort out what was race and what was other stuff. And what is next for her as a leader. Whatever move she chooses, internal resilience will serve her well.

A key to resilience is to choose an organizing principle. In Kendra's processing after the debacle with Jim, we can see both her ***differentiation*** of her inner state from the Context, and her ***connection*** to an organizing principle around which to mobilize.

Kendra makes meaning

When we discussed Kendra's experience, I asked her to become aware of her emotions and sensations. As she described the incident, she reported rage, a knot in her belly, anxiety, intense shame and a desire to run and hide.

Kendra saw how vulnerable she had felt in her first board meeting when she wanted to make a good showing. She knew the decision to hire her had not been unanimous, and she wanted the whole group to have confidence. Her Identity as a capable, resourceful, unifying leader was at stake.

She had seen that Jim's question was a trap. She could see how strongly she had been affected by what she experienced as a personal attack. This reaction was amplified by discovering that her new job was yet another Context where she would be questioned because of her race, presumably forcing her to prove herself doubly.

Kendra was eager to learn from this very painful experience. These strategies proved enormously helpful:

- *Kendra saw that she had effectively ceded power over her inner state to Jim. She had been unable, in the moment, to tolerate the intense discomfort of this major historical trigger and had essentially collapsed. While she was still furious with Jim, she also had a deeper appreciation for how a lifetime of experiences led to her entire nervous system reacting to a shallow and mean-spirited question.*

- *She saw that she could have taken some time to breathe and center before responding. A pause for state-shifting might have allowed a more creative and skillful response.*

- *She identified several skillful tactics for responding to the question that she could have used had she been able to resource herself.*

- *Kendra also saw that Jim was probably needing to prove his own worth at Kendra's expense. Whether or not this was actually true, it was helpful to Kendra because it provided a different narrative and allowed some compassion for Jim. It also suggested some different approaches to future interactions.*

Most importantly, Kendra chose to frame this setback as an opportunity. Kendra chose the perspective that this incident, and her relationship with Jim, offered her a developmental opportunity to resource herself under fire. Overbearing white men threatened by strong black women were a perfect and rather predictable foil for her to practice with. While she actually didn't care that much about Jim, whom she saw as old school and insecure, she did care deeply about her own power and effectiveness in an important role.

She immediately got back on the horse by scheduling another meeting with her board. She trusted herself, knowing that it was likely that there would be challenges next time as well, and she made a promise to herself to meet those challenges from a firmer inner foundation.

Resilience-Enhancing Strategies and Practices

Resilience results from the capacity for directed attention and choice, no matter what's going on around us. This is, in principle, available in any moment. In practice, it can be devilishly difficult. We have been so deeply conditioned to be responsible for, and reactive to, what is going on around us that we don't even see how we have become hooked into the system, and thus, unable to lead effectively. The liberating realizations of the previous sections sound good on paper. But when we are triggered, we are triggered, and Frankl's experience in the concentration camps of Nazi Germany seems hardly relevant.

Yet, Frankl speaks deep truth into the human condition. Our knowledge about attention, embodied learning, and capacity building shows us conclusively that specific perspectives and practices can increase our access to resilience. Investing in our capacity for resilience will dramatically increase the likelihood that we can access the liberating realization of choice when the stakes are high or triggers particularly strong. Practice over time, and we will discover how our attention is the doorway to our innate resilience.

Here are some strategies and practices that draw from conversations Bev Wann[58] and I held with many remarkable people who were able to access resilience under extraordinary conditions. The following four perspectives and strategies will increase your fluidity in accessing resilience.

> ## FOUR RESILIENCE STRATEGIES
>
> Here are a few ways to scaffold the realization of resilience:
>
> - See triggers as opportunities
> - Build tolerance for discomfort
> - Recognize and expand moments of stillness and choice
> - Build a repertoire of proven state-shifting practices

See Triggers as Opportunities

One strategy to build resilience is to change our perspective on the very things we experience as challenging. You can choose your relationship with difficulties in your Context, inhabiting a perspective that enhances, rather than detracts, from your resilience.

Here's a lovely story that illustrates this principle:

Atisha and the Bengali tea boy

When the great Buddhist teacher Atisha went to Tibet… he was told the people of Tibet were very good-natured, earthy, flexible, and open. He decided they wouldn't be irritating enough to push his buttons. So he brought along with him a mean-tempered, ornery Bengali tea boy. He felt that was the only way he could stay awake.

The Tibetans like to tell the story that, when Atisha got to Tibet, he realized that he need not have brought his tea boy: the people there were not as pleasant as he had been told! [59]

The fact that major spiritual teachers have deliberately chosen to hang out with jerks in order to fast-track their own enlightenment should mean something to you. Jerks can reliably provide an accelerant to your own resilience practice if you choose the appropriate perspective, just as Kendra reframed the dynamic with Jim as a practice opportunity for her own resilience and power.

In your own situation, surely there is an irritating "Bengali tea boy." Who do you find frustrating? What dynamics in your environment are difficult? Probably you didn't choose these triggers. But, in Complexity, the universe can usually be trusted to provide plenty of triggers, unbidden. You don't always get to choose the situation, but you can always choose your perspective on it.

How can you use that triggering? What is there for you to see in your own reactions to things? How might you, in the face of these triggers, practice tolerating discomfort, staying centered, and making wise leadership moves?

Seeing our obstacles as teachers and catalysts for development is an important perspective shift.

Build Tolerance for Intense Experience

A second strategy is to learn to tolerate our discomfort by not acting on it. We simply stay present to it. [60] States, even highly uncomfortable ones, arise and pass. Sometimes, the move is simply to stay with our intense internal experience, including strongly activated emotional states, as they arise and pass.

Our relationship to our emotions is often complex. Emotions are not welcomed in many organizations; they are seen as some sort of alien force that threatens to weaken the objectivity upon which all good decisions are theoretically based! And they can feel overwhelming when they arise, especially where the Context does not support the expression of emotions.

Thus, where emotions are not welcomed, we may try the opposite strategy of stuffing them. This doesn't work: stuffing or denying emotions actually strengthens them, gives them power and freezes them in place. Longer term, it leads to all kinds of health consequences and diminishes resilience.

In between stuffing emotions and being overwhelmed by them is the middle ground of allowing and observing them at the same time. We don't get to cherry-pick the particular feelings we are willing to feel while tuning out the others. We stay present to all of it. We feel what is arising within us, and at the same time we keep enough distance to name and describe our experience. We allow ourselves to participate in our emotions, staying present to them. We allow our experiences to follow the natural trajectory of any emotion or experience, which is to arise and inevitably pass, like clouds moving across the sky.

With the realization that emotions arise and pass, just like all experiences, the power they have over us lessens. We don't act to avoid feeling difficult experiences, nor do our attachments to happy experiences drive us into unskillful actions. Presence means allowing the flow of all experience to move freely through us. We realize that we can tolerate unpleasant experiences without being driven by them to unhelpful actions.

I repeat my early caveat here. Resilience is not the Olympics of tolerating intensity! There's no gold medal for the endurance of triggering. ***Not everything should be tolerated.***

Building resilience is not simply a matter of building tolerance for discomfort, especially when doing so requires overriding vital discernment about the source of the discomfort. Some kinds of triggering are indicators that it is time to leave a relationship, team, or organization within which you cannot be healthy. Or time to take a stronger stand for what you care about. Other kinds of triggering are indicators of trauma or unprocessed psychological material that requires therapeutic support. These situations are common and beyond the scope of this book.[61]

Recognize and Expand Moments of Stillness and Choice

A third strategy is to exercise the muscle of choice through presence, however minuscule the opportunity might seem at the time.

I was an intense little boy and had a bit of an anger management problem as a child. My mother, with all too much frequency, would tell me that when I was mad, I should count to ten before saying or doing anything. While there's nothing magic about the number ten, there is definitely magic in remembering that in any given moment I have choice. My mother was on to something.

Again, from Frankl: "Between stimulus and response there is a space. In that space is our power to choose our response. In our response lies our growth and our freedom."[62] This space is precisely the stillness we have been talking about.

Counting to ten created a moment of choice. I had no theory to back this at the time, but it actually worked. By the time I got to ten, the wave of anger had often passed, or at least diminished. I had already made the choice to count, rather than punch. I could make another choice.

In this moment of stillness anything is possible. My poor brothers, seeing I was mad, didn't know what would be next. Neither did I. But the space, the breath, the moment of choice allowed a much greater range of possibilities than did my immediate and nearly overwhelming action urge. Recognizing and practicing with these moments of choice, however small, creates stillness when nothing is settled and much is possible.

Kendra, with hindsight, saw the missed potential moment of stillness and choice in her meeting, and it became an important part of her preparation for her next encounter with Jim.

Build a Repertoire of Validated State-Shifting Practices

A fourth and final strategy for cultivating resilience is to build a range of practices that you have experimented with and personally validated for yourself as helpful.[63] After practicing and building this repertoire, you can access any of them as needed.

As you look over these common practices, you might note that some are already in your leadership toolbox and you are quite familiar with them. Others will be new. Some of these can be done in seconds, others take some time and investment.

This is often a new perspective. Whether or not you have thought consciously about "state-shifting practices" or have ever inventoried what you know about shifting your state to access resilience, you likely already do some of these instinctively. I will wager that you have a far more extensive resilience skill base than you have previously made explicit to yourself.

In Chapter 8, I offered four core state-shifting practices that can be used in the moment to resource ourselves:

- Centering
- Grounding
- Stabilizing breath
- Stillness

Doing these with regularity over time will produce noticeably greater access to more resourceful states under pressure. Here are some others for use when we need to decouple our inner state from the Context immediately. These may seem trivial, but state-shifting is neither complicated nor high drama. Simple is good:

- Counting to ten
- Taking a few deep breaths
- A quick use of humor
- Changing body posture or physical environment
- Continuing a conversation but shifting the venue or going outdoors
- Shifting perspectives, which often produces a state change

Now, a few practices that require more time. These are perfect for stepping out of a situation and reentering it later, after a few minutes, a few hours, or a few days. Again, the practices are simple and you've heard them all before. Contextualizing them as state-shifting practices for resilience changes them:

- Getting a good night's sleep
- Exercising with a strong physical workout, run, or fast walk
- Getting into nature
- Talking to someone outside the situation who can listen well
- Taking time away from a problem and coming back to it later
- Eating a good, healthy meal
- Taking time away from someone we're having difficulty with and returning later
- Playing with kids or grandkids
- Grabbing a double espresso
- Reconnecting to what's most important to you
- Taking a vacation!

All of these shift our state in various ways and on different timescales. You are assuredly familiar with the benefits of some. I encourage you to become more intentional about using these in situations where you can benefit from resourcing yourself.

Resilience Is Pragmatic

Resilience—our Being—is core to our leadership. Becoming more resilient is to reclaim our innate capacity for choice and resourcefulness in a situation that often perversely seems to deny it to us.

Rajeev invests in resilience

Rajeev began to experiment with self-regulation and state-shifting. These strategies were really intended to reduce his reactivity and to allow his people to begin to step up.

Rajeev knew that moving away from the village of his birth, attending college, and then pursuing a successful and meaningful career had taken both pluck and luck. However, he had not fully recognized the cost to himself and the team of his self-imposed mission to save as many others from poverty as possible. These mutually reinforcing dynamics—a Context and mission to which he was deeply committed, and a passionate Identity predicated on achievement and doing good—had taken up persistent residence in his Soma as a constantly driven and hypervigilant inner state. The behaviors of his team members, which he had labeled as sluggish and lacking initiative, became powerful mirrors for his own impatience, and reminders about what he needed to change as a leader.

Rajeev worked with decoupling his inner state from these larger issues. In India, he had been a regular yoga practitioner. He had dropped this practice, but resumed it now, which was enormously helpful in settling himself and focusing his attention. Now, he could see constriction and activation in his Soma as an opportunity to practice stabilizing breath to settle himself, whether in yoga or in meetings.

He also engaged in a consistent practice of seeking perspectives. His impatience and sense of urgency had always seemed noble, but he was coming to see it as compulsive and even tyrannical. Pauses and silence that had seemed like wasted time became stillness within which new thoughts and possibilities might emerge.

Rajeev was on the way to decoupling his inner state from the Context of his organization's mission, and how the mission triggered his own Identity. This began slowly, but some experimentation and practice began to reveal new and significant organizing principles around what mattered most to him.

These are ways to shift your Being en route from Sensing to Acting. Resilience is the insertion of presence and choice into this in-between realm of metabolizing energy and information. Resilience allows creativity, resourcefulness and skillful Acting regardless of what is going on around us.

Experiment 9.1:
Identify Your Resilience Practices

Take a few minutes to respond to these questions:

- What specific dynamic in your Context has been a particular challenge to your resilience?
- How has your Identity been entangled with the Context?
- How has your inner state been coupled with the conditions in the Context?
- What do you Sense now about how your Soma is triggered by these challenges? What happens inside you?
- What are three resilience strategies, based on the material in this chapter, that you could experiment with for restoring your resilience in this situation?
- What specific experiments or regular practices will you now commit to?

CHAPTER SUMMARY

This chapter challenged you to realize the interconnectedness of your Context and your inner state. You saw that you (like all of us) are relentlessly being triggered by what's going on around you, that it is natural to incorporate the condition of the Context into your own Soma. Triggering and your identification with the Context reduce your resilience. When your inner state is an enmeshed component of the system, you are unable to take perspective or act in useful ways.

The core realization of this chapter is that it's possible to decouple your inner state from the Context. Resilience is the innate, always available capacity to be creative, resourceful and able to take skillful action regardless of circumstances. You build resilience as you liberate yourself from an inner state conditioned on that Context and invite one grounded in an organizing principle of your own choosing.

Important stepping stones from this chapter include the realizations that:

- Your inner state will **always be influenced** by what is going on around you but will **never be determined** by it.
- Decoupling your state from the Context liberates your attention and awareness for new organizing principles of your choosing.
- Accessing resilience isn't always easy, but it is always possible. It is particularly challenging, and particularly necessary, when you are strongly triggered. Pausing to stay present with your own fierce experience is key.
- Stepping stones include a growing palette of state-shifting practices that you can use

on various timescales. These practices support decoupling and produce resilience, creativity and resourcefulness no matter what's going on around you.

- Supporting strategies include reframing triggers as opportunities, building your tolerance for discomfort, recognizing and expanding moments of choice, and increasing your repertoire of state-shifting practices.

These pragmatic strategies, all enabled by directed attention, support the profound realization that resilience derives from mastery over your inner state, producing tremendous freedom in the moment. This presence-based resilience is available in any circumstance: a phone call, a difficult conversation, a conflict, a battlefield.

To be present is to be resilient.

Take some time to reflect on what you now realize as a result of this Pane.

- What do you understand differently?
- What are you now curious about?
- What experiments might you try?

✍ PRESENCE PAUSE ✍

	CONTEXT	IDENTITY	SOMA
SENSING	Observe The System	Recognize Identity At Stake	Attend To Experience
BEING	Decouple State From Context	EMBODY WHAT MATTERS	Regulate Inner State
ACTING			

Being an Identity: Embody What Matters

*The body always leads us home . . . if we can simply learn
to trust sensation and stay with it long enough for it to
reveal appropriate action, movement, insight, or feeling.*

– Pat Ogden

*Everyone has been made for some particular work, and
the desire for that work has been put in every heart.*

– Rumi

IN OUR JOURNEY TOGETHER UP TO NOW, you have been focused on Sensing
and Being in a world that is unpredictable and sometimes overwhelming.
By Sensing in new ways, and by self-regulating and decoupling your inner
state from the Context, you are acquiring a resilience and potential for
influence in the system around you in ways impossible to access if you are
entangled with it.

This is freedom. Freedom for what, you might ask? Freedom, as Kendra found
on examination, to replace a triggered reaction to dynamics in the system with
a centered, grounded internal organizing principle of her choosing. Freedom to
choose the attitude to see Jim, her baiter on the board, as a foil for her practice
of resilience and power.

On a grander scale, it is freedom to imagine and to lead towards optimistic futures that are literally invisible from within a particular Bell Jar and/or Context.

Facing and negotiating with your reactions as present-moment phenomena frees you not only from the constraints of your history but also—and sometimes most importantly—the limitations of what the present seems to allow. The freedom you are beginning to access is the freedom to embody and create results that matter.

Mandela embodies a future

Through decades of repression and imprisonment, Nelson Mandela had been the leader of the anti-apartheid movement in South Africa. During his release, election as president, and subsequent inauguration, South Africa was a country riven with fear, mistrust and violence. Many in the African National Congress would have been understandably happy to wreak revenge on the white minority who had oppressed black South Africans for so long, and Mandela himself had more than enough justification for bitterness, resentment and rage.

Mandela became, famously, the symbol of an integrated, peaceful and harmonious South Africa. His moral standing was impeccable. Mandela was loved by black South Africans, but also feared by many whites. Mandela understood that the future of the nation depended on healing deep and painful divisions. He also understood, and empathized with, the powerful currents that were pulling in the opposite direction: the easy and tempting road of revenge.

Mandela embodied the future of a united South Africa. Whatever the odds, he knew that it began with him. His consistent grace, compassion and integrity sent a strong message about this future.

One notable story has Mandela, on his inauguration day, spontaneously getting out of the limousine and walking up to the Afrikaans head of his security detail. He told the man, "Colonel. I just wanted to tell you that there is no more you and us. You are our police. I am your president."⁶⁴ This out-of-the-limelight comment was one of countless and congruent leadership moves that brought the future alive in the present, helping a nation heal and move forward.

Mandela embodied a future that was not yet real. Through the instrument of his Identity, he acted consistently with this future, inviting it to emerge in the present.

To bring in Mandela here—in this final chapter on Being—is itself a declaration of the power of presence for leaders. At this moment, we make a significant pivot. This pivot has been hinted at throughout. Now I will make it very explicit and pragmatic.

You have learned to *differentiate* your inner state from what's going on in the present around you. Now you will *connect* it to a future you care about through the process of embodiment. This process of building an Identity that is congruent with what matters most is the essence of embodied leadership.

This chapter is about how humans turn minute firings of neurons into dams, books, trips to the moon, lasting relationships, financial success, and social justice. A future to care about. A culture of curiosity and experimentation. A world that works for all.

⚞ PRESENCE PAUSE ⚟

Two Conditions for Embodied Leadership

It's important to be able to distinguish and to Sense, within ourselves and in others, the difference between this kind of embodied congruent leadership and the conventional though well-intentioned leadership that sometimes leaves us wanting. I find two conditions to be essential in a presence-based approach to leadership in complexity:

- *The articulation of a future, a direction in which to move.* This sense of direction, and the articulation of some alternative future that matters, is the fundamental act of leadership.

- *An internal congruence with that future.* Here, a leader's Soma, Identity, actions, thoughts, and behaviors are internally congruent with the articulated future. And, this congruence is consistent and palpable by others.

Let's explore what leadership might look like when these conditions are absent. Embodied leadership is not simply a matter of behaving our way differently to the same future, nor more skillfully driving for results. Rajeev's continuing story will illustrate the difference between tactical new leadership behaviors and embodying a new leadership Identity. Here he is again, working hard to become a better leader.

Rajeev tries new means

Rajeev was on the edge of a significant developmental shift. To his credit, he was able to recognize that his drive and urgency were counterproductive, stifling ownership and creativity among his people. Yet there had been little shift in his core Identity, the headline of which was "It's up to me to save the world."

Due to Rajeev's self-regulation and other experiments, meetings were better, there was a new energy on the team, and Rajeev himself seemed more relaxed and open. This was rather tactical, however, and his people could still sense his underlying urgency. Rajeev's new behaviors also seemed to require a considerable assertion of will and patience to sustain. Rajeev eventually felt frustrated, as if he were straining at the end of a leash, and didn't like the feeling of having to rein in his prodigious energy to take care of others.

In essence, the embodiment of a new Identity was still a way off. His behaviors were not yet underpinned by internal congruence and a new organizing principle. He liked the idea of a highly collaborative organization, but this was not yet embodied. Rather, he was simply managing himself more skillfully towards the same business results.

Rajeev's laser focus on results, and his working to relax and open his behavior and his Being, were both commendable. Yet there was a tension, a certain incongruence, that Rajeev could sense within himself. Others could also sense this, though they appreciated Rajeev's evident changes, and didn't have the language or distinctions to name what still seemed somewhat "off."

Rajeev was working hard, both at the business results and at changing himself. In his very efforts at self-improvement, he was still driving himself hard. Development as a leader, becoming more relaxed and collaborative, had simply become another project to manage, to drive, to succeed at. His underlying achiever Identity had co-opted his intentions to be a different kind of leader, and this internal incongruence was subtly palpable to all.

A Radical Possibility

I am proposing that our intended future can come to live in our body in the present. The future can come alive through us. This is both radical and audacious. The perspective offered by this Pane is that in the swirl of unpredictable Complexity, we ourselves can serve as an organizing principle for what we care about.

I know this sounds like a stretch. For now, consider Nelson Mandela and Rajeev. Mandela's consistent, stable, and optimistic direction towards unification was the embodiment of a future that was far from assured. And his reliable internal compass informed and shaped actions by himself and others that shepherded South Africa through a very perilous transition.

Rajeev has a mental picture of what an inclusive, relaxed, and facilitative leadership style response might have been in his situation, but it is not yet embodied. For him, so far, this has the feel of an experiment, the testing of a possibility. It makes sense to him, and he knows what to practice, but it is not yet an embodied set of internal conditions from which he can reliably lead.

Direction as Organizing Principle

In traditional wedding vows, two people make vows to each other to love and cherish each other. We promise to stay the course, regardless of a diverse and specified set of conditions (e.g., richer, poorer, sickness, health, better, worse…) until "death do us part."

In fact, when we get married, we haven't a clue how we will actually do this, nor likely what those vows even really mean. Our financial goals, career aspirations and timelines are not prescribed in our wedding promises. But deeply held vows can provide powerful guidance and orientation for the countless unforeseeable circumstances that will inevitably make it difficult to follow them.

Marriage, of course, is a Complex system. Vows provide a ***stabilizing directional force*** that transcends the ups and downs and challenges of daily life to provide an organizing principle for a lifetime of partnership.

Organizations often work towards futures via the declaration of specific commitments, goals, measurable results, and outcomes. Such rigor is helpful, and very useful in many situations, especially when the challenges we face are Obvious or Complicated, per the Cynefin distinctions in Chapter 1. When problems are largely Complicated, and outcomes are relatively predictable and knowable, detailed planning is well-suited.

However, in Complexity, we might Sense patterns, but the Context and future remain elusive and unpredictable. Goals and metrics can actually be anti-helpful. Detailed planning prescribes actions, based on assumptions about what ***will happen***, that actually reduce our range of potential creative responses to what ***actually happens***. Plans focus our Sensing; we assess performance and information only through the lens of the plan. We likely (unconsciously) filter out rich additional information that could inform us whether the system is actually working.

We must inoculate ourselves against the reassuring but false belief that sufficient effort and planning can enable us to predict, control, and fix our way into the future. Not having our hearts set on a particular destination, however, does not mean we cannot set intentions about the general *direction* of the change we are trying to lead. We might notice that a general direction may feel less satisfying to hang onto. Or, we experience it as lacking rigor in the traditional (Complicated) sense. Yet, this notion of direction is very enabling in Complexity when flexibility, responsiveness and creativity are essential conditions.

Leading in Complexity means beginning with great clarity about the direction we are heading and about the future we intend. We Sense, and then embody, the broad direction, the outlines of the shore upon which we aspire to land. Preserving flexibility and spaciousness, this overall direction becomes an organizing principle. Then, we trust our creativity, and nourish the resourcefulness of those around us, in order to navigate and adjust as new information becomes available. We work together to create the conditions for this future, rather than engineering a set of business outcomes.

Internal Congruence

Think of a leader whom you implicitly trust, with whom you believe you can find the way together, who in some way possesses an internal way of Being that invites participation. This leader is aligned with the future she intends. You likely find yourself wanting to share the journey with her.

For sure, this leader takes skillful actions. She knows her stuff.

But, almost certainly, there's also something inward that complements her actions and that draws you. This subtle but palpable quality is *internal congruence*: an alignment of body, heart, thought and action that is coherent and consistent. It is both present within the leader's internal state and palpable by others. Internal congruence results from having declared a future that matters, and from having integrated that future possibility into who we are now. Congruence is attractive: Others are drawn to these leaders.

An embodied future, and an explicit direction towards that future, serve as organizing principles around which we can develop internal congruence. The more compelling, the more the future matters, the more we are emotionally connected to where our direction leads, the more powerful the organizing principle. Direction doesn't tell us how we will get there. Just where we are going.

Acting follows, naturally and spontaneously, once appropriate internal conditions have been created and stabilized.

≈≈ PRESENCE PAUSE ≈≈

Integrating Direction and Congruence

We all have mental pictures of some future we intend for ourselves and for the Context around us: an accomplishment, business success, making a contribution that we care about. And given the uncertainty and complexity in the world, there really are no guarantees of success. There are, however, ways to tilt the odds in our favor. This tilting of the odds begins with *shifting the conditions within our own self-system*.

Embodied futures begin as explicit statements or visions about the future we intend, which we then incorporate into our Identity and our psychobiology. We cultivate, through practice, inner states that are congruent with this future. These inner states become integrated into our Being such that we *live from that future in the present. We are essentially reshaping our Identity—our self-system—around a new organizing principle*. Thoughts, meaning-making, and actions that arise from the internal conditions of an embodied future are naturally and consistently aligned and consistent with this future. This makes the manifestation of this future far more likely.

And, by organizing ourselves around what we truly care about, we are far less likely to waste our precious life energy on the relentless and myopic pursuit of results that actually don't matter to us much at all.

Ed Catmull's wonderful book about creating a sustainable creative culture at Pixar is a rich study in Complexity, in particular about how Pixar built a shop that reliably produces deeply human films with leading-edge animation technology.[65] Doing so requires addressing both the Complicated and the Complex, each in service to a clear overall direction. And, it requires the presence-based capacity for trust and collaboration that is built through the integration of congruence and direction.

Pixar nourishes human-scale creativity in a mega-successful studio

Ed Catmull, long-term CEO of Pixar and now of Disney Animation, which owns Pixar, imagines his role as the ongoing creation of a sustainable culture of technical innovation and artistic creativity. Pixar's thirty-one Academy awards, consistent box-office successes, leading-edge technology, and track record of deeply human and beloved films attest to the success of this complex undertaking.

Running a studio is a Complicated thing. Catmull describes "the Beast" at Disney as the growing "infrastructure of the studio… to service, market, and promote each successful film." The Beast needs to be fed, accelerating the need for "more product in the pipeline." A well-run studio needs to budget time, money and resources in appro-

priate amounts at appropriate times; coordinate production, financing, and marketing; and do intricate and complicated planning on the basis of an idea that, at the outset, exists only as a glimmer in someone's imagination.

Yet, the making of a delicate, nuanced, full-length animated story is also a creative and Complex thing. In an early catastrophe, Pixar discovered that the initial approach to Toy Story 2 *had gone so far off the creative rails that they had to start over, at great financial and emotional costs. No less devastating were compromises designed to "feed the Beast" at Disney, resulting in a long period of lower quality films that privileged creation efficiency over creativity itself.*

Catmull describes a number of approaches for holding the direction towards creative, deeply human, and financially successful films. One is the tradition of "Braintrust" meetings during the development of a movie. These periodic gatherings bring together the company's best directors, artists and storytellers to review each project along the way.

The direction of these Braintrust meetings is pointedly stated: to move an embryonic creative project from something that "sucks" to something that "doesn't suck." It involves an assumption that every film starts off ugly and will take many months and iterations to become great. Egos are left at the door, and the meetings are characterized by a precious blend of "frank talk, spirited debate, laughter, and love." Trust is built because all these supersmart creative people have the best intentions for each other and for the film. This level of trust and shared commitment allows everyone in the room, regardless of rank, to share their views on what works and what doesn't work about the film. Trust and candor are conditions that emerge from the shared direction in the room.

At Pixar, there is still plenty of need for goals and metrics, for budgeting and scheduling resources; much of what there is to accomplish resides in the Complicated space. At the same time, many of the subtle but crucial cultural elements that have made Pixar great could only emerge in the realm of Complexity.

In Complexity, a broad direction for moving towards the future is far more useful than a specific performance goal. Rigor is required to note the human tendency to narrow toward concrete finish lines when a broader direction will be more enabling and less frustrating. The internal congruence of leaders, and a shared sense of future direction, nourish the innovation and creativity and resilience that are so essential when the Context is unpredictable and uncontrollable.

With these distinctions in mind, and with the newfound freedom from Chapter 9 to liberate our inner states from the Context around us, we will imagine futures that matter deeply to us, discern the direction to move, and embody both to become an organizing principle in the system. By the end of this chapter, we will see how this approach created a major shift for Rajeev and his organization, including much greater ease and joy for himself. And, how this might happen for you.

EMBODYING A FUTURE: IDENTITY AS A STAND FOR WHAT MATTERS

We can see the natural arising of congruent action in the story of Mandela expressing the future of a unified South Africa through a spontaneous aside to the Afrikaner head of his security detail. This was not part of a plan. It was a creative moment that arose, spontaneously, from the internal conditions of an embodied future.

So, how do we get there ourselves? How do we cultivate, and then embody, an Identity that will naturally and creatively move us in our intended direction?

Experiential Neuroplasticity

Let's take a deeper look at how embodiment really happens.

We can harness the same developmental forces that made us who we are in order to become the leader we choose to be. *Neuroplasticity* is the tremendously exciting focus of groundbreaking scientific research and the subject of a rash of books.[66] Plasticity refers to changeability; neuroplasticity to the phenomenon of how our nervous system can encode a wide range of capabilities for later ready access. Neuroplasticity explains how we learn and grow and evolve at all stages of life, and how we can embody this learning in our neural circuitry on a semi-permanent basis.

Whether or not you have ever heard of neuroplasticity, you are already a master at it: you've been practicing since before you were born. Now you will learn how to use this inherent biological capability intentionally in order to embody chosen directions that matter to you.

Permit me a moment to refresh your memory. In Chapters 2 and 3, we explored how development proceeds through a series of stages. In this process, physical capabilities as well as capacities for holding Complexity, meaning-making and taking multiple perspectives increase. We learned how new capabilities are embodied at each stage, only to be disrupted when the requirements of our Context, and/or our internal development impulse, propel us into new territory.

Some habitual states (experienced as particular moods, familiar behaviors, strong memories, habits, triggers, etc.) have what we might experience as a gravitational pull. They have become, internally, an organizing principle. This is because neuroplasticity—

meaning "neurons that fire together wire together"[67]—has stored these frequently accessed states in long-term memory. Neurons associated with each other through this prior experience acquire a semi-permanent predisposition to fire together, encoding patterns that lie latent in our circuitry, perpetually poised for activation.

The good news is that these capabilities have become instantly available. The bad news is that our Bell Jars have become embodied, drastically limiting our resilience and creativity.

Crucially, because this is how our psychobiology was conditioned in the first place, *neuroplasticity is also how we can recondition our psychobiology now in service to what the future is asking of us.*

Experiential neuroplasticity is my affectionate term for the intimate process of "sticky" physiologically supported embodiment through the skillful direction of our attention into our immediate experience. Our active engagement and focusing of attention on precisely what we choose is the key to embodying new organizing principles. And for sustainable and consistent internal congruence with what we care about. The attention practices in Chapters 8 and 9 took advantage of these principles. We now turn to harnessing this same fundamental process in service to what we care about as leaders.

Richard Strozzi-Heckler writes, "The human body is incapable of not practicing. And what we practice we become."[68]

Through attention-directed neuroplasticity, we can build new patterns—even a new Identity—that can then be available in service to the future we care about. Embodying a future as a present-moment, optimistic, aspirational inner state is the key to leadership. Experiencing this fully, across all channels of our Awareness Map, begins to encode permanent neuronal networks of this state.

"Practice makes permanent."

PRESENCE PAUSE

Core Practice 10.1:
Take in the Good

Here is a simple embodiment practice. You have seen others in the previous chapters of Part Two. However, you will now add the awareness that, through your attention, you are literally changing the physiological foundation for your inner state. You are creating subtle but real shifts in what your psychobiology will tend to produce.

Rick Hanson writes about a practice called Take in the Good,[69] based on research that shows thirty to forty-five seconds of sustained attention is sufficient for the nervous system to initiate neuroplastic change.

- Sit or stand with an erect posture.
- Use the centering practice from Chapter 8 to become present right now. Align yourself with the dimensions of length, width and depth.
- Take several deep breaths, inhaling and exhaling strongly. Pause, sensing the stillness and the shift in your state. Be rigorous and precise in your attention.
- Invite the awareness that, in this very moment, the quality of your attention tells your hippocampus that this specific state is important enough to encode for future access. The inner state of center is being telegraphed across your entire nervous system. You are actively initiating the process of neuroplastic change, creating associations between neuronal networks of this state, in order to record it in long-term memory.
- Hold this state, and the awareness that you are actively shaping your psychobiology in real time, for a minute or so.
- Sense appreciation and gratitude.

Seeds for an Embodied Future

I would love to claim that we can simply decide on the future we want, make a declaration of the direction to get us there, and ride that horse all the way off into the sunset! If it were only so simple!

Rather, embodiment is a biological phenomenon: the development of a new set of internal conditions. Initially, as with Rajeev above, this kind of deep change begins as an idea. It is likely to feel tentative and awkward as we do new things in ways that are not yet practiced and embodied. Yet, our self-system is both complex and emergent, and there is much we can do to nurture our internal congruence.

> ### SEEDING A FUTURE
>
> Here are four mutually reinforcing elements that bring alive a possible future:
>
> - We imagine an optimistic and aspirational future.
> - We find language for our future: an easy-to-remember, concise direction.
> - We connect our direction to a purpose.
> - We invite the future to come alive in us now.

Putting the pieces together, we glimpse four elements of how this iterative evolutionary process might work for us.

We Sense into the big picture, inviting a more inclusive perspective on what is important to us and what we care about most in the big picture. We look beyond the immediate discomforts of unsolved problems and schedule delays, allowing ourselves to *imagine an optimistic and aspirational future.* We relax about the specifics of how we get there, choosing rather to focus on what this future will feel like when it arrives. We bring this alive in our imagination.

We formulate memorable language, orienting towards this aspirational future with an an *easy-to-remember, concise direction.* This language is available at a moment's notice as a reminder of what we stand for, what we want more of, or what we want less of. This direction is an organizing principle. The language is an activator, a "quick link" into our nervous system, serving to remind us of meaning and purpose when the world becomes unpredictable or even perverse.

We *connect our direction to a purpose.* We ask ourselves: Why is this important to us? Who is this direction serving? Who will benefit in this future? Considering and responding to these questions gets us looking outside ourselves to a bigger sense of meaning for our direction. If answers are not forthcoming, something might still be a good idea, but it is unlikely to activate our caring and thus our emotional circuitry. We want to ignite our passion and our caring and our highest self; these questions help us to reawaken our caring.

We *invite the future to come alive in us now.* We listen to how our interior state responds. If our future is important to us, it will awaken sensations of aliveness and energy and optimism, emotions coupled with a narrative of why it matters and a sense of how it will connect to and benefit others. Specific action urges may be present, or simply a sense of forward pull. If this organizing principle feels "off," our body tells us it is incongruent or it lacks meaning; this is also important data. When all the channels of the Awareness Map connect in some way to the principle, our experience of it becomes holistic and inclusive, which furthers embodiment.

These four elements are mutually reinforcing. They are the seeds of embodiment, and can be watered over time through practices that wire them ever more deeply into the substrate of our Being.

When my colleagues and I teach together, we always ask each other before the start, "So… why are you doing this?" We pause, we face each other. We center, and then each of us in turn responds to this question, from the heart. The answer is fresh, different and real every time. And it orients us back to the purpose for what we do, regrounds us in what we care about, and brings alive, in the present moment, our embodied organizing principle. It changes how we begin our work. This is a practice for us.

Now, here's an experiment that invites you to create language for a future and a direction. This will provide a starting point for your own ongoing iterative process.

Experiment 10.2:
Clarifying a Direction

There are countless approaches to identifying a direction, and the process could be rather elaborate. I am going to suggest a quite simple process that will get you started, one you can redefine later as your relationship to the direction evolves.

The inner state from which you Sense a future direction is important. The language and the feeling of the process will be very different if you are present and energized than if you are tired and just going through the motions.

This is a key experiment, and it anticipates the pivot to Acting in Part Four of the book. Please give this the time and space it needs.

Preparation:

- Create a special space: outdoors is good, or an indoor space that is private and inspirational.
- Include something inspiring: symbols of who and what you care about.
- Go for a run or get vigorous exercise of some sort to get your body alive and energized and oxygenated.
- Give yourself plenty of time, even several sessions.
- Center yourself. Ground. Bring yourself present using state-shifting practices.

With this preparation, take your time and explore the following questions. Consider writing this out longhand, which encourages involvement of both sides of your brain. Or, speak into a recording device. Or, inquire out loud with a skilled listener who will gift you with their presence and attention. Allow yourself to feel emotions and sensations, not focusing solely on language and words. Recenter yourself as necessary.

This is a lived experience, not just a thought experiment. Sense yourself and what comes alive in you at every step along the way.

- What is most important to you in this Context? (Go big here. This is about bringing in a longer view and larger Contexts, accessing optimistic futures and a greater span in your Sensing of what matters to you.)
- What is the overall direction in this challenge? (Remember, direction, not goals: more of X, less of Y, etc.)

- Why is this important to you?
- Who will benefit from this direction?
- Who will you be when this direction is fulfilled?
- What else will be different when this direction is fulfilled?
- Now, express this in a concise, easy-to-remember *direction statement* that can be a "quick link" in the future to bring you into the felt sense. (E.g., "I am increasing the interdependent well-being of our borrowers and our team." "We are increasing the willingness of our engineers to challenge orthodoxy." "I am bringing forward this book.")
- Find opportunities to share this direction statement with others, speaking it in an embodied way in appropriate contexts.

You have created language that you can now experiment with, practice with, try on, and live into. As you do so, know that you will be changing yourself, as well as changing the conditions around you. You will notice when this direction feels energizing and helpful; you will also notice when it feels daunting or provokes resistance from others. All of this is of course grist for the mill.

Watering Seeds: Practices for Embodying a Future

Development is usually rather messy. Our self-system is complex and emergent, and development takes time to unfold. The assumption that we can change ourselves through the combination of a simple decision and willpower is often a setup for disappointment and frustration.

Rather, mastery requires giving an embodiment process the necessary time and attention. I am promising sustainable, physiologically supported development; this embodiment only takes place through *practice*.

There are several powerful ways to practice towards connecting your Soma and Identity with your intended future. These are strategies for developing and embodying Being. Because of the dynamic relationship between your Identity and your Context, these will also have subtle (or not) effects in the system around you. For now, your focus is on incorporating your intended future and chosen direction into your Being. Acting will follow in Part Four.

First, *state your intended future and direction publicly*. Be clear what you intend. The purpose is not to get everyone to jump on board. Rather, practicing the language, and seeding this future in the vocabulary of those around you, will change you and will open possibilities in the Context. *Mandela's simple comments to the policeman, impromptu and spontaneous, spoke worlds. Mandela saw the possibility of this action and felt the urge to manifest it, precisely because he had previously embodied the future of a unified South Africa, and thus was able to recognize a simple opportunity to bring it into being.*

Act consistently with your direction. Actions send a stronger message than words. Actions that are congruent with direction build trust as well as your own embodiment. *If your direction is "increasing attention to our own personal lives and balance," then leaving the office at five o'clock and taking your vacation time is the embodiment of this direction. Not doing so is incongruent and sends the message that the direction is just words.*

Say yes to what is congruent with the direction; **say no to what is not congruent.** This is a practice in aligning decisions, which reinforces the direction itself. *Key creatives at Pixar built trust and shared commitment to the Braintrust process by inviting challenging and direct feedback that required major rework because it served the project, rather than defending and justifying decisions into which they had already invested significant time and emotional energy.*

Cultivate whole-person inner states that are congruent with the future. Couple your language of the future direction to creative and resilient inner states. This associates elements of experience from across the whole Awareness Map. It is possible to build, through the doorway of language, new default neural networks. *A senior leader of a nonprofit agency, who is also a runner, declared before and during*

NEUROPLASTICITY AND PRACTICE

Neuroplastic change is most efficient in optimal conditions. These five are crucial:

- **Do a practice repeatedly.** Frequent repetition over time supports embodied memory.

- **Do practices with full attention.** Presence and intensity matter.

- **Include all channels** of the Awareness Map in your attention.

- **Create emotional immediacy.** Connect the practice to who will benefit, people we love, or values and principles. Practice because it matters.

- **Do practices in a healthy body.** Nutrition, exercise and sleep all make a big difference in the physiology of embodiment.

lengthy runs, "I am running to build the capacity and stamina to refocus this agency towards our veterans in need." The felt experience of stamina, of patience, and of trusting his capacity became increasingly available to him as a default way of Being through a difficult transition that required saying no to some existing projects they cared about and redirecting resources towards their core work with veterans.

Do **somatic practices that are metaphorically relevant** to capacities required by the direction and that support embodiment.[70] *An insurance executive, challenged by delegating work to others that was developmental for them but also needed to be done right, used the tennis court to practice serving the ball to others at a level that would challenge but not overwhelm them. A quality assurance officer, committed to partnering more skillfully with operations, enrolled in ballroom dancing classes to practice leading with grace and partnership, rather than through command and control.*

Organizing Principles and Stability

Recall that we just spent the previous chapter decoupling (**differentiating**) our inner state from the Context around us. This was liberating.

Now we are intentionally recoupling (**connecting**) our inner state with a specific declared direction.

Clarifying and embodying a future that we deeply care about is immensely pragmatic. It means cultivating an Identity coupled with an internal organizing principle over which we have some level of control and agency, even in a crazy world. This new Identity will naturally give rise to actions and choices that bring this future alive.

Like the heavy keel on a ship, our embodied future is an organizing principle. It helps us to stay upright, to steer a straighter course in the direction we want to go and to be less subject to the buffeting of wind, currents and waves along the way. We are not trying to avoid rough waters; we are simply cultivating the centered presence and organizing principles for stability as we travel through a fluid, swirling world.

This stability is the basis for taking a stand. As leaders, our embodied future helps us sustain a clear sense of the direction we are heading in, as well as the internal conditions that support that direction.

Rajeev embodies a new future

Continued focus on development led Rajeev to a new direction. The business outcomes remained unchanged—that the organization capitalize on the new micro-lending strategy. But coaching and conversations with his people about their personal aspirations revealed that his team also cared deeply about the mission of the organization. In fact, they actually didn't need his personal story as a motivation, or his stress- and resentment-producing urgency.

This awareness resulted in a markedly changed internal state. That his people cared so much about the same things as he touched him. He discovered that he cared deeply about his team's fulfillment.

As Rajeev worked with himself to soften his exterior appearance, his intensity became discussable, and his relationships with his team began to warm. He enjoyed this, as did they. Collectively, they began to have different conversations; a greater sense of connection and shared commitment begin to emerge.

A couple of months into this, Rajeev sensed that his direction was evolving. He had been working to change himself in order to reach their business goals. Over time, Rajeev came to realize that these practices were actually changing his perspective. He had the realization that his dedication to a better world explicitly included building a better organization and team culture. He saw the incongruence of trading his well-being, and that of his team, for the well-being of those they served, however desperate and deserving they might be. Rajeev's developmental shift was to see that **being committed to the mission and also to each other were not mutually exclusive, but actually complementary.** They were a polarity.

Rajeev's new organizing principle affected him profoundly. As always, he took it on with the zest and tenacity with which he did everything else. He publicly articulated his commitment to the well-being and development of his team in parallel with his commitment to the financial goals for the program. Privately, he spoke this new and broader direction to himself every morning before his yoga practice and before meetings: "I am organizing myself towards the interdependent well-being of our borrowers and our team."

Rajeev invoked this as a constant theme in all meetings and announcements about the strategy. He articulated publicly and explicitly how this would look and what it meant in terms of meetings, relationships and investments in development and learning.

This new direction became a constant reminder to him. He became more present and aware of how his relationships with people either supported or detracted from this new and expanded mission. New behaviors were no longer tactics to reach the existing goal, but natural expressions of a new and deeply felt organizing principle that he now lived as an ongoing practice that had become transformational for him.

Core Practice 10.3:
Embodying a Future

Design and commit to an ongoing practice for the embodiment of this direction. This is an embodiment practice and thus should incorporate the conditions outlined in the Neuroplasticity and Practice call-out (page 201): repetition, attention, emotional valence, healthy body and connection to purpose. (Notice that the previous experiment also established some of the foundations for this.)

Draw from several of the suggestions in the Embodiment Practices section (page 200). Consider how you might include all of the following elements in practices you commit to moving forward:

- A regular, preferably daily, somatic practice that you can do with consistency
- Communicating the direction in some public fashion
- Connecting the language of your direction to creative, resilient and optimistic inner states
- The ongoing iteration of your understanding of the direction that allows it to be both stable and responsive to changing conditions, the importance of which we will be exploring deeply in Part Four.

CHAPTER SUMMARY

The core realization of this Pane is that you can harness the very same neuroplasticity processes that created your current Identity to forge the Identity that the world now needs you to become. You can articulate a direction towards a future that matters and then build the internal congruence and Identity that can bring this future alive in you now. Embodying, then acting congruently with this future also makes it significantly more likely to manifest.

You developed new stepping stones for Being in service to what matters. These include:

- Realizing that embodied leadership requires both a clear future direction and internal congruence
- Articulating this future as a broad direction, an organizing principle that is connected to purpose, and then bringing it alive in the now
- Creating the conditions for neuroplastic change (repeating practices, attending to all channels of the Awareness Map, linking practices to what matters, doing practices with presence, maintaining a healthy body)
- Engaging in ongoing embodiment and resilience practices explicitly linked to your direction

Just as your embodiment of historical experiences makes them available in the present, you can embody an intended future now so that it becomes increasingly available to you down the road. "You are what you have practiced; what you practice now is what you will become."[71]

Presence enables the moment-by-moment awareness to respond to the dynamism around you in ways that bring that future alive now.

Take some time to reflect on what you now realize as a result of this Pane.

- What do you understand differently?
- What are you now curious about?
- What experiments might you try?

⁓ PRESENCE PAUSE ⁓

PART
FOUR

Acting

*No ray of sunlight is ever lost, but the green which it
awakes into existence needs time to sprout, and it is not
always granted to the sower to see the harvest. All work
that is worth anything is done in faith.*

– Albert Schweitzer

YOU MIGHT BE THINKING THAT, AFTER ALL THESE HARD-TO-GRASP CHAPTERS
ON SENSING AND BEING, finally you actually get to DO something!
That said, the Identity-based desire to take what you're practicing and apply
it in the world can quickly slide into the comforting historical mindset of driving
change. "How do I take all this inner stuff and make the things happen that I
care about?" Unwittingly, you could lose your hard-earned focus on creating
different internal conditions for what matters to you. This is insidious and
subtle, so I want to be very explicit and deliberate as you and I move into this
fourth part of this book.

I trust, by now, you realize that bringing attention and intention and choice
to the realms of Sensing and Being produces a strong foundation for action.

Actions arising from the work of the previous six Panes are far more likely to be congruent with what we intend. This is a good thing. But pent-up energy for action may also be present, and to dissipate those urges heedlessly could result in actions unhelpful for Complexity.

Let's take a look back and see how we got here. We have the Nine Panes framework: a perspective, or a map of the territory. The Panes are interdependent and dynamic, each affecting and being affected by the others. We can take the perspective of looking at the whole, or we can double-click on any one of the Panes.

There is a logic I have followed in unveiling the Panes. This is not to imply that there is a determined sequence of passage through them; the sequence simply makes them easier to understand. Indeed, it's crucial to understand that they also are integrative: They co-arise, and any one can be an entry point.

You explored *Sensing* by starting with the Context: You are accustomed to trying to make sense of what's around you (Chapter 5). Then, you looked at the elements of Complex systems, and at how your Identity might be challenged by the Complexity around you (Chapter 6). Third, you Sensed your own inner experience, accessing data about how you actively protect and defend your Identity. You realized that you can observe and pay attention to how your psychobiology, or Soma, organizes itself to defend that Identity (Chapter 7).

In *Being*, you pivoted from Sensing your Soma to the realization that the act of Sensing actually changes what is being sensed. Observing your inner state changes your inner state. You developed this through the next three Panes into a set of presence-based capacities for regulating your state (Chapter 8), finding resilience by decoupling your state from what is going on around you (Chapter 9) and embodying a future you care about (Chapter 10).

With the above realizations (and nothing else), you are likely realizing how your intentionally generated internal congruence will naturally give rise to new actions congruent with what you care about. The big takeaway, of course, is that *we must become present in order to cultivate the internal congruence out of which right action will emerge*. That is the power of *Presence-Based Leadership* and of its expression in Action.

So now you turn to the next three Panes. You might see them as logical extensions of the first six. Who would argue with the power of *Extending your Leadership Presence* to create resonance and connectedness with others (Identity)? Or, with the importance of *Scaling Awareness* to create Complexity-capable cultures (Context)? And then there's the matter of the criticality of ongoing investment in *Tuning Yourself as Instrument* (Soma). This is what you have been after the whole time!

Yet it's too easy to fall into a Complicated mindset. With the above distinctions in mind, you might reasonably revert to the old habit of designing distinct actions for the Context, as an Identity, and on your Soma. You might act on the levels of system separately, as if they were not connected, in your very eagerness to engineer the change you want.

In the process of writing this book, I have witnessed many times my own tendency to fall into this mindset. It has only been through the candid feedback and challenging questions of beloved collaborators that I've woken up several times to my own tendency to fall into the very traps that I predict. Earlier drafts of Part Four were unconsciously hijacked by my own need to help you by concretizing the deliverables of this book in a pragmatic toolkit for how to implement all of this in your world. How easy it is to fall back into a Complicated mindset, as if sufficient planning and proper execution, organized around this new meaning-making framework for Complexity, could assure the future we intend!

Lest you yourself go back to sleep at the wheel, I am going to take a non-intuitive pivot here that I hope you will find both paradoxical and powerful. We will inoculate against the ever tempting and Identity-driven urge to make Complexity knowable. We will avoid the trap of directing energy at the various levels of a Complex system without seeing them as a whole.

How will we do this inoculation?

I intend to highlight four cross-cutting conditions that focus how we can act in Complexity-appropriate ways, rather than organize the next three chapters around the three Acting Panes. These cross-cutting conditions are:

- Attitude
- Connection
- Fluidity
- Stability

These four particular conditions are necessary and crucial for Complexity. They are not the only ones we could choose. We could talk about trust, boundaries, shared purpose or any number of other conditions. Many, including these four, have been implicit throughout the book, and written about by others.

In a sense, the entire book so far has been about cultivating internal conditions. Now, in Acting, you will focus on cultivating conditions of connection, fluidity and stability at all levels of scale—Context, Identity and Soma—simultaneously.

Here's how we will proceed together through the consummating Acting part of this book.

Chapter 11 explores an *attitude* for Action in Complexity and, in particular, how you might begin to play with *experimentation* as a means for discovering more about the multiple levels of system you are engaged with. This is how you cultivate a self that is increasingly Complexity-capable across Context, Identity, and Soma.

In Chapter 12, you will look at the condition of *connection* and how connection supports your leadership in Complexity at the levels of Soma, Identity, and Context.

Chapter 13 dives into the condition of *fluidity*, including the related aspects of agility and responsiveness. Again, you will apply this at all three levels in a way that is integrative and whole.

Chapter 14 explores the condition of *stability* at all three levels.

Of course, it will be helpful to recognize and articulate how each of these conditions actually draws upon, and energizes, each particular level of the system. I promise that I will continue to make these linkages explicit in the process. The Nine Panes will continue to be an orienting framework.

At the same time, in the spirit of disrupting your meaning-making process, the Nine Panes will recede into the background, but will not disappear, as we explore how to act in and on the system as a whole with these conditions as stepping stones.

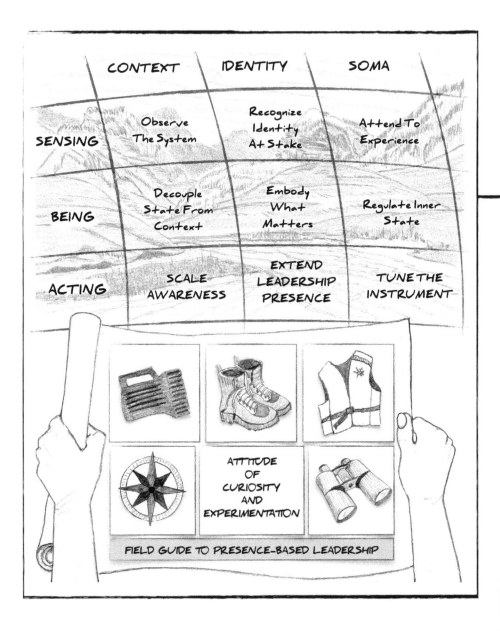

	CONTEXT	IDENTITY	SOMA
SENSING	Observe The System	Recognize Identity At Stake	Attend To Experience
BEING	Decouple State From Context	Embody What Matters	Regulate Inner State
ACTING	SCALE AWARENESS	EXTEND LEADERSHIP PRESENCE	TUNE THE INSTRUMENT

ATTITUDE OF CURIOSITY AND EXPERIMENTATION

FIELD GUIDE TO PRESENCE-BASED LEADERSHIP

212

CHAPTER 11

An Attitude of Curiosity and Experimentation

The whole globe is shook up, so what are you going to do when things are falling apart? You're either going to become more fundamentalist and try to hold things together, or you're going to forsake the old ambitions and goals and live life as an experiment, making it up as you go along.
– Pema Chödrön

Be patient toward all that is unsolved in your heart and try to love the questions themselves, like locked rooms and books that are now written in a foreign tongue. Do not now seek the answers, which cannot be given you because you would not be able to live them. Live the questions now. Perhaps you will then gradually, without noticing it, live along some distant day into the answer.
– Rainer Maria Rilke

YOU HAVE DONE A LOT OF EXPLORATION THROUGH THE FIRST THREE PARTS OF THE BOOK. Congratulations on staying the course so to build a foundation of principles, as well as to engage in the stretchy and elusive inner work of Sensing and Being. I acknowledge, and honor, your probable urgency to "get to the point."

Acting is certainly intrinsic to leadership. At the same time, it takes ongoing attention and focus to suspend historical and anti-helpful habits in order to act in ways better suited to the territory of Complexity.

Practicing a Complexity attitude, infused with curiosity and the spirit of experimentation, is counterintuitive to many leaders—and yet remarkably well-adapted for leading in territory for which we have been ill-prepared.

Susan faces an immediate challenge

Remember Susan from way back at the beginning of Chapter 1? Susan was the new minister at a mainstream church in the Midwest and the first woman ever to lead this church. Her charge was to turn around both the declining congregation and the stagnating church finances due to organizational stasis. While she felt vulnerable for many reasons, she also recognized both the challenge and the opportunities.

The difficult dynamics in her Context were abundant and obvious. While she had strong ideas for bringing more participatory spirituality into the church community, doing so risked alienating the older (and wealthier) sustaining members. On the other hand, if she didn't attract new and younger members, the decline would also continue. The tension between these imperatives felt like a tightrope, with her Identity on the line.[72]

Susan had ministered to other churches. She had read and studied much about leadership, and specifically about change processes in churches. She was eager to jump in, but also daunted by the tightrope and the weight of responsibility for the future of this century-old religious community that seemed to rest on her shoulders. She felt called to act. She wanted to be successful, she wanted results. She wanted to prove to the church hierarchy, to the congregation, and most of all to herself that she was the right person.

Susan was eager to begin. But where to start?

I'm anticipating that this question—where to start—has been on your mind in your Complexity Challenge. I hope that you are eager to try some things out, if still a bit daunted about how this applies to you.

This chapter offers you a nonconventional attitude that you can try on for size. You can *experiment*—with the understanding that your own attitude is a crucial part of the conditions in the system. From the foundation of that curious, experimental attitude, different actions emerge.

Here's a view of our path. In this chapter, you'll anchor your approach to experimentation with a brief exploration of the final three Panes before placing them in the background. Then, you'll explore this attitude of curiosity and experimentation to inoculate you against the inherent tendency to use Acting as cover for defending Identity and driving for results. ***Rather than driving for results, you will experiment with creating the conditions that produce results.***

You will close the chapter with a sense of how you can use these stepping stones to support your continued awareness to moving through Complexity with wisdom and presence.

THE THREE ACTING PANES

The biggest challenges for me in writing this book have been in the Acting part.

Sensing, Being, and Acting are in constant and dynamic interaction. Action arises from Being. Being is shaped by our Sensing. And, every time we Act, we change the world a little bit, and therefore change what there is to be Sensed, which changes our Being state, which changes the Action that follows from it.

Like the children's story of a tiger chasing its own tail around and around a tree until it turns into butter,[73] it's impossible to find the point from which our leadership, and any human experience, actually arises. In frustration, we might throw up our hands in despair, say "Screw it!" and jump into action because it feels so good to dissipate that tension, thinking that we actually can control what future emerges through our own disciplined planning and skillful execution. (Note how tempting those words might feel to your Identity!)

However, doing so, no matter how tempting, would require discarding much of what we've learned so far. Let's slow down and tease this apart, seeking to illuminate how awakened and presence-based action might avoid some of the frequent unintended consequences that happen in the midst of Complexity. And, simultaneously might create conditions for what we care about most to emerge.

A Light Pass Over the Three Acting Panes

We pay due homage to the three final Panes in our map. Then, in the next several chapters, we will explore how we might actually address all three Panes simultaneously by focusing on the cross-cutting conditions that make our system more capable in Complexity.

First, and following with ease the previous chapter around Embodying What Matters (Identity), comes Extending Leadership Presence. Acting

AS an Identity means that we invite and extend our particular embodied state into our communications and into our actions. It becomes clear what we stand for, what we care about, what our organization principles are. In essence, our internal state becomes available as an organizing principle with and for others around us. We *act AS an embodied Identity*, intentionally extending our internal congruence into our relationships. This is the pane of *Extending Leadership Presence*.

THREE ACTING PANES

The three final Panes are how we behave our embodied commitments into the world. They include:

- *Scaling Awareness:* We *Act WITH our Context* to nurture teams, organizations and families that can Sense, Be, and Act in complexity-capable ways.

- *Extending Leadership Presence:* We *Act AS an Identity* to build resonance and connection with others, in service to what we care about. This is the foundation of relatedness.

- *Tuning the Instrument:* We *Act ON our Soma* by investing in our development. We embody ever-greater capacity to hold and navigate complexity.

Second, we *act WITH our Context*. We offer our attitude of curiosity and learning and practice to other members of our teams and organizations. We invite others to join us in experimentation, and we collectively explore and learn through the realizations of Sensing, Being and Acting. We generate more information, collectively held, about the Complexity in which we are operating. Over time, we cultivate, together, a Complexity-capable culture on the level of team, organization, family, community. This pane reveals strategies for *Scaling Awareness*.

Third, we *act ON our own Soma* by recognizing our development as a lifelong and fundamental commitment. We practice to deepen and to embody the meta-competencies of Sensing, Being, and Acting. We seek practice partners, get coached, foster communities of practice, read this book, and seek out developmental opportunities. Making an ongoing investment in becoming the leader we are asked to be is *Tuning the Instrument*.

The Seduction of Planning

Logic dictates that, given a green light to act at the three levels of scale—Context, Identity and Soma—we would now shift into designing strategies for Scaling Awareness and Extending Leadership. And we could now create new development plans for ourselves (to Tune the Instrument).

But let's be both humble and honest. We've all created development plans for ourselves, which we have followed more or less consciously, with mixed results. As well-intentioned as we are, some of our signature flaws have persisted for years or even decades after we became aware of them! (Our Soma is deeply committed to stasis and to what it has embodied: Ask your spouse if you lack concrete examples!)

We have learned communication and feedback and listening skills, and sometimes we remember to use them, but often we don't. Our Identity and our relationships remain Complex, and our colleagues and loved ones often don't show up in the ways we want. Nor do we.

We have all been involved in strategic planning, SWOT analyses and projecting the future based on the past. And some of that has played out in the ways we intended, but even so, we have never fully controlled how our Context became what it is right now.

Through all of this we have persisted, sadly and gloriously, as ourselves: fully human and shaped thoroughly by our practiced patterns and habits.

We cannot engineer our way to the future. Much as this runs counter both to our training and to our Identity-preservation system, Complexity offers no "right" strategy, no optimal set of actions or moves. Reality will appear in ways that none of our imagined scenarios can reliably anticipate. The bad news is, to the extent that our Identity is linked to the comfort and illusory certainty of a good plan, reality is likely to ensure the fundamental collapse of our Identity-construction processes!

That good news is that this collapse liberates us to deal with reality as it is. It gives us the freedom to experiment.

Acting in Complexity is, frankly, rather a crapshoot. This is where a Complexity-appropriate attitude can be extraordinarily helpful. We can rein in our anti-helpful craving for reliable action and predictability and replace it with curiosity, spaciousness and a spirit of experimentation.

A Pivot

How might we engage in action differently? With less certainty, perhaps, and more faith and trust? With a deeper grounding in our own resourcefulness and that of others, and with less energy put into futile efforts to control that which can't be controlled?

A brief experiment

Please stop reading and go to the kitchen for a beverage or a snack. Or, even both. You deserve it.

Yes… I'm serious. Please place this material in the background, and let yourself mull it over as you literally get up, walk to the kitchen, grab a snack or a beverage or a treat. Then come back….

I'll see you in a minute…

～ PRESENCE PAUSE ～

Welcome back! Take a moment to center and be present.

Sense how this brief transition into physical action shifted your perspective. You put this abstract discussion of Complexity, and the myriad implications for your challenge, into the background.

And, simultaneously, you actually DID something specific and concrete. You were in action, purposeful, accomplishing the goal of retrieving a beverage or snack.

Notice how this action, and the simple and direct task of navigating the round trip to the refrigerator, was fundamentally rewarding in two ways. First, presumably you got something that gave you pleasure. Plus it feels good to take "obvious" action that produces a clear result.

It also changed your perspective. What did you consider as you made your round trip to the fridge? How is your relationship with this material any different now? How is your inner state different from having taken a concrete action?

Taking concrete action towards specific results is relatively simple and stimulates the reward centers of our nervous system. Yet any action also forecloses other options; a commitment to do X is also a commitment to not do Y.

As leaders, we have built our Identities, our careers and our organizations based on results. It is natural, even inevitable, that we would organize around what has worked in the past. We can focus intensely on results, wanting to be seen as committed and willing to sacrifice. We are likely to be appreciated and rewarded for this, and we might even be rated "excellent" for our results focus.

Yet, this focus on results can be a real stumbling block since Complexity guarantees only that the future is unknowable.

While results are obviously crucial, results always arise out of an underlying set of conditions. Having a plan can be very useful, as long as we don't focus on it so tightly that it becomes a constrictive Bell Jar.

We can't control much, but we can do some pretty simple (if sometimes difficult) things that are likely to foster the conditions for the results we care about. Cultivating these conditions is also far more likely to lead to the results we intend than the conventional "drive for results" attitude that so quickly narrows our view and excludes critical information about how the system is actually functioning in the present.

Moreover, experimenting with these conditions has triple benefits: Not only does it invite shifts in the Context around us, it invites them also in our own Identity and Soma.

While it may feel frustratingly indirect, our ***Acting is wise when it cultivates particular conditions across Context, Identity, and Soma that are well-adapted to Complexity***. As a first step toward cultivating these conditions, we will focus on an overall attitude for leading in Complexity, which is itself a condition!

BE CURIOUS: EXPERIMENT WITH CONDITIONS, AND RESULTS WILL FOLLOW

What can help us remain mindful and aware as we move into action? Here are some mental stepping stones that can help us focus on creating the conditions for what we want to emerge. Here are six realizations, originating as concepts, but ultimately living in us as felt experiences that we can embody in a Complexity-ready attitude.

Complexity Is Normal

We might think that VUCA (volatile, unpredictable, complex and ambiguous) represents a new set of conditions. Certainly the intensity of our world, and the felt sense of risk, are increasing.

Still, Complexity has been around forever. It's not new, it's not unique to us and our Context, and it most certainly is not personal. We might actually know more about how to navigate it than we give ourselves credit for.

The bad news is that our worlds really are unpredictable, particularly when other human beings are involved, and particularly when our own reactions to things tend to overpower all rational intentions. We can't plot a reasonably reliable pathway much beyond where we will have dinner tonight, and the worthwhile and reasonable goals we (or others) have set for us to accomplish are maddeningly elusive.

The good news is that it's always been this way. Nearly everyone we know is wrestling with something Complex. We have plenty of company.

Complexity feels paralyzing because there's so little to hang on to. Whatever we try to lean into shifts, and no planning really assures the results we want.

However, we can Sense what is going on around us, and we can tease apart what is Complex from what is Complicated or Obvious. The latter domains can often be dealt with in more traditional ways. If it's Obvious, take care of it! If it's Complicated, get the right kind of help, work through it, and implement a Complicated solution.

There is usually some low-hanging fruit to be found. Take care of it. File your taxes. Keep your boss in the loop. Hire the right expertise to address Complicated things. Doing so frees you to focus on what really is Complex.

Not Knowing Is Liberating

Even though Complexity is normal, there is no reason that anyone should expect us to be skillful at leading in Complexity. The situation in which we are leading has never existed before. And our neurological wiring, together with our training and preparation, is designed for a predictable world.

Yet we drive ourselves incessantly, comparing ourselves to impossible standards. We judge ourselves as if we should be good at everything. What novice tennis player would expect to challenge Serena Williams? What budding saxophonist would reasonably expect to improvise like John Coltrane? Yet, as leaders, we absurdly expect ourselves to perform masterfully without the countless hours of practice that Williams and Coltrane put into learning the foundations of their art.

In leadership, as in tennis and jazz, we can build a strong foundation of self-confidence and competence through practice. This foundation allows us to meet unpredictable and fast-moving realities with grace, ease and fluidity.

The problem is that many of us learned that we are supposed to know the answers and to be good at whatever we touch. If this is the case, our Identity will be threatened every time we don't, or aren't. This is a big downside of a culture in which every kid has to be a star, self-esteem is next to godliness, and failure feels existential.

From another perspective, we can see ourselves simply as a leader doing the best that he or she can in a brand-new situation. With this more spacious view, vulnerability is simply transparency. There is nothing to defend. We are open, unpretentious and curious. We are available to reality as it actually is.

In this perspective, *not knowing* is a liberating realization.

The embracing and embodiment of *not knowing* liberates us from our incessant quest to know and have the answers. It also happens to be a great strategy for Complexity because not knowing supports our attitude of curiosity and experimentation, allowing more openness, creativity and fluidity to enter and to become manifest.

With the acceptance of not knowing, everything we do becomes practice. Everything we do is an experiment. Everything we do provides learning. I don't mean that there aren't real consequences to the choices we make. *Simply, the perspective is available to us that everything we do can be done with the attitude of a learner.*

SIX REALIZATIONS FOR A COMPLEXITY ATTITUDE

Complexity requires a different attitude than do Complicated and Obvious domains. A spacious, curious attitude is a condition that supports wise action and learning through experimentation.

These realizations support this attitude:

- Complexity is normal.
- Not knowing is liberating.
- Direction provides an organizing principle.
- Results *reveal* underlying patterns and conditions.
- Curiosity and experimentation *probe and shape* conditions.
- Attitude itself is an emergent condition.

Direction Provides an Organizing Principle

Of course, our curiosity and experimentation require both a purpose and a direction. Lewis and Clark intended to find a navigable route to the Pacific Coast. While the specific route and even the overall viability were unknowable, there was an overarching direction, an organizing principle that guided daily tactical choices.

In your Complexity Challenge, you will have established your own organizing principles and broad directions (Chapter 10). These organizing principles are flexible enough to allow for improvisation and emergence, yet clear enough to provide some boundaries. They keep us on track, pointing in the right direction.

Results Reveal Underlying Patterns and Conditions

Results matter. We are all committed to results.

Yet, one of the most counterintuitive and elusive realizations for leaders in Complexity is that a myopic and relentless driving towards future results actually reduces our ability to see patterns in the present.

Results always arise out of a set of conditions. Understandably, when patterns and interactions in a Complex system produce results different from what we intend, we get frustrated. Instead, it is crucial to see how problems reveal priceless information about how a system actually behaves and what it primarily tends to produce. Beware the lens of Identity, which interprets problems as yet another frustrating failure and a justification to work harder and control things more.

Chapter 5 explored how we can begin to Sense patterns and tendencies. We can learn to explore how the system works and how it is producing the actual results we have been seeing (even when they are perversely different from what we intended!). This is not an easy thing: Pattern recognition isn't a given for leaders who have been strongly focused on achieving results through command and control. Yet, this new and more subtle Sensing is absolutely essential for navigating this new territory.

Curiosity and Experimentation Probe and Shape Conditions

The Complexity literature is full of references to "**safe-to-fail experiments.**"[74] These are small-scale, cheap experiments that probe how the system works and that are interesting enough that we will actually do them! We design experiments that can be amplified if they reveal something worthwhile. Plus, they have very little downside if they don't.

Safe-to-fail experiments are like scouting in unknown terrain: They probe to gather additional information at low cost, and they illuminate the territory sufficiently to design another round of experiments. A viable pathway is revealed piece by piece over time, when it would be impossible to anticipate and plan it all in advance.

Safe-to-fail experiments reveal the nature of reality and accelerate realization. In Complexity, curiosity and presence can often take us further and faster than driving results through inflexible plans and metrics and quantified goals.

Experimentation is the vehicle for this discovery. Experiments might amplify one condition or dampen another: We have a hypothesis; we try something that is quick, easy, interesting, and fun (safe-to-fail); and we learn from the results.

Whether or not the results are consistent with our direction, we have learned something about how the system works. Then, we can design a new experiment, or we can expand or dampen the changes in conditions, depending on whether we like what happened.

Attitude Itself Is an Emergent Condition

Our attitude is also a condition. Attitude arises internally from our conditioned psychobiology and then expresses itself through our Identity, altering the conditions outside us in the Context as we touch others with our attitude and perspective.

Our attitude is an element in the Complex territory through which we are adventuring. It is (theoretically) one of the elements we are most likely to be able to control. Yet, it is also affected by events outside us, highly vulnerable to the attachments and aversions that keep our Identity in place.

Attitude is an emergent phenomenon; cultivating a particular attitude intentionally takes awareness and practice. While it is always possible, it is not so easy to simply decide on an attitude and thereby make it solid and fixed.

More realistically, we read something in a book, we have some insight or realization, we have a moment of clarity, and then we re-enter our Complexity challenge. In spite of our best intentions, we might sacrifice our newfound attitude of curiosity, losing the opportunity to cultivate and validate it for ourselves the first time we get challenged by the system about producing results.

Attitude is itself a set of internal conditions. It is emergent and will require some level of courage to cultivate and maintain in the face of a culture that might or might not be supportive. It also may take experimentation and practice over time to create the conditions for embodying this attitude as a leader.

Susan tries on an attitude of curiosity

Susan, though eager to get going, was aware that she had never led a change process of this magnitude before. Conventional wisdom prescribed first getting to know the people, the lay leaders and the community. Then, a few months in, she could convene a visioning and planning process, building consensus for a new strategy with strong involvement from lay leadership and then implementing a plan. That's what research told her would lead to success.

She had colleagues who had done this, and there were funds available from the hierarchy to bring in consultants and facilitators. But this approach and the situation seemed increasingly daunting, complicated and not much fun. Also, her research did not reveal many reassuring predictors of success. In fact, as she discovered when digging in deeper, most orchestrated change efforts had been remarkably unsuccessful. Maybe others, even those who offered themselves as experts and facilitators, didn't know much more than she? Perhaps there was no silver bullet?

Susan believed deeply that there existed some pathway to the future that she, with the congregation and lay leadership, would be able to discover together. She knew that it was important for her to provide leadership and organizing principles for a process that would likely be messy at times and had no guarantee of success.

Susan saw herself as a microcosm of the congregational culture. Like the church, she would need both to change and stay true to her core. If she expected the church to embrace transformation, she needed to model that transformation herself, while simultaneously reassuring old-timers that traditions were honored. She would need curiosity, a spirit of adventure and a lot of presence and improvisation.

Not having reliable pathways to follow meant that she was free to experiment. This perspective came as a relief. Now eager to begin, Susan was also wise enough to recognize that her own urgency to get into the job and create the changes she wanted was in itself a trap.

Susan saw that the initial organizing principle for her leadership was to slow down, to stay curious, and to engage fully in the process, firmly grounded in the present. Suspending her urges for some grand process meant trying small experiments with the culture of the church and trusting that the results would follow in time. This attitude required a leap of faith.

A SAFE-TO-FAIL EXPERIMENT PRIMER

The rest of Part Four, starting here, will focus on extending this attitude into action through safe-to-fail experiments. We will explore, together, how ***this counter-intuitive approach, while focusing directly neither on business results nor on the Complexity capabilities of Scaling Awareness, Extending Leadership Presence and Tuning the Instrument, actually creates the conditions for all of them.***

This will not be a road map that guarantees results and solutions to the obstacles that will inevitably arise. It is, however, a pragmatic application of the attitude we have been cultivating. And it will create change—in you, in those you touch, and in the system around you. Like Lewis and Clark, you will discover a way.

Five Questions: Stepping Stones for Safe-to-Fail Experiment Design

This section, and the next three chapters, will conclude with instructions for safe-to-fail experiments that you can play with or adapt as you wish.[75]

Experiments are best designed as integrative, such that they engage all three levels of system: Soma, Identity and Context. The conditions that we seek to develop, as you will see, are relevant on every level of system, and each supports the others.

These experiments are where the rubber meets the road. There is no right way to do them, and for many who are used to driving Complicated processes for measurable results, the whole notion of experiments will seem soft and elusive. A premise of safe-to-fail experiments is to allow "ideas that are not useful to fail in small, contained and tolerable ways."[76]

For the following experiments, the instructions may seem more elaborate than for the other experiments in the book. Please feel free to take substantial liberty with the guidance I provide. My intention is to provide enough structure to scaffold your own experiment designs through these five guiding questions

> **EXPERIMENT DESIGN QUESTIONS**
>
> Safe-to-fail experiments are how we probe the system, and how our complexity mindset translates into action on the ground.
>
> Questions to address:
>
> - **Direction**: What direction do we intend?
>
> - **Hypothesis**: What do we suspect about conditions?
>
> - **Design**: What can we try together?
>
> - **Safety**: How can this be safe enough to try?
>
> - **Learning**: How will we learn?

Direction: Experimentation begins with the direction, or organizing principle, in which we want the system to move. ***What direction do we intend?*** We are asking: What do we want more of? Less of? (For example: "more conversations with marketing during new product design," "more stories of Joe having learned something interesting from Sally," "fewer instances of hearing engineers complain about sales being out of touch," "more accountability for follow-through on our decisions," "less wasted energy on pet projects with little potential," or "more engagement by the community we are serving.")

Hypothesis: What do we suspect about conditions? Next, based on our Sensing and our embodiment of our intended direction, we likely discern that there are conditions present in the system that might be helpful either to amplify or to dampen. We might discern that we need, for example, more connection to support engagement by the community we are serving, or we might need to dampen the fluidity that is revealed when decision after decision gets second-guessed and never implemented. This is not hypothesis-driven problem-solving; it is curiosity-driven probing of how the system actually works. We welcome having our hypothesis proved wrong, because anything we learn means better information. Useful questions here: What conditions are we seeking to change in service of our direction? What results might we anticipate? How would these results link to the overall direction?

Design: Now we design safe-to-fail experiments to probe how the system responds. We seek to discover what happens when we increase or decrease the qualities of connection, fluidity, stability or any other system quality or element that is of interest. Who might be fun to play with? What conversations might inspire experiments? *What can we try together?* (Think cheap, interesting, fun, engaging, within your scope of authority and not going right to the knot of the system's problems, but rather playing around the edges.[77]) Remember, this is different from a pilot initiative, in which we hope to prove some concept that we can then scale.

Safety: Safe-to-fail means it feels safe enough to try. Different people of course have different tolerances for risk. We might all agree that the possibility of crashing the entire online ordering system for a day makes an experiment not safe. But for others, the threshold for safety might preclude being embarrassed in front of bosses, risking the judgment of others, etc. Note that Identity is closely involved here; "safety" is a relative term. *How can this be safe enough to try?* Explore with those involved what safety means, given your experiment. Consider what would make it *not* safe enough to try. (E.g., an experiment that puts existing commitments at risk, where negative results would jeopardize a career or run counter to organizational values.) Work with the boundaries of the experiment until there is sufficient safety that those involved are really "in." Where there are concerns, it might be helpful to identify, in advance, indicators that the experiment should be ended. The definition of safe-to-fail is subjective, and the de facto indication that it's safe enough is that we can move forward with enthusiasm and try something!

Learning: How will we learn?
It's important to consider how learning will result. Our curiosity, recall, is not about whether the experiment "succeeds" or "fails." Our experiment is not a prototype, a pilot or a proof of concept. Our experiment is research. Embedded in our fifth question is our core attitude of learning about the system. What do we expect to happen, and how will we know? What might be the effects of tweaking this or that condition? What evidence will we pay attention to? How will we know if what happens is supporting our overall direction?

When we learn from our experiments, then we see what's next. Maybe another experiment? How else might we create conditions for what we want? But we don't need to anticipate these questions now... they are down the road. We simply try things out, trusting that we will know what's next when it's time.

A SECRET RESOURCE

Shhh! A secret Appendix C at the end of the book offers a range of safe-to-fail experiments.

But: Complexity doesn't lend itself to cookbook solutions. Rather, it lends itself to curiosity and presence. Beware of these...

...temptations:

- Cherry-picking ideas
- Thinking this is a copy-and-paste menu of possibilities
- Skipping the creative messiness of design.

... and, suggestions:

- Center yourself
- Be willing to struggle a bit
- Get curious about what experiments you might create
- Save the Appendix for later.

Experiments as a Strategy

Please be alert for becoming hijacked by the idea that experiments are pilots. A pilot, while also based on a hypothesis, is a proof-of-concept. If it "works," we intend to replicate and scale this. Pilots are a great way to do this. By contrast, experiments are simply dedicated to probing the reality of the system and learning how it behaves. If we enter into it with the hope, however subtle, that we will prove something that we can then scale, we are going down the slippery slope of allowing our attachment to results to hijack our curiosity.

Experiments are experiments. Experiments are not objective observations of a static system that enable us to put together a strategy. Rather, experiments are themselves a strategy. Not *the* strategy. *A* strategy.

Complexity is ongoing, and our experimentation is also ongoing. Experimentation is an attitude and a way of life. It is a means through which we simultaneously learn about and create change in the systems around us, in our relationships and within ourselves.

We ourselves are part of the system, including our Identity and our Soma. We are constantly generating creative ideas for experiments, getting anxious about trying something new, thinking we should be perfect and deciding whether or not it is actually safe-to-fail. *In order to design and conduct experiments, we must change the internal conditions within ourselves. Experimentation is therefore also an intervention in the way of Being of the experimenter.*

Our enlivening perspective on experimentation is that it engages all three levels of system: Context, Identity and Soma. The act of observing changes both what is observed and also the observer.

Experimentation is, in and of itself, a strategy.

≈≫ PRESENCE PAUSE ≪≈

Experiment 11.1:
Amplifying the Conditions for a Complexity-Adapted Attitude

Please consider what attitude shifts might be useful for you, both personally and for others in your system as you move forward into Acting. Grounding yourself in an open, creative perspective on your challenge can be a powerful antidote to the problem-solving mindset so pervasive in most organizations yet so poorly suited to Complexity.

Attitude is itself a foundational condition for Tuning the Instrument, Extending Leadership Presence and Scaling Awareness. You can design safe-to-fail experiments for yourself around the condition of attitude. Plus, I encourage you to extend the experiments beyond yourself; experimenting with others around attitude is a fabulous opportunity to practice. Either way, experimenting is a system intervention.

If your Complexity Challenge and direction are not crystal clear in this moment, please return to page 199 and work through Experiment 10.2 again. Having this clarity is the essential starting point for this experiment, as well as for the next three chapters.

It is now time to engage with others as you extend your internal conditions into the world. Please read through these suggested questions. I have written the instructions assuming you will find some colleagues to play with. Of course, with slight modifications, all of these questions can also be used for self-experimentation.

1. What ***direction*** do we intend?
   - What is our Complexity Challenge as we currently understand it?
   - What do we want more of?
   - Less of?

2. What is our ***hypothesis*** about how a Complexity attitude might be helpful for us?
   - How might curiosity and experimentation support our direction?
   - How might the six realizations in the previous section help us normalize and navigate complexity?

3. What can we ***design*** and try together?
   - What is cheap, interesting, fun and possible to do within our authority?
   - Who might want to play?
   - What design conversations might we have?
   - What might we try?

4. How can this be ***safe enough to try***?
   - What's the worst that could happen?
   - What is at stake for your Identity?
   - How can we make this safe enough to try?

5. How will we ***learn***?
   - What do we expect?
   - What evidence might we see?
   - When and how will we reflect on what we learned?

Now, make this real. Talk with people. Convene design conversations with people who may want to play. Experiment with attitude and the six realizations together. As you do so, stay present and grounded: use Being as an organizing principle. Maintain your Complexity attitude during these conversations, staying curious and open. How does it feel to do this?

What do you notice about how the conversation changes the relationships you're in?

Conduct your experiments. Learn from what happens. Then, talk about what's next. What else might you learn?

You're on your way.

CHAPTER SUMMARY

The core realization of this chapter is that Acting in Complexity is fundamentally different. Rather than focusing on results and driving specific outcomes, you gain clarity about the overall direction and then cultivate an attitude of curiosity, experimenting to see what else can be discovered about the territory. You can be optimistic, curious and persistent. You experiment, and you learn from what happens.

This is, of course, counterintuitive to many. You are likely accustomed to leading processes that "make things happen." You learned to assert as much control as possible over the Context in which you lead. And, for sure, you are accountable for the results you get (or fail to get).

I understand. By all means, where you find yourself capable of exercising control and making things happen (as will be true in many aspects of your leadership), then have at it! You should act where you are reasonably able to predict what those actions will accomplish. Not everything is Complex, and keeping important and relatively predictable work moving forward frees up attention for working with what is not at all predictable.

However, where Complexity reigns, what happens is often not at all what you intended; unpredictability often means that what you know to do isn't actually what is needed.

In Complexity, then, you cultivate presence and an attitude of curiosity and experimentation. This attitude is anchored in the principle that if we *experiment with conditions, results will follow.* It is supported by these explicit realizations, attitudinal stepping stones that you can validate for yourself through experimentation:

- Complexity is normal.
- Not knowing is liberating.
- Direction provides an organizing principle.
- Results *reveal* underlying patterns and conditions.
- Curiosity and experimentation *probe and shape* conditions.
- Our attitude itself is an emergent condition.

Grounded in a Complexity-appropriate attitude, you can translate the inner work of the previous six Panes to extend your internal congruence into the world. You Tune the Instrument, Extend Leadership Presence and Scale Awareness simultaneously by experimenting with the conditions that support these final three Panes.

Safe-to-fail experiments are system interventions that simultaneously engage Soma, Identity and Context. These five questions serve as stepping stones for the sometimes-elusive process of designing experiments that both probe the system and intervene in it at the same time.

- *Direction*: What direction do we intend?
- *Hypothesis*: What do we suspect about conditions?

- ***Design***: What can we try together?
- ***Safety***: How can this be safe enough to try?
- ***Learning***: How will we learn?

You can invite others through your Embodied Leadership Presence. You can Scale the Awareness you are building within yourself into your Context. And you can invest in your own ongoing development. However, you do these indirectly, through using the stepping stones of a Complexity attitude and experiments with the qualities of connection, fluidity, and stability.

Take some time to reflect on what you now realize as a result of this chapter on an attitude of experimentation.

- What do you understand differently?
- What are you now curious about?
- What experiments might you try?

ᴿ PRESENCE PAUSE ᴿ

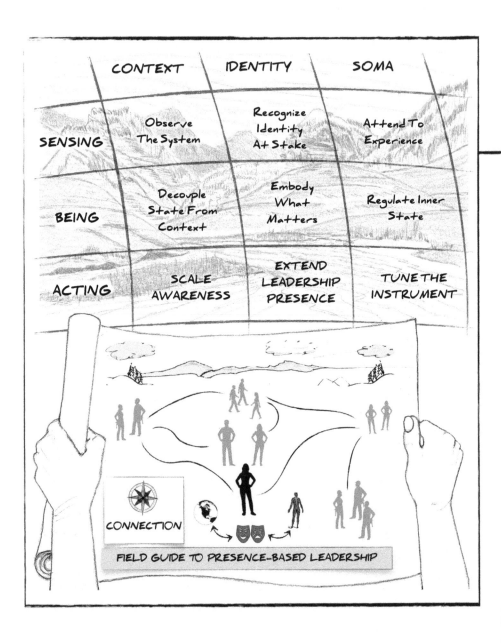

	CONTEXT	IDENTITY	SOMA
SENSING	Observe The System	Recognize Identity At Stake	Attend To Experience
BEING	Decouple State From Context	Embody What Matters	Regulate Inner State
ACTING	SCALE AWARENESS	EXTEND LEADERSHIP PRESENCE	TUNE THE INSTRUMENT

CONNECTION

FIELD GUIDE TO PRESENCE-BASED LEADERSHIP

Acting for Connection

*In organizations, real power and energy is generated
through relationships. The patterns of relationships and
the capacities to form them are more important
than tasks, functions, roles and positions.*
– Margaret Wheatley

*We cannot live only for ourselves. A thousand fibers
connect us with our fellow men; and among those fibers,
as sympathetic threads, our actions run as causes, and
they come back to us as effects.*
– Henry Melvil

*We are like islands in the sea, separate on the surface
but connected in the deep.*
– William James

I MET MY FRIEND PETER INDALO ON A TRIP TO KENYA IN 2010. An Anglican priest, twenty-five or so years before we met he had been helping with relief work in a severe famine in the north of Kenya, delivering food and medical supplies and ministering to the dying.

Out of the throngs of desperate people, a starving woman approached this tall, gentle priest and placed her dying baby in Peter's arms, telling him that she'd already lost her other child and could no longer keep her baby alive.

In the face of overwhelming tragedy, Peter declared, "We're not losing this one!" and somehow nursed the baby back to strength, found the mother and returned her baby to her. That moment was catalytic for Peter, and he committed to living his faith not through preaching, but through working at the roots of famine.

Peter spent the rest of his life seeding projects that connected people and encouraged them to become self-sustaining. Until he died in 2013, he served as the informal hub of a network of committed people changing the face of the Migori area of southwestern Kenya. Peter's patient, persistent and bold work was instrumental in improving standards of living.

One example was women's circles, in which groups of eight to ten women formed an interdependent circle to share scarce financial resources. They were taught rudimentary group and decision-making skills, and explicitly encouraged to be creative, to experiment and to try things out and discover what worked. Peter might have had ideas on what would have been most useful, but the women were most in touch with their needs. Peter wisely understood that the most responsive ideas to their needs emerged within the incubator of the relational, connected space between these women.

The women met monthly, each time contributing the Kenyan equivalent of a dollar. That might not sound like a lot, but in a matter of months, they had enough together to purchase a shared *posho* mill: a grinder to make flour out of grain. They would pass the mill around the circle, and each woman would grind her grain, with the opportunity to grind the grain of others for a small fee. Together, sharing resources, they began to leverage what they had in order to produce more resources.

The circle sometimes experimented with making group purchases, like the mill; other times with loaning money to one member, who would then repay the loan after newly purchased chickens began to lay eggs, a goat had kids, or a crop came in. Connection allowed them to transcend the limitations of operating as independent economic units and to build much greater independence and resilience. These women's circles were profoundly successful. We visited one extraordinary woman who proudly showed us her own water well and functioning car, solar cooker, cow and flock of chickens. This was wealth indeed! And, this wealth resulted from experimenting with connection.

Part Four is entirely about Acting. In the previous chapter, you explored an attitude for action that is appropriate to Complexity. An attitude of curiosity and experimentation will help you stay spacious and creative when historical approaches to problem-solving and detailed planning seem to be anti-helpful. It also will support your nourishment of the conditions of connection, fluidity and stability, the topics of these three final chapters.

In this chapter, you'll experiment with how connection builds capacity on distinct levels of Soma, Identity and Context, as well as integrating across these levels. You will act through pragmatic safe-to-fail experiments that probe the system for learning, intervening also in your Complexity Challenge. You'll act by amplifying the condition of connection and staying curious about what happens.

CONNECTION

Connection is critical for leading in Complexity.

We can see connection explicitly in many previous parts of the book. We can see it, for example, with Soma as we connect through awareness with our internal experience and connect with what matters most in order to embody a future we care about. Connecting through our Identity fosters resonance and understanding in conversation with others. And connection appears in relation to Context, as we recognize how our inner state becomes coupled with the state of the system around us. Connection is everywhere.

What's less obvious is that connection also requires differentiation. To talk about connection is also to talk about differentiation: after all, distinctions have allowed new observations throughout our work together. For example, in order to decouple our state from what's going on around us, we differentiate internal and external conditions. And disentangling our Identity from the Context is a process of differentiation as well.

Without differentiation, connection is meaningless.[78] In fact, the connection of differentiated parts is precisely what makes sex fun! It is why this book is a meaningful transmission between the writer (me) and the reader (you) across time and space. And it is how anything at all useful happens.

It's this integrating connection between clearly differentiated parts that makes a functioning system out of a collection of parts. If you were to take all the chemicals that make up your body (water, bone, DNA, dopamine, bile, etc.) and put them into separate jars, the total inventory of the jars would be the same as of your body: exactly the same amounts of all the components. However, the same materials in separate jars wouldn't be reading this book. It's the relationship between these distinct components, and the connections between them, that allow your body to function as a self-organizing system.

Connection invites creativity and emergence. This is true on all levels of scale, from the interactions of subatomic particles to the collisions between massive galaxies, each containing hundreds of billions of stars. And it's true on the levels of scale we have been exploring in this book: Soma, Identity and Context.

Let's explore what this means and how you might experiment with connection on these levels of scale. This dynamism of connection and differentiation has been implicit throughout the book; we will now make it explicit and pragmatic.

Connected Soma

When we explored the Awareness Map in Chapter 7, we differentiated aspects of our awareness: cognition, emotions, sensations, stillness. We can recognize all of these differentiated components in the memory of some childhood experience that brings up a visual image, the name of a person who we saw, the emotions of that experience, and sensations of the scent of flowers or somebody's perfume. Those phenomena are inextricably **connected** in the neuronal network of our nervous system. But they also are **differentiated** because we can direct attention to any one of them.

Later, in Chapter 9, we saw how our inner state became coupled with what is going on around us: We take on the stress of the system. This results from our **connectedness**: We care, we pay attention, our Soma is constantly connected with what's around us. The antidote, of course, was to **decouple** our state from the Context: dampening connection and increasing **differentiation**.

Connection across the system in which we are leading begins with connection to ourselves. **Internal congruence** is when our whole somatic inner state, and our expression of this inner state as Identity, are coherent and aligned with what we seek to cultivate in the system. Congruence greatly reduces the cross-currents and mixed messages when leaders say one thing but embody something very different.

Scaling Awareness might include fostering conditions of greater connection in the system. However, if we disconnect from ourselves, focusing urgency externally on changing the system ("driving for results") but losing touch with our own internal awareness and aliveness, we are already out of congruence. We have disconnected from ourselves in order to encourage connection "out there!" While this is absurd on the face of it, it is an easy myopia to slip into when we focus on changing the Context but completely omit our Identity and Soma from consideration.

Connection thus begins internally: in the Soma. Fortunately, as we move into Acting, we have built a solid foundation through many chapters on Sensing and

Being, as well as the previous chapter on attitude. We have practiced connecting our attention to the various differentiated realms of our experience, including our emotional life, the realm of internal sensations, and cognitive processes. Having new distinctions, such as the Awareness Map and the various channels of awareness, allows us to connect our awareness to the granular experience of our aliveness that arises moment by moment. This is how we maintain congruence between our Soma and the conditions we are fostering in our Complexity Context.

Do this now. Take a moment to connect with your own interior experience. Notice how quickly available this connection is (at least, when you remember to take this time, this pause…).

PRESENCE PAUSE

In this example, a wise leader recognizes how important it is to begin with herself. Changing the way she contributes and leads begins with the Soma.

Ingrid and self-awareness

It was important to Ingrid to make real contributions in the senior team she had just joined. This was a new cross-functional level of responsibility, and she was eager to hold her own.

Ingrid noticed how often she was attuned to others' moods and ideas in meetings. She tracked the fast-paced exchanges well, but also noticed how this tracking of others seemed to disconnect her from what she herself was feeling or thinking. She could formulate ideas, but by the time she had language for them, the moment had often passed. She found herself uncharacteristically quiet and feeling like an outsider.

Ingrid hypothesized that being more connected to her inner state, and tracking what she herself was thinking, would create the conditions for quicker and more useful contributions.

She experimented with bringing explicit attention into her internal state during meetings. She worked with tracking her physical sensations, her emotions, and specifically the ideas and questions that were constantly bubbling up. She was committed to staying connected to herself—and to watching how many contributions arose from this deliberate internal attentiveness. She quickly noticed how much of a difference this made in what she knew she had to contribute.

Connected Identity

Leadership presence is the extension of our inner state into the world: the outward expression of our internal congruence as experienced by others. Having first cultivated the inner conditions for Acting, leadership presence is how our internal organizing principle becomes a magnetic force in mobilizing a dynamic, complex web of relationships.

Leadership presence is a means to cultivate conditions for collaboration with others, particularly when our positional authority is limited or absent. The Identity we build in our relationships with others, the internal state from which we engage, and what we include in the spotlight of our attention—all these are crucial to our efficacy. The more embodied our presence and the more congruent our inner state, the stronger the organizing principle we become in our Context.

Influence is one possible result of leadership presence. However, at the core, the primary tangible result of leadership presence is *connection* with *differentiation*. Our relationships are, at core, interactions between distinct biological systems. To pretend that communication is simply a matter of getting our words right ignores millions of years of biology and a lifetime of accumulated experience.

Relational fields are the invisible, yet palpable fields of energy[79] and consciousness that connect us when we are in relationship with someone. The field is present, whether or not we are conscious of it, in one-on-one interactions, meetings, presentations, and mob scenes. Everyone present influences, and is influenced by, the relational field. We can sense the field changing when we step outside into nature as well.

Skillful leadership has a level of attunement: the kind of presence that builds relatedness and connection between unique and differentiated individuals. In communicating, we focus on being receptive and on deep listening, not just on transmission. We extend our energy outward, not simply to influence, but to receive. We can imagine extending our attention, like the unfurling of sensitive antennae, to receive what is coming back. Rather than the traditional heroic leader acting *on* her Context and shaping it according to her intentions, we thus begin to shape our selves around the deeper process of embodied connection *with* and through the relational field.

Consciously or not, we shape, and are shaped by, the fields around us. *Biological co-regulation* is the process through which the state of one Soma is transmitted through the relational field to influence the condition of others' Somas. Richard Strozzi-Heckler writes, "When our conscious attention touches someone and informs our perceptions, there's a dynamic interplay, a reciprocal encounter at a very intimate level, between the perceiver and the perceived. Extending in this manner is both touching and being touched."[80]

Co-regulation is the dance of two or more nervous systems, each shaping and being shaped by the others. Presence is contagious. Because we are connected through the relational field, our internal state is in dynamic relationship with the internal state of others around us. Co-regulation is the means by which we transmit our state. It is the means by which we, as leaders, can share our internal spaciousness and optimism in service to our team's capacity and growth. Through the relational field, our internal congruence becomes contagious and palpable to others. Our stability and consistency have a stabilizing effect on others; our reactivity and stress do the opposite. Being spreads.

I cannot overemphasize the importance of this dynamic interplay. It is present in every meeting, every phone conversation, every encounter with a loved one, rival, boss, or customer. Bringing awareness to this will explain a lot of the mysteries of human relationships!

Allison claims space

Allison is a small woman in a fiercely competitive, largely male-dominated line of work. In meetings, she was often the only female and was frequently interrupted by others with strong points of view who also physically towered over her. It took a lot of energy to hold her own in this testosterone-laden environment, and she often found herself having to fight for airtime in ways that didn't feel true to herself.

Allison's safe-to-fail experiment on the level of Identity began with her Soma: with accessing an internal state that she experienced as more resourced, which she then extended out into the room. In meetings, she grounded and centered (Chapter 8), took up more space by sitting tall in her chair, and opened her chest and shoulders to take up more width.

Then, when she spoke, she did so from a more congruent body and voice. She expected to be listened to. She noticed that this erect and expansive posture seemed to get the men's attention far more often than previous, more aggressive efforts from a contracted body. Plus, it simply felt better. Extending Leadership Presence was on her terms. She glimpsed a new Identity, one that both felt truer to herself and that initially seemed notably more effective in a tough environment.

Connected Context

Ours is a collaborative species. Shared connection and learning were an early and fundamental evolutionary advantage of early *Homo sapiens,*[81] allowing us to quickly accelerate the numbers and sophistication of our species to become, for now, the most powerful on the planet. (The jury is still out on this particular safe-to-fail experiment, by the way!) In fact, enforced disconnection from others (e.g., in solitary confinement and long-term isolation) produces debilitating psychological effects, as the lost connection with others deprives us of both social stimulation and validation of our Identity.

We have a deep historical Context for connection as an organizing principle for Complexity. Complexity, of course, on the Serengeti in Africa three hundred thousand years ago looked and felt very different than it does in today's fast-paced organizations. Yet, connection is still essential for collectively addressing Complexity in useful ways.

In Complexity, it is our innate biological disposition towards connection and collaborative learning in teams and organizations that allows unexpected, nonlinear innovation to arise. Our creativity nourishes and is nourished by that of others.

Complexity-capable cultures also pay attention to differentiating the parts of a system. After all, too much connection and insufficient differentiation is also unhealthy. Consider the loss of resilience when our inner state becomes coupled with the state of our Context, or when biological co-regulation with toxic people becomes overwhelming. Differentiation is the antidote.

Complexity-capable cultures foster linkages and connections between differentiated parts, as well as to the relational field that underlies all interactions. Connection, in turn, is the antidote to the excessive focus on the reductionism and compartmentalization (i.e., excessive differentiation) that paralyze Complicated approaches to Complex challenges.[82]

The inner work of the first six Panes cultivated a connected, present, resilient inner state ready to act in service to our embodied organizing principles. At core, Acting in Complexity might take the surface form of actions we have historically taken. However, now these actions are taken from a sense of connection and with awareness of the relational field, thus executed with more purpose. They are expressions of a curious, experimental attitude. Importantly, they now arise from an internal congruence with what we care about most.

From the grounding of internal congruence and purposefulness, consider how these actions not only may create a resonance with the immediate people with whom we are in conversation but also may catalyze the connections necessary for a Complexity-capable culture on a bigger scale. Some examples of your connection-conscious actions might include:

- *Offering perspectives and information* as an act of generosity. Sharing information that might have been held in isolation supports others. For example, sales and engineering might have very different kinds of information, but both are necessary for appropriate customer service and product design. Offering unsolicited information increases the capabilities of other parts of the system to respond to emergent issues.

- *Requesting perspectives and information.* Each part of a system exists in its own Bell Jar. Inviting perspectives and information from across boundaries provides the opportunity for others both to support and challenge us.

- *Instigating creative conversations across system boundaries* (levels, functions, units). Conversations are inherently connecting. New kinds of conversations might explore synergies across boundaries, reveal what each part can learn from others, and stimulate creativity and learning across the system. Conversations build the field of connectedness, out of which surprising possibilities or questions might emerge about the downstream impact of our decisions on the larger Contexts of society and the Earth itself.

- *Asking new questions* that invite new kinds of Sensing and meaning-making within your group or across boundaries. New questions can be provocative and can disrupt perspectives and assumptions.

- *Testing assumptions.* The act of including different perspectives from outliers (e.g., customers, people with different histories or expertise, and other nonmainstream viewpoints) really is crucial for exposing the assumptions that we can't see because we are too comfortable or because we surround ourselves with people who see the world in the same way.

- *Inviting others into safe-to-fail experiments.* Try stuff. Cheap, interesting, fun, provocative stuff. Probe the system around you to see what works and what doesn't. When we discover something that seems to move the system in the direction we intend, we can expand and amplify it. Likewise, when we discover something that moves us in the opposite direction, we can declare, "Oh, how interesting! That produces these unintended effects!" We have learned something, and we can change or dampen it; we can try a new experiment.

There are countless others, of course. I simply invite you into the realization that Acting in Complexity is both about the **nature of the actions** that you take (e.g., creating connection at levels of Soma, Identity and Context) and about the **consciousness and presence that you bring to these actions**.

Scaling Awareness can be an organic and emergent process, and thus may seem counterintuitive if you have participated in or designed elaborate culture-change initiatives. In fact, you may need to forget what you already know about changing culture (which is highly likely to derive from an expert-driven, Complicated mindset) in order to rediscover the joys of curiosity and experimentation.

Culture change might be more likely to emerge from a series of small experiments and the building of collective curiosity, as groups of people begin to shift the ground of their own Sensing, Being, and Acting together. It is possible, too, that our most profound influence on our Context might result from our presence in the most mundane of encounters. The key shifts are an embodied presence and a sense of purpose that touches and invites others.

Mira experiments with listening

Mira was a software engineering director in a hugely successful and disruptive technology company. Customers were often frustrated because the company culture was notoriously secretive, and core capabilities were often being tweaked right up until new product releases. Last-minute surprises meant that customers couldn't plan around capabilities in advance. Moreover, sales believed that innovations reflected what engineers found cool and new but not what customers actually wanted or needed. It was an innovative, engineering-driven culture, but the disconnect with the customer base was growing, and engineering was increasingly seen as arrogant and out of touch with the market.

This created ongoing tension between the global sales force who represented commercial customers for the company's product suite and the world-class engineers whose innovation had driven the success in the first place.

Mira got together a small group of sales and engineering leaders to talk about the problem. Rather than looking for a fix, they initiated a safe-to-fail experiment where a few engineers (including Mira herself) visited field offices and customer sites around the world. These visits generally lasted a week or so and were fun and interesting. The sales folks were delighted to design the itineraries, all too happily bringing engineers to customers to hear their perspectives directly. This took the sales folks out of the middle: the point was simply to listen, to be curious, and to understand the end users of their products and the difficulties created by the product-design process.

Over time, these visits eventually led to significant changes in the innovation pipeline and the involvement of customers. At the outset, it was simply an experiment.

Fostering Connection Across a Nested Complex System

The previous sections focused on cultivating the conditions for connection on each of the three levels of system. We explored how we might Tune ourselves as Instrument through the connecting power of awareness. We explored Extending Leadership Presence and how the relational field supports building resonance and connection with others. And we got curious about how connection might serve as an organizing principle in Scaling Awareness for Complexity.

Connection is valuable within all three of these distinct levels of system. That said, focusing experiments at any level runs the risk of reinforcing the belief that they are separate and distinct.

Context, Identity and Soma are interrelated and dynamically interdependent levels of system within a complex, emergent whole. Recall Figure 4.1, in which we see all three levels of a nested system continually and dynamically influencing the

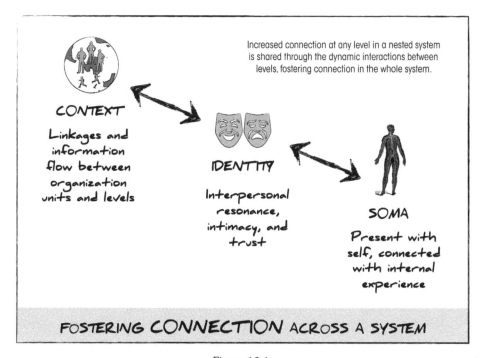

Figure 12.1

others. Now, in Figure 12.1, we see that the conditions of connection at any level of our nested system also foster connection on the others. Our connectedness in our own Soma expresses itself through our Identity to produce more connection in the Context. Similarly, a connected Context influences downward in ways that influence everyone, and that aware members will sense in their own Somas. Experimentation at any level produces shifts at all levels; the intentionality of including all levels as you design experiments enhances this integrative effect.

When we attend to the whole system, we simultaneously access connection at all levels. We are centering and bringing ourselves into the present moment. We are extending leadership presence out. We are inviting people into safe-to-fail experiments that create shifts in our Context. *In short, we are connected and present with ourselves, we are connected and present with each other, and we are inviting connection and presence collectively within the larger Context.*

These are not separate phenomena. We experiment with connection as an organizing principle across the levels of system, as well as within each of them. We do this intentionally, consciously. We don't disconnect from ourselves in order to create resonance with another. We don't badger people into safe-to-fail experiments around connection. We can't engineer intimacy and resonance.

Rather, we embody and practice connection simultaneously at all levels of scale so that the conditions of connection integrate vertically across the nested systems.

Susan fosters conditions of connection

Susan recognized the importance of revitalizing the congregation and its finances, but orchestrating change really wasn't her thing. In a word, she needed to connect with others, and connect others with the community and its goals. Susan was kind and introverted by nature, but she was also conflict- and risk-averse. Enabling connections would play to both her strengths and her weaknesses.

Susan focused first on experiments with connecting to her own Soma, understanding that her own embodiment of connection would serve as both model and invitation to the congregation. She began a regular sitting practice, and worked with grounding and self-observation practices to become more connected to her inner experience. She did this with the intention of observing how she might become less reactive to criticism and more relaxed in the presence of people who were initially skeptical of her.

This inner work was, surprisingly, both fun and interesting. She quickly noticed how often she felt anxious, which would creep into her voice. She also discovered that she could take that experience of anxiety and shift into more centered states, even though she still felt challenged by self-consciousness in social situations.

After the practices became more familiar, she worked with extending this new aspect of her Identity—including a nascent settled presence—into her personal conversations with lay leaders and members, focusing on staying grounded, curious about them, and warm. Susan didn't intend for these conversations to persuade or get people on board change. Rather, she simply wanted to experiment with how extending her own presence might build connection.

The pulpit also gave Susan an additional great practice opportunity. Not a naturally charismatic speaker, it challenged her Identity to be personal and vulnerable in public. Her voice became stronger, deeper, and clearer.

Susan talked about her self-experimentation publicly. She explicitly used her experimentation as a metaphor for the change in the church, then invited the congregation to connect with each other and share their own experiences of change. She then went further, approaching potential conflict directly. Susan experimented with informal personal connections by gathering traditional members who liked things just as they were with younger members who saw the need for change. She didn't advocate in these small gatherings, but neither did she avoid the tension. She became known in the congregation for her accessibility and curiosity, and for being "real." They saw themselves in her and felt connected and increasingly relaxed, even as she challenged them to be more and more authentic in their own spiritual expression.

Susan's experiments with the conditions of connection were beginning to Scale Awareness.

It's now time for you to design an integrative experiment directed toward Scaling Awareness. I am inviting you here to integrate the somewhat abstract book content into your specific Complexity Challenge. I want you to create something new and energizing and custom tailored for you.

As with Susan, tools are available, but you ultimately have to find your own way.

Trust me on this. Take a minute to shift your state from the focused mental intensity of reading to connect to a more fluid, creative space from which you might imagine new action. Center yourself, relaxing and grounding in your intention to design something that's interesting and useful.

Yes, now.

⇗⊘ PRESENCE PAUSE ⊘⇖

Now, from this more creative resourceful state, imagine your own experiment.

Experiment 12.1:
Experimenting with Connection

Tuning the Instrument, Extending Leadership Presence, and Scaling Awareness are related and interdependent. Your experiment will include all three levels of system. Experimenting with connection within and across all three levels is a fun and powerful approach to creating conditions for Complexity.

Bring to mind your Complexity challenge and direction. If they are not clear to you, and freshly in mind, please revisit and update Experiment 10.2, on page 199.

Begin with your Soma. Center yourself, connecting internally to an organizing principle. What is most deeply important to you in your Complexity Challenge? (By the way, this centering itself is a safe-to-fail experiment with Soma!)

Then, consider the following questions. (You can refer to Experiment 11.1, on page 228, for more detailed questions that you can translate for connection. This set is edited for brevity.)

1. What *direction* do you intend?
2. Connection is not an end in itself. Where are there disconnections? What is your *hypothesis* about how amplifying connection might serve your direction?
3. What can you *design* and try, with others?
4. How can this be *safe enough* to try?
5. How will you *learn*?

Now, convene conversations with others. Experiment with connection, together. As you do so, stay present and grounded, connecting with your own Soma, and connecting through your Identity with others as you design together! Engage all three levels of system to build congruence and connection.

What do you notice about how the conversations and experimentation create shifts in your relationships?

Learn from what happens. Then, what's next?

CHAPTER SUMMARY

In this chapter, rather than organizing your exploration around the bottom three Panes, you took an indirect and counterintuitive approach.

The core realization of this chapter (and the two that follow) is that experimentation can amplify or dampen underlying conditions that are present in all systems in support of the direction you have declared and embodied. As in earlier chapters (Chapter 7, in particular), what you focus on tends to grow. By focusing here on connection, you can simultaneously Scale Awareness in your Context, Extend a signature Leadership Presence, and Tune your psychobiological Instrument as the substrate for your leadership in Complexity.

I acknowledge that this may seem counterintuitive to you. After all, you are likely a leader accustomed to taking direct action and expecting certain results to naturally follow.

Of course, that is precisely the trap that you are trying to avoid with this counter-intuitive approach. You are placing into the background the very results you are rightly committed to! In its place, you are putting into the foreground three necessary conditions for Complexity: connection, fluidity and stability. ***This shift enables you to focus more and more on creating the underlying conditions that nourish those desired results over time.***

Via this chapter, you focused on the condition of connection, and its opposite of differentiation, and on integrating the two for your Complexity Challenge. We also explored how you might use safe-to-fail experiments with connection to probe the whole system for information about how things work in reality, while simultaneously intervening in all levels of the system simultaneously. It is highly integrative.

Stepping stones for building connection include:
- Maintaining a Complexity attitude
- Being aware of the relational field as a substrate for all conversation and for language
- Developing consistent practices that foster internal connection within yourself
- Creating connection with others through your leadership presence
- Creating safe-to-fail experiments that build connection within the larger system
- The realization that experimentation both probes for new information and changes the system at the same time

Take some time to reflect on what you now realize as a result of this chapter on connection.
- What do you understand differently?
- What are you now curious about?
- What experiments might you try?

≋ PRESENCE PAUSE ≋

	CONTEXT	IDENTITY	SOMA
SENSING	Observe The System	Recognize Identity At Stake	Attend To Experience
BEING	Decouple State From Context	Embody What Matters	Regulate Inner State
ACTING	SCALE AWARENESS	EXTEND LEADERSHIP PRESENCE	TUNE THE INSTRUMENT

FLUIDITY

FIELD GUIDE TO PRESENCE-BASED LEADERSHIP

Acting for Fluidity

*It must be obvious...that there is a contradiction in wanting
to be perfectly secure in a universe whose very nature is
momentariness and fluidity.*
– Alan Watts

*The physical reinvention of the world is endless, relentless,
fascinating, exhaustive; nothing that seems solid is. If you could
stand at just a little distance in time, how fluid and shape-
shifting physical reality would be, everything hurrying into some
other form, even concrete, even stone.*
– Mark Doty

*The biggest job we have is to teach a newly hired employee how to
fail intelligently. We have to train him to experiment over and over
and to keep on trying and failing until he learns what will work.*
– Charles F. Kettering

W E HAVE SEEN HOW CONNECTION ON THE LEVELS OF SOMA, Identity and
Context supports the conditions that enable resilience and capacity
for Complexity. And we have seen how experiments with connection,
across the three levels of scale, serve to integrate the whole, in service to what
we care about.

In this Acting chapter, we explore ***fluidity*** and the stepping stones it offers
for creating the conditions for navigating Complexity.

A "team of teams" in Iraq

In 2004, the Joint Special Operations Task Force of the U.S. military was losing an unconventional war in Iraq.

By any measure, the U.S. military was the most efficient, powerful, and well-resourced organization in the history of human endeavor; the task force coordinated the elite special operations units from across the branches of service.

As powerful as the military machine was, it was also Complicated. General Stanley McChrystal describes helicopters returning from combat missions to be loaded on transport planes minutes later, then replaced by newly tuned helicopters just flown in from bases in the U.S. The entire operation was an astounding exercise in Complicated logistics.

But this compartmentalized and hierarchical decision-making, however efficient, was no match for fluid terrorist networks coordinating via cell phone, "martyrs" willing to die for their cause, and highly mobile groups that arose and dissolved into their environments at a moment's notice. A finely honed Complicated machine was fighting a rapidly evolving war for which it was not designed.

In his excellent description of Complexity, McChrystal describes how the mindset and organizational practices of the task force needed to radically change in order to meet an unconventional threat. He writes, "Few of the plans... unfolded as envisioned. Instead, we evolved in rapid iterations... The environment in which we found ourselves... demanded a dynamic, constantly adapting approach." [83]

Over time, a series of experiments radically changed the culture and structure of the task force. Evolving experiments included the creation of an open meeting space, with representatives from all agencies sitting at the same table and sharing the same information. Up to seven thousand people conferenced in from around the globe for a two-hour daily meeting, and the task force changed its default operational process to fluid and open sharing of information, rather than maintaining traditional secrecy that shared information only via formal channels. High-quality and timely information across agencies and functions and geography made the meetings valuable for everyone; breaking intelligence could translate into a special forces raid hours later, which would procure new intelligence that could be quickly scoured for relevant information that, then, could be brought to the next day's meeting.

The result was, as McChrystal termed it, a "team of teams": a structure vast in capabilities, yet also nimble and responsive. One of the keys to this fluidity was the connection across units, levels, and branches of the service. Connection and "shared consciousness" of the mission created the conditions for fluid and responsive action.

In this chapter, you will explore fluidity at each of your three levels of system. Out of this exploration, you will design a safe-to-fail experiment at using fluidity as an organizing principle to integrate across scales in your own Complexity Challenge.

Fluidity

Fluidity. The image comes up of a river roiling down out of the mountains. It pours around rocks and boulders, flowing towards the sea. Obstacles arise, but the fluidity of water assures that the overall trajectory moves in the direction it is destined to. Disruptions, cross-currents, eddies, and rapids are part of the journey. From the perspective of the water, however, these are simply features of the game, not existential threats to its nature or to the journey itself.

Complexity is like this. There is an overall direction (an embodied future, an organizing principle, a direction). Disruptions and obstacles will certainly arise: This is the nature of unpredictability and the perversities of Complexity.

Yet, if we were water, we wouldn't take these things personally. We would stay relaxed, curious, open to the countless alternatives that we know are available for the discovery but haven't yet seen. We would experiment and see what might work. When something didn't work, we wouldn't persist. Rather, we'd be pleased at our realization that we learned something else that didn't work. Effortlessly, we would try something else. Celebrating our inherent fluidity, we would appreciate our nonattachment to some rigid and predetermined plan for how to get to the ocean. If we were but water!

Really, then, what might we learn from this metaphor? How might fluidity support the conditions for our direction, in service to what we care about most?

The unfreezing of habits and defaults, our letting go of an obsessive clinging to structure and to what's worked in the past, begins on the level of Soma.

Fluid Soma

In your attention practices, you have likely experienced some elements of fluidity. Thoughts, sensations, emotions arise and pass. In the absence of some focusing and organizing principle, our internal experience at times resembles a "shrieking madhouse on wheels"[84] as the incessant chatter of our psychobiology generates seemingly random bits and bytes of experience.

Disorganized and random, this kind of experience seems to serve little purpose; we experience it as distractibility, lack of focus or disregulation. With practice, however, we can witness our lightning-fast and unconstrained flipping of attention.

On the other end is rigidity, in which recycled thoughts occupy our minds, a persistent mood or emotional state takes up residence, or we stay stressed and tight for hours, days (or years) on end. This also isn't particularly useful and, in the extreme, can lead to real neurosis and psychosomatic illness.

In between these poles, the structuring and directing of our natural flow of experience is crucial for our functioning in the world. When this structuring is foreground, we call the resulting conditions *stability* (and we will focus our entire next chapter on stability[85]). When our focus is on the flow of creativity, intuition and openness to new possibilities, we call it *fluidity*. Here, we are water.

In fluidity, we can shift perspectives easily, accessing multiple perspectives that arise moment by moment. We can experience emotions, but we don't attach to them: They rise up, and they pass, like images on a movie screen. We have sensations, and we notice them, but they are always changing and shifting. There is no internal friction, no slowing or resistance to the natural fluidity of our creative intelligence as it arises.

Presence expressed as fluidity frees our capacity to respond to what is arising around us in new and creative ways. Several times in the writing of Part Four of this book, my Identity-based desire to offer you elegant toolkits bogged me down. I lost my fluidity in the desire for comforting structure. With hindsight, I can see that letting go of previous drafts was both humbling and necessary. It was only through investing tremendous energy into experiments that revealed how *not* to write Part Four that I could step into unknown territory and discover a pathway that feels right.

The river has to flow through boulders and obstacles to find the way, and water doesn't judge itself at all for the path it takes to the sea.

◈ PRESENCE PAUSE ◈

Even fluidity can be actively cultivated and practiced. In fact, the work we have already done around Sensing and Being offered extensive attention, state-shifting and resilience practices specifically designed to amplify the internal conditions of fluidity.

Improvisational theater artists, jet-fighter pilots, basketball players and rap musicians embody fluidity and harness the power of presence in their arts. So do leaders of innovative and creative organizations.

Leticia plays with fluidity in perspective

Leticia was a VP at a commercial bank in Latin America. She was enthusiastic but sometimes impatient when she thought she knew what needed to be done and others were slow to arrive at a plan. She knew there was value in talking it through and considering all perspectives, but it came at the cost of efficiency.

She experimented in meetings that she was not actively leading. Staying present to herself, Leticia practiced accessing as many perspectives as possible. These included the perspective of the whole room, the point of view of specific meeting members, the point of view of someone not present, the perspective of customers, or of someone hearing about this conversation a year from now, etc. She found it fascinating to see how many different perspectives she could touch into; she even practiced holding multiple perspectives at the same time without making any of them wrong.

Practicing this way gave Leticia the internal experience of fluidity. Like water, her perspective proved able to shift easily and flexibly, and she became increasingly able to access and reconcile different viewpoints without driving so hard.

Fluid Identity

We each have a variety of roles that we can use in service to others and to our purpose. To the extent that we identify with a particular role, we are likely to unconsciously use it as a default. Doing so, after all, reinforces the very Identity that perpetuates our reassuring sense of self.

However, this slip into a default position radically reduces our fluidity by producing behaviors and actions that privilege the preservation of Identity over what is actually most useful in the moment. (If you are familiar with my previous work, you will recall the seven Voices, or roles, that leadership coaches play with clients. My first book[86] explores how we might cultivate fluidity in our roles in service to what we care about.)

By bringing mindful awareness to the attachments and aversions that hold these Identity-driving behaviors in place, we bring more fluidity and choice to our leadership. For example, I have a lot of Identity as a teacher, which serves me in good stead writing this book but sometimes undermines my coaching of leaders if I habitually offer expertise when a good penetrating question would be of greater service. I have to watch myself lest my Identity needs, perpetuating a fixed and reassuring sense of self, narrow my presence and resourcefulness.

We all have multiple roles that we play: mother, supervisor, strategist, facilitator, provocateur, queen, comforter-in-chief. Choosing wisely what role is helpful at any given moment and offering ourselves in that role without attachment requires fluidity.

Sometimes our Identity hijacks our fluidity. We conflate who we are with a particular role, coming to believe that we actually *are* the set of behaviors, attachments and aversions that come with the role. When this happens, we lose our fluidity. We become rigid, predictable and not at all resilient. Like ice, not like water.

As long as we recognize that this role is not fundamentally who we are, we are free to shift fluidly, like water, as the circumstances demand.

Odede, the grasshopper, survives through fluidity

I met a remarkable young man in the slums of Nairobi. I will call him Odede, Luo for grasshopper.

In his early twenties, Odede had grown up in extreme poverty. His parents had brought him as a young child to the city; the family lived under a sheet of plastic held up by sticks. They soon died of AIDS, leaving four children to fend for themselves.

Now sharing a rented room, Odede and his siblings had survived the endemic violence, raw poverty, and grittiness of the slums for nearly their entire younger lives. His older brother became a shell after the ravages of hardship, drugs and alcohol; Odede, meanwhile, was one of the most resourceful people I have ever met. He had accepted the responsibility of keeping his siblings alive, even putting his delightful younger sister through school. Odede had a cell phone with which he generated sufficient income through anything that might work: a tiny barbershop, fixing radios, running errands. He knew everybody.

Odede was the embodiment of the attitude of experimentation and learning: consistently upbeat, positive, and radically entrepreneurial; trying anything and everything. With a big smile and boundless energy, he was as water, constantly probing for possibilities and trying something new in his dangerous and seething Context. If something didn't work, he let it go. If it did, he did it more. From everything I could tell, Odede was thriving through fluidity, in spite of the lousy hand he had been dealt.

Fluidity of Identity—optimism, flexibility, doing what is needed and appropriate in the moment for the greater good—allowed the charismatic Odede to contend successfully with a Complex life situation. It was also a means to Extend Leadership Presence into the relational field, creating and strengthening connections with family and with the larger community. It also benefited others around him, who were drawn to him and learned from him in their own ways.

Fluidity, like so many other aspects of presence, is contagious.

Fluid Context

Introducing fluidity into the Context level of system arises as a result of individual leaders liberating themselves from their own unconscious processes for constructing and maintaining Identity. The Joint Task Force in the leadoff example is a rich example of Scaling Awareness through this kind of fluidity. McChrystal writes about *shared consciousness* as the connectivity (and what in our language would be *relational field*) that allowed a vast organization to mobilize with agility, fluidity and power against a radically inventive and determined adversary. When leaders—from the top on down—can embody this creative fluidity and extend it into the relational field, awareness begins to scale.

We feel this happening when multiple people across levels and units begin to access fluidity. The energy is unmistakable. The effects of focusing and aligning towards a shared direction become exponentially greater. Cultures that share purpose and direction work collaboratively with much less wasted energy. They can Sense and Act on creative possibilities, and they self-organize with much greater ease.

Consider how these leadership actions may build the conditions for fluidity so necessary in a Complexity-capable culture on a bigger scale:

- *Model letting go.* When we, as leaders, visibly let go of an idea, a project, an agenda that we have previously been attached to, it sends a strong message that there are larger organizing principles than an individual's fixed ideas. Nonattachment is contagious, and we make explicit what's more important.

- *Stimulate creativity by asking skillful questions* that reveal untested assumptions or challenge constraints. Conversations and meetings in many organizations are more characterized by advocacy than by inquiry. Skillful and intentional questioning can bring more information into the room, loosening the boundaries that constrain fluidity and creativity.

- *Eliminate a constraint.* Jack Welch's "speed, simplicity and self-confidence"[87] initiative across GE in the 1980s was intended to eliminate bottlenecks and bureaucracy so that people closest to the work could respond with self-confidence and fluidity to emerging situations.

- *Invite multiple perspectives.* Offering or, better, generating multiple perspectives together expands the space and information available in a particular issue or meeting. Accessing multiple legitimate and powerful perspectives internally is also a fluidity practice; when we do it with others, it becomes a way to Scale Awareness.

- *Contextualize obstacles in the long game.* This is itself a perspective shift. Holding, together, the perspective that obstacles are opportunities to find a different pathway brings the water metaphor alive in the collective awareness. It reorients our attention on the overall direction, rather than on an obstacle channeling us into "fixing" mode.

- *Design safe-to-fail experiments in fluidity.* The process of designing and conducting experiments with conditions of fluidity probes the system to see how it might respond. Experiments simultaneously generate information about the system and are interventions in the system.

These are, of course, samples. Fluidity in your Context begins with fluidity in you. Note our attitude again here: We see Complexity as normal. We embody an attitude of curiosity and experimentation. We have fun doing small things, not in running pilots for major institutional change initiatives. No speeches necessary (though a fun and inspiring speech about why fluidity is relevant to what we all care about might also sometimes be just the thing!).

Conditions of fluidity change culture

The culture survey at a prominent health-care organization looked terrible. I sat at the table with the leadership team as the results were discussed; long faces expressed shock at the unanticipated negativity. Clearly, the team was out of touch with staff's concerns. And just as clearly, senior leadership assumed it was up to them to fix the culture. Staff expected them to. This felt paralyzing to an already overwhelmed senior leadership team.

The mood and perspective changed radically when I asked the question, "What if staff were the solution?" This questioned the tacit assumption that it was up to senior leadership to fix the problem. The question introduced a new fluidity into the conditions of the meeting.

Out of this very different conversation emerged a small, safe-to-fail experiment. Two members of the senior team would meet with four staff members. This short-term, ad hoc group was invited, within explicit boundaries of money, time and policy, to try out any means they chose for addressing a concern of their choosing from the culture survey.

The experiment was wildly successful. Staff was thrilled to be given authority and to sit at the table with senior leaders. They were committed to contributing and had lots of ideas. In the first experiment, the group created their own experiment with staff-driven communication about upcoming initiatives to the whole staff.

The energy unleashed inspired other experiments around diversity and inclusion, friction between departments, and efficiencies in organizing work. While specific innovations were discovered by the work of these ad hoc experiment groups, the real power lay in the groups themselves. The increased fluidity, possible by bypassing the usual structures of planning, empowered those most interested in a problem to experiment with finding new ways to address it.

Complexity-capable cultures emerge from the interactions of Complexity-capable leaders with others. We connect with others in creating the conditions for fluidity; this is a means for responding to the perversities of Complexity.

Fostering Fluidity Across a Nested Complex System

We have explored how fluidity arises on the three levels of system, and a bit about how we might experiment with cultivating fluidity on each.

Fluidity is relevant within each level of system. At the same time, it is most valuable as an organizing principle if we see the interdependence of our three levels of system, with fluidity as a means to integrate these three levels into a coherent and responsive whole. Figure 13.1, on page 259, shows how fluidity at each level of system invites it on the others.

Scaling Awareness begins small, through your embodiment of a direction and conditions you care about. Fluidity arises when the collective is provided with the "minimum critical specifications"[88] of direction, mission, and purpose and with the express support and power to do what's needed in service of that direction. These conditions, embodied by influential leaders and communicated through resonant leadership presence, encourage the fluid emergence of results that matter.

FAVI's grand experiment

Belgian author and consultant Frederic Laloux describes a lovely example involving Jean-François Zobrist, CEO of FAVI, a French manufacturing company that is a model of self-management.[89] *FAVI had made significant progress towards pushing authority down, yet Zobrist still saw entrenched mindsets that perpetuated excessive control, rigidity and mistrust.*

As an example, the production down time required to authorize and procure a new pair of gloves cost ten times what the gloves would have cost. This was antithetical to the fluid and creative culture that Zobrist believed was possible but that seemed difficult to engineer.

Before shutting down the plant for the Christmas holidays, Zobrist called the entire company together and announced several major policy changes to start after the holidays. The supply room would be open to all, the pay system would be replaced by salaries that did not include deductions for behavior control, and managers would no longer have their own dining room. Everyone would eat together.

When asked how things would be run, he responded: "How will we operate in the future? To be perfectly honest, I don't know. I'm convinced that you deserve for us to work together differently, but I don't have an alternative model. I suggest that, together, we learn by doing, with good intentions, common sense and in good faith."

From Zobrist's perspective, this was a safe-to-fail experiment. Rather than continuing to push organizational systems to foster the culture he envisioned, Zobrist experimented with eliminating controls in order to amplify fluidity and connection. Zobrist invited all to the experiment, as if the workforce were both responsible for, and capable of, designing itself. Which, given these conditions, it then developed the capacity to do!

We can see, reflecting on this, that Zobrist's bold and public experiment in the Context also included his internal state of trust and confidence, as well as the embodiment of an Identity that extended trust and didn't need to control much. He identified what was "safe-to-fail" and started from there. He openly expressed this internal congruence with the direction they were taking by acknowledging their collective capacity to "learn by doing, with good intentions, common sense and in good faith."

Others might see this as a bold or even irresponsible adventure with unknowable outcomes. In a sense, that is true. At the same time, Zobrist had become impatient with the status quo—frustrated that he couldn't move the culture from the top as far and fast as he wanted. He had moved past the illusion that he could personally orchestrate what was needed and build the internal conditions for this bold move over a period of time. Soma and Identity were very much at play here, though others, watching from outside, would only have seen the announcement at the preholiday meeting.

Integral to the experiment were not only eliminating organizational structures of control, but also the transmitted confidence and trust that they could together find their way forward. Tuning the Instrument, Extending Leadership Presence, and Scaling Awareness are mutually reinforcing domains within the same whole system.

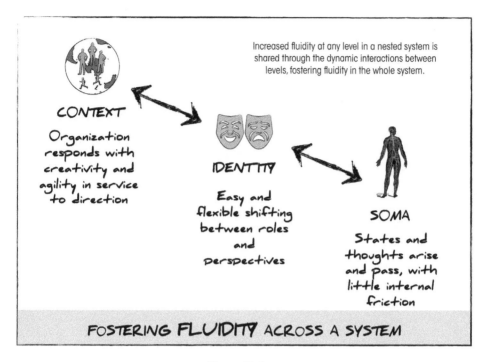

Increased fluidity at any level in a nested system is shared through the dynamic interactions between levels, fostering fluidity in the whole system.

CONTEXT

Organization responds with creativity and agility in service to direction

IDENTITY

Easy and flexible shifting between roles and perspectives

SOMA

States and thoughts arise and pass, with little internal friction

FOSTERING FLUIDITY ACROSS A SYSTEM

Figure 13.1

Susan experiments with fluidity

Susan developed a better self-care regime, including more exercise than she had done in years. This helped her unwind, oxygenated her body, and energized her nervous system. In addition to her regular sitting practice, she began a regular tai chi *practice to develop an internal sense of fluidity and flow within her Soma. She enjoyed the reassuring and relaxing flow that this practice began to generate and wanted to see how this internal practice might affect the ease of her interactions with others.*

From the pulpit, she embodied fluidity, her body sometimes animated and sometimes still and deep. Aware of the field she created and held in this role, she experimented with switching frequently in her sermons between scripture, stories about renewal among families, communities, and nations, and personal sharing about change and flexibility of perspective. Her hypothesis was that her expression of fluidity in language, perspective-taking and body would create different conditions for the informal conversations that took place between members of the congregation.

Susan extended her embodied fluidity into the relational field. First she issued an open invitation for church members to join experimental conversations

about the church, its history, and its future. Some of these conversations were spontaneous after services, others were scheduled lunches. She intentionally both asked for and validated very different perspectives in these conversations, listening to and reinforcing a wide range of viewpoints. She intended to learn from these conversations what conditions encouraged active sharing and deep listening. The warmth and accessibility she was cultivating took effort and attention; others noticed and followed. She also experimented with stepping out of the conversations in the middle so that the exchanges were less dependent on her.

Soon members, with Susan's support, began to invite each other into new kinds of conversations. Experiments, seeded by Susan but led by members, included an alternative religious practices class, as well as circles to identify and hold up long-standing traditions.

Susan never explicitly connected inner practices like tai chi *and self-observation with the increasing fluidity within the church community. Yet she was publicly and frequently transparent about how she was working on herself.*

In Susan's mind, her own inner work and the beginnings of a culture shift in the congregation were intimately connected.

Experiment 13.1:
Experimenting with Fluidity

Time for another experiment. Again, recall the integrative value of including all three levels of system in your experiment. And, recall your Complexity Challenge and direction from Experiment 10.2 (page 199); revisit as necessary to refresh yourself.

Begin with your Soma. Take a couple of minutes to access your own internal fluidity. Stand up, flap your arms, move your entire body in ways that are fluid and creative and unpredictable, bark like a dog, laugh, be ridiculous for a minute or two. Really. You are taking yourself awfully seriously! Loosen up!

Center yourself, connecting internally to an organizing principle. What is most deeply important to you in your Complexity Challenge? (By the way, this centering itself is a safe-to-fail experiment with Soma.)

Then, consider the following questions, referring back to more detail in Experiment 11.1 (page 228) as needed:

1. What *direction* do you intend?
2. What might fluidity enable? Where is fluidity lacking? What is your *hypothesis* about fluidity?
3. What can you *design* and try, with others?
4. How can this be *safe enough* to try?
5. How will you *learn*?

Convene conversations and play with fluidity, together. As you do so, stay present and grounded, fluid within your own Soma, curious and nonattached to your own views and perspectives. Extend fluidity through your Identity as you design experiments together! Engage all three levels of system to build congruence and fluidity.

How do these conversations, and your experiments, shift your relationships?

Learn from what happens, and then explore what's next.

CHAPTER SUMMARY

You built on the foundation of the previous chapter on connection, seeing that connection allows fluidity.

Fluidity is a powerful quality for Complexity, in the same way that a river finds its own course to the sea, moving with a clear direction regardless of the obstacles that arise.

The core realization here is that fluidity can be actively cultivated at all three levels of system: Soma, Identity and Context. Your fluid Soma expresses itself in a fluid awareness, unattached to particular positions or Identity, free to access intuition, creativity and your innate resourcefulness. Your Leadership Presence in relationships invites fluidity and creativity with others. And, together, by cultivating fluidity across all levels, you create the conditions for creative and agile innovation throughout the whole contextual system.

Stepping stones for continuing to explore and embody fluidity include:

- The spaciousness and curiosity of the Complexity attitude from Chapter 11
- The metaphor of water: flow, flexibility, finding a way within an overall direction
- Practices that foster fluidity within your Soma: perspective shifting, body practices, observing states arising and passing, letting go, state-shifting
- The expression of fluidity in your relationships through extending leadership presence
- Experiments in fluidity within the larger Context
- The realization that experimentation both probes for new information and changes the system at the same time

Take some time to reflect on what you now realize as a result of this chapter on fluidity.

- What do you understand differently?
- What are you now curious about?
- What experiments might you try?

≈ PRESENCE PAUSE ≈

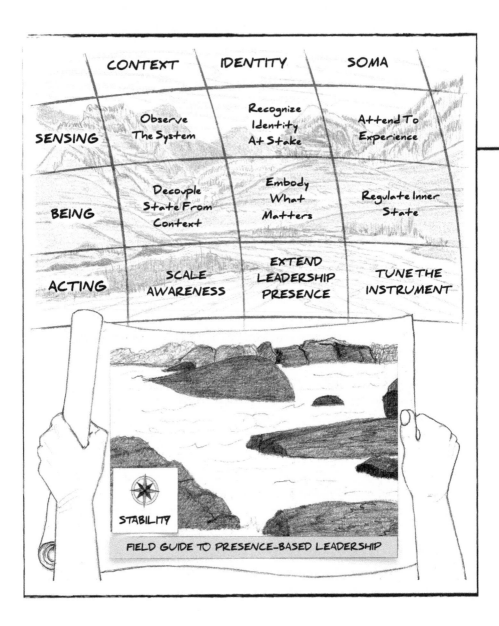

	CONTEXT	IDENTITY	SOMA
SENSING	Observe The System	Recognize Identity At Stake	Attend To Experience
BEING	Decouple State From Context	Embody What Matters	Regulate Inner State
ACTING	SCALE AWARENESS	EXTEND LEADERSHIP PRESENCE	TUNE THE INSTRUMENT

STABILITY

FIELD GUIDE TO PRESENCE-BASED LEADERSHIP

CHAPTER 14

Acting for Stability

*We may be floating on Tao, but there is nothing wrong
with steering. If Tao is like a river, it is certainly good to
know where the rocks are.*
– Ming-Dao Deng

*People are looking for stability in a shaky world. They
want something they can get hold of that's firm and sure
and an anchor in the midst of all of this instability in
which they're living.*
– Gordon B. Hinckley

*The stability we cannot find in the world, we must
create within our own persons.*
– Nathaniel Branden

THROUGH PART FOUR SO FAR, you have been approaching the last three Panes
rather obliquely. While Extending Leadership Presence, Scaling Awareness,
and Tuning the Instrument are still the Panes of Acting in your map, you are
approaching them through an attitude of curiosity and experimentation. You
are cultivating conditions, internally and externally, that support creativity and
capabilities for Complexity.

You first experimented with Acting to foster conditions of connection
across the three levels of system. And next you have seen how fluidity is
also a necessary condition for responding to unpredictability with creativity
and resilience.

Now, you will experiment with another condition essential in Complexity: that of stability.

Leadership on the brink

The Fukushima Daini plant is the sister plant to Fukushima Daichi, the site of the post-tsunami nuclear catastrophe in Japan. Daini was similar in design and six miles to the south; the tsunami knocked out power to three of the plant's four reactors. Without power to cooling pumps and other critical equipment, core meltdown was a certainty.

According to Charles Casto, the Nuclear Regulatory Commission's senior executive responding to the Fukushima disaster, the skillful leadership of Daini's site superintendent, Naohiro Masuda, was crucial to stabilizing the crisis, achieving a cold shutdown and preventing a second meltdown.[90]

The Daini situation could have gone either way. Casto shared with me that Masuda's calm leadership presence was instrumental in mobilizing workers to obtain information, act rapidly and efficiently and adapt to constantly changing conditions, including new problems at every turn. Eventually, they were able to achieve the Herculean task of running nine kilometers of replacement cables from the only functioning generator to the cooling pumps during the short window before pressure in the containment vessels would likely have caused explosions.

Barking orders and jumping into crisis problem-solving would likely not have worked in the immediate chaos after the tsunami. The plant staff was overwhelmed with existential realities (magnitude 7 aftershocks, no power, "sharks in the parking lot," uncertain fates of loved ones, possible core meltdown, etc.). In fact, Masuda and his team did very little in the first hours after the tsunami. As Chaos settled into Complexity, they tracked incoming data about aftershocks, watching them lessen in intensity and frequency. Masuda stayed calm, allowing each member of the staff to process their reaction to the enormity of their situation.

Masuda responded to the tsunami not with immediate action, but rather with Sensing the Context around them, the state of the plant's staff, his own interior condition. He invited patience and the calm and grounded sharing of information, simply waiting until the immediate chaos had settled down so that staff members' own meaning-making processes and Being could catch up to the realities. Ultimately, they needed to, and could, move with remarkable fluidity and speed as a dynamic and rapidly changing Context necessitated about-faces and fluid improvisation.

What might have seemed to some a slow reaction to a crisis situation with an emphasis on Sensing and Being actually was crucial to building the connection and stability for Acting fast and efficiently, thereby coordinating a rapidly changing situation with high stakes and limited resources.

In Complexity, much is unpredictable, and the plant staff was understandably overwhelmed, shocked and terrified in the immediate aftermath of the tsunami. However, Masuda's internal stability affected everyone in the control room, facilitating the remarkable accomplishment that saved their plant from the fate of the sister facility up the coast. Restoring stability at the level of the Fukushima Daini nuclear plant was enabled by stability within the Soma of the plant superintendent and, through his Leadership Presence, within his staff.

At the beginning, stability was desperately lacking. Masuda saw that the extreme fluidity and peril of the circumstances actually required the restoration of stability before anything useful could happen. Fluidity and stability exist in dynamic balance; both are essential in Complexity.

In this final chapter, you will explore how the cultivation of stability in the midst of Complexity allows everything else to work. You will design experiments in stability across the levels of scale, cultivating the conditions of stability where it is needed, creating another means for integrating the whole system and accessing the final three Panes.

STABILITY

If a useful metaphor for fluidity is the water of a river flowing to the sea, the metaphorical corollary for stability is stone. The course of the river is determined by the interaction of the water and the boulders around which the water flows. Massive, solid stone provides a reliable stability. Its very immobility is a requirement for water to be fluid.

Stepping stones throughout this book have provided stability and pragmatism in the constantly shifting territory of Complexity.

In Complexity, much is changing and unpredictability is everywhere. We have explored how disturbing this experience can be. Our Identity is founded to a large degree on predictability and stability, so it is profoundly threatened by their absence. Our psychobiology can even interpret instability as an existential challenge to survival.

This is important to see. Yes, fluidity in our Soma, Identity and Context is vitally important to responding skillfully to emergent challenges. Without the balancing conditions of sufficient stability, however, we are unlikely to be able to access the creative fluidity crucial for resilient, resourceful action.

The risk of excessive stability is when we get stuck in a habitual pattern of activity intended to perpetuate the illusion of predictability and control. This is actually only a way to preserve the felt experience of stability for the benefit of our Identity, rather than a useful stability within which we can assess the situation and ourselves in order to decide on a wise course of action.

Knowing this, wise leaders preempt this cycle by finding places to cultivate sufficient stability proactively. While cultivating connection and fluidity, leaders also recognize that an excess of fluidity, or the absence of stability, is problematic. Masuda instinctively knew this, and while this must have been extraordinarily difficult, he found stability within himself as the first step towards stabilizing a nuclear plant in the midst of disaster.

Stability begins from the inside, in the Soma, through the stability of our focused attention and presence. We then extend it through the relational field and our Leadership Presence to others. And, we create conditions of stability in the larger Context that we, and others, find reassuring, and that then provide a foundation for the fluidity and resourcefulness required by our Complexity Challenges.

Stable Soma

By now, it is not a mystery that directing our attention inward shifts our inner state. The act of observing changes the observed. In fact, focused attention and *the presence produced by Sensing ourselves in the moment is itself inherently stabilizing.* Truth is clarity and is stable.

Additionally, specific practices—particularly grounding and stabilizing breath practices (page 165) are intentionally and explicitly designed to produce conditions of inner stability when we recognize these are needed.

In Part Four we are transcending the notion of cultivating resilience and resourcefulness in response to what is coming at us (e.g., state-shifting, decoupling our state from the Context, embodying directions), and now including in our larger perspective that, over time, we can Tune the Instrument to embody core capabilities for how we lead. This ongoing training and cultivation of a self is a long-term view. It builds on the work of Embodying what Matters, expanding this to a lifelong commitment to self-development.

We practice when the stakes are low. We design safe-to-fail experiments around our own development. Over time, through practice, our core inner stability is available to us when the power goes out, a gun is pointed in our face, someone challenges our integrity, or we make a mistake with grave consequences. Our unshakable stability is gold in these circumstances.

Jeffrey sits on his hands

A coaching client of mine was known for being impatient, often interrupting others. To say the least, his behaviors invited conditions unconducive to open exchange of ideas.

After receiving tough feedback, Jeffrey began a simple experiment on the level of Soma. He sought to change the conditions within himself and was curious to see if stabilizing himself internally would affect the room. The experiment was simply to sit on his hands every time he felt the urge to interrupt, accompanied by the stabilizing breath from Chapter 8. He did this religiously for two weeks. He still interrupted occasionally, but less out of impatience and irritation.

After this Tuning the Instrument experiment, Jeffrey really noticed the difference in his interior conditions. Additionally, he thought he noticed a greater level of engagement in the room.

When stability is lacking, it's important to find it someplace: with a simple and obvious action, a principle, a fact that we actually do know. Identifying the few known things in an interminable field of the unknowable is stabilizing and reassuring. Even facing and accepting the fact of not knowing can paradoxically be stabilizing (see Chapter 11).

When we feel internally too fluid, or overwhelmed by ambiguity and unpredictability, the leadership move is to recognize this and get creative about how we can resource ourselves into stability.

Stable Identity

Biological co-regulation, recall, is the process of physiological synchronization between the states of distinct nervous systems. It is an interpersonal means of connectedness through which a mother transmits love to an infant. It also is the way intimacy and trust are built in relationships, how we might influence without authority, how Susan built authentic relationships with her parishioners, and the restorative practice through which Naohiro Masuda's calm, grounded presence helped his anxious staff find stability in the terrifying and lonely hours after the tsunami.

An inner stability, cultivated in the Soma, can be transmitted to others through the relational field. We first embody, and then convey, stability in our way of Being. In this, we actually become a source of stability for others in the Context.

Any organizing principle can be a source of stability. Stability is introduced by declaring a direction ("more attentiveness to customer concerns," "we deliver the package, whatever it takes"), a value (generosity, inclusiveness, power) or a particular future (buying a house, a launch date, the completion of a book). These organizing principles provide a basis for Acting and are a helpful source of stability in the midst of disruption.

A Red Cross example

In the hours and days after the 9/11 attacks, many Red Cross blood centers nationally were overwhelmed by thousands of volunteers spontaneously moved to donate blood. Lines a block long formed outside donation centers. Nurse staffing was inadequate; supplies had to be moved where needed and processing services were disrupted in significant ways. Nobody had been prepared for this outpouring of support.

Others told me afterwards how stabilizing the calmness of certain nurses had been for them. Some of these natural leaders were later told things like: "I don't know how you did it, but somehow seeing you calm helped me relax myself."

This sense of optimism, calm, and purposefulness spread from nurse to nurse. Stability is contagious. As the day wore on, a strong sense of pride and accomplishment infused the staff. Many would later describe this powerful experience of coordination, teamwork and dedication as among the highlights of their career.[91]

A primary emphasis of Chapter 10 was to make available, through embodiment, the stabilizing conditions of an embodied future. Through neuroplasticity, stability becomes incorporated into our psychobiological structure. Through training and practice, it is thus always available.

Extending Leadership Presence sometimes means taking a stand for what we care about. Leadership requires stabilizing an internal organizing principle (a value, direction, quality or inner state) within ourselves. From this internal congruence, this core stability, we express it externally such that we literally become the organizing principle in our relationships. Others hear this in our language, and they Sense it in the relational field.

Stable Context

Organizations need to be innovative and responsive to disruptions and to unpredictable changes in their markets and environments. Agility is the watchword of the day, which speaks to the importance of fluidity.

An exclusive focus on creativity and innovation and boundarylessness, however, is problematic. Fluidity without the counterbalancing of stability is a recipe for disaster. Our consulting firm was once asked to help a prominent utility undo the damage caused by their well-intentioned experiment with self-managed teams. In an effort to access the energy of "empowerment," they had done away with significant management processes and controls, setting up teams with undefined roles and responsibilities that in theory would have the flexibility to identify and solve problems. But nobody knew what to do, and fluidity, instead of producing the intended benefits of agility and ownership, brought work to a standstill.

Leaders begin by stabilizing conditions within themselves, then expressing this stability externally through their congruent leadership presence, and then inviting others to experiment with creating conditions of stability on the levels of Context outside of themselves.

Mayors take local initiative in stabilizing climate change

Perhaps the most complex, existential and seemingly intractable complex challenge we face is that of human-induced climate change. President Trump's withdrawal of the U.S. from the Paris climate accord was only a particularly egregious example of most national leaders' failures to make significant progress. "Right now it will be cities in the U.S. that lead our country's fight against climate change. Fortunately, cities are in a great position to fight climate change and protect the environment because we are able to innovate quickly."[92]

Mayors from over ninety of the world's greatest cities have organized the C40 organization as a means to create connection in support of local, urban climate initiatives. Four cities (Cape Town, Paris, Washington DC, and Sydney[93]) happen to have women mayors who are deeply committed to local action on climate resilience. All are part of the C40 initiative to share information (connection), foster innovation (fluidity), and support pragmatic initiatives on the ground that anchor progress (stability). All four have had major weather events in the past few years with significant health and economic consequences.

These four mayors are leadership exemplars for experimenting in great Complexity with approaches that can stabilize emissions, establish green space, reduce heat capture and increase resilience. In Cape Town, a green entrepreneurship competition was won by a young man growing organic vegetables in the city; a grant followed, helping him scale and stabilize this replicable model. Washington established a green bank for financing new clean-energy projects, and solar job training for energy installations that in turn reduce utility expenses for low-income residents. Paris is experimenting with urban agriculture, tree-planting, green roofs, and pedestrian zones. Sydney is planting trees, investigating reflective roofs, building bicycle lanes and experimenting with a range of emissions-reduction efforts inside of a long-term direction towards net-zero emissions.

Each of these women cites very specific roots for her commitment to local climate leadership, mostly catalyzed by seeing the suffering produced by environmental degradation and extreme events. With each, we can see a leader's embodiment of a future, expressed in bold work that increases stability on multiple levels of Context: residents, city, and the global community.

In these four cities and countless others, committed local efforts are creating conditions of stability for individual residents through jobs, higher quality of life and reduced cost of living. On the city level, these initiatives are creating stability by reducing vulnerability to extreme heat swings and energy disruptions. And, these cities, along with many others, are taking leadership in stabilizing global climate for all of us.

Stability is an essential element for our psychological well-being. It is also an essential component for any reason-based thinking about the future. Don't fear stability: In our efforts to respond skillfully to an unpredictable and complex world, it is tempting to see inertia and stasis as the enemy, instead rushing wholesale to create conditions of nimbleness, agility and resilience (rolled into fluidity here). This is understandable but insufficient: We must simultaneously seek and maintain conditions of stability where it is possible to do so.

It is through the skillful navigation of the dynamic tension between these two seemingly opposed organizing principles that we access the benefits of both.[94] Too much fluidity, or too much stability, and we have big problems. Attending to both has the potential for resilience with ground, nimbleness with a core foundation.

Jessica cultivates stability in a dicey classroom

A very close friend, Jessica, is a retired early-childhood educator. She tells the story of her first job, in a small rural school in a very poor county in the South. She was told, the day before she entered her special education class, that the students were impossible and that five different teachers had quit the same job in the last two years. Sure enough, she walked into class the first day of school, and kids were standing on their desks, throwing stuff and guessing how long it would be before they got the next teacher to quit.

Jessica didn't bat an eye. She neither made any effort to discipline nor sought to control the wilder ones. Rather, she smiled at all of them, greeted them warmly and walked around, simply handing little torn pieces of paper to the kids who were sitting down or who were listening.

Jessica never explained what the tokens meant or how to earn them, but any time a kid did something that was helpful, responded to a request or exhibited self-regulation and positive behavior, she'd give that student a token. She just piqued their curiosity.

Students got curious; getting tokens from the teacher became an organizing principle in the class. She never took one away, but constantly sought opportunities to reward them. Students tried to discover how to get tokens, and as tokens built a certain status in the class, the game began to shape the collective behaviors of the group. Token technology changed from torn pieces of paper to cut-out cards to plastic poker chips. Jessica was learning too; the experiment evolved over time.

After a few days, with a surging interest in tokens, Jessica experimented with providing rewards. Students would ask for a pencil or a notebook, and Jessica would provide it in exchange for a token or two. In this community, many kids came from abusive homes or didn't have plumbing at home. Kids could exchange tokens for toothbrushes, a shampoo in the classroom's hot-water sink, or donated clothing. In the impoverished community where Jessica taught, these were big things. Students, without quite understanding how, were enrolled into Jessica's safe-to-fail experiment with creating conditions of stability, both behaviorally in the classroom and, for these marginalized special-needs students, in their lives at large.

By Christmas, the tokens had served their purpose and the experiment ended. Jessica had earned their trust and the students actually enjoyed being cooperative and attentive. Forty years later, Jessica thinks back on this as one of the most rewarding teaching experiences of her career.

From a behavior-modification perspective, Jessica simply created an alternative currency, and students were being paid to behave.

From a Leadership-in-Complexity perspective, Jessica's safe-to-fail experiment illustrates everything we are talking about. Jessica's experiment created the conditions for stability in what had been an overly fluid and dis-regulated Context. Dramatic stabilizing effects were evoked by a simple, cheap, easy series of experiments that evolved over time as conditions changed. Part of the experiment, of course, required Jessica to stay calm and positive and resistant to being triggered into Identity-based control behaviors. This took some inner work. Then she had to extend this positive regard and appreciation to the students through her Leadership Presence.

These integrative elements supported radical change in the conditions for stability and learning in this particular class.

Soma. Identity. Context.

FOSTERING CONDITIONS OF STABILITY ACROSS A NESTED COMPLEX SYSTEM

Up to now, we have seen the conditions of stability as they manifest at each of the three levels of the system. We can Tune stability within ourselves as Instrument and we can Extend our Leadership Presence in order to stabilize others in a group, team, or situation. We can identify crucial opportunities to increase stability in an excessively fluid Context as we practice Scaling Awareness.

Context, Identity and Soma are interrelated and dynamically interdependent levels of system within a complex, emergent whole. This final section of this chapter will encourage you to view stability as a cross-cutting organizing principle. Of course, you will never arrive at the "right" amount of stability at any level of the system, let alone across the entire multilevel system of which you are a part.

Whether connection, fluidity, or stability is lacking, your Sensing of when and where certain conditions might usefully be amplified is an essential aspect of Presence-Based Leadership.

An integrating leadership perspective includes scanning for stability or its lack. We scan within ourselves, between ourselves and others, and across the Context. We Sense instability, or its opposite, rigidity, only when we have the distinctions and we have trained ourselves to do so. The same, of course, is true for Sensing the presence (or lack thereof), of connection, fluidity or any other needed condition.

Figure 14.1 represents this simultaneous cultivation of the condition of stability at all three levels of scale. Clearly, our attention to stability at any level invites changes on that level. Also, because of the dynamic interdependence of the levels, each always and continually affecting the others, *an investment in stability at any level invites increased stability at the adjacent levels as well.* A wise leader is attentive to all three levels, and intentionally works with all three simultaneously for maximum congruence across the system.

As exemplified by Masuda, presence allows us to Sense and to respond to the need for stability where it is needed across the levels of system, as well as within each of them. We embody and practice stability as an integrative leadership practice.

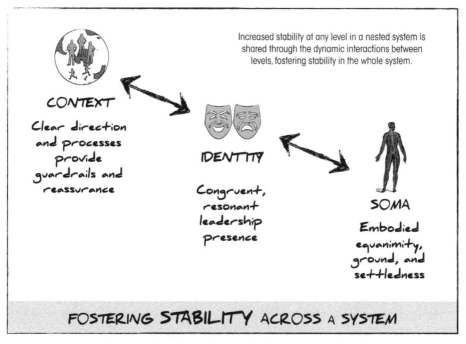

Increased stability at any level in a nested system is shared through the dynamic interactions between levels, fostering stability in the whole system.

CONTEXT

Clear direction and processes provide guardrails and reassurance

IDENTITY

Congruent, resonant leadership presence

SOMA

Embodied equanimity, ground, and settledness

FOSTERING **STABILITY** ACROSS A SYSTEM

Figure 14.1

Susan gets the paradox of fluidity and stability

While Susan's experimentation and invitations were refreshing to many in her troubled parish, at the same time, her transparency and willingness to experiment made others nervous.

As in any institution, some of the congregation's leaders had been there for a long time; they had a vested interest in stasis. These Identities, thoroughly reinforced by the status quo, also happened to be some of the bigger contributors to the church's finances. Alienating them risked the financial stability of the church, one of the key measures upon which the church hierarchy would assess Susan's performance.

In the cross-currents of change and tradition, Susan personally needed stability. She experimented with building her somatic foundation through regular tai chi *and grounding practices. (Previously, I told you that she used* tai chi *to cultivate fluidity as well. Yes, such a practice really can do both. It depends on what you pay attention to!) This gave added support to her evolving Identity, historically deeply introverted and risk averse.*

Susan's stable presence was reassuring to others. The older and more traditional congregants, in particular, needed reassurance. She paid attention to Extending a calm, settled Leadership Presence in conversations with these traditionalists. People

who came into conversations upset about issues or anxious about the future found themselves feeling more relaxed simply by being with her. In sermons about renewal and transformation, she experimented with dropping and slowing her voice, with feeling her own ground as she spoke. She embedded the sermons on change within time-honored service structures that included scripture and other traditional elements.

Explicit about honoring traditions, Susan familiarized herself with church history and mentioned predecessors and significant lay leaders from the past by name. She invited small safe-to-fail experiments like conversations about commonalities between old and new religious traditions, as well as exchanges in which old-timers shared what they liked that was new and newcomers talked about the traditions they thought were important to keep.

This emphasis on stability and tradition actively built trust. Together, the traditionalists and the rest of the increasingly diverse congregation Sensed they were moving forward. Financial contributions stabilized and improved slightly even as younger families joined, attracted by a sense of community, openness to new ideas and new experiments with outreach and service. A more promising future was emerging, and not through a complicated planning process.

The church itself, supported by Susan's low-key and attentive approach to leadership in Complexity, was experimenting its way into a more promising future.

Experiment 14.1:
Experimenting with Stability

Time for the last experiment in this book (and the next in a lifetime of experimentation)!

Again, recall the integrative value of including all three levels of system in your experiment. And, recall your Complexity Challenge and direction from Experiment 10.2 (page 199); revisit as necessary to refresh yourself.

Begin with accessing stability within yourself. Stand. Shift your state. Ground yourself. Feel your feet. Shift around, pressing your feet down into the floor. Feel your weight, dropping your attention, and exhaling slowly, pressing your exhalations firmly down into your lower belly.

From this grounded state, consider how is stability important right now in your Complexity Challenge? What do you stand for? What do you care about most?

Then, consider the following questions, referring back to more detail in Experiment 11.1 (page 228) as needed:

1. What **direction** do you intend?
2. Where is there excessive fluidity and uncertainty? What is your **hypothesis** about how stability might serve your direction? Stability of what? Of whom?
3. What can you **try**, with others?
4. How can this be **safe enough** to try?
5. How will you **learn**?

Now, engage others in conversation, and design experiments together.

As you do so, stay present and grounded, stable in your Soma, committed to your values and organizing principles. Extend stability through your Identity as you design together! Engage all three levels of system to build congruence and stability.

What do you notice about how the conversation and experimentation changes the relationships you're in?

Conduct your experiments. Learn. Then, talk about what's next. What else might you learn?

CHAPTER SUMMARY

Stability is the felt sense of stone: massive, grounded solidity that a person can Sense and lean into. The core realization of this chapter is that stability is always present and available at all three levels of system: Soma, Identity and Context. In fact, the clarity of Sensing and accepting reality is the beginning point for stability.

The inherent stabilizing influence of directed attention creates conditions of stability in your Soma. You then express this grounded and centered Identity through a reassuringly stable Leadership Presence that regulates others. You embody what matters, and the stability of your embodiment affects those around you. You sense where stability is needed, and you are willing and able to experiment with amplifying it in the Contextual system around you.

Cultivating stability at each level of system propagates it as a condition throughout the whole system. You realize how connection supports stability, and how fluidity and stability are interconnected, each requiring and supporting the other.

Stepping stones for stability include:
- The Complexity attitude of Chapter 11
- The metaphor of stones, boulders, mountains and the earth itself
- Practices that foster stability within your Soma: sensing yourself as you are, grounding, stabilizing breath, somatic practices of settling
- Expressing stability in your relationships with others through Extending Leadership Presence
- Experiments in stability to Scale Awareness in the larger Context

- The realization that experimentation both probes for new information and changes the system at the same time

Take some time to reflect on what you now realize as a result of this chapter on stability.

- What do you understand differently?
- What are you now curious about?
- What experiments might you try?

 PRESENCE PAUSE

Epilogue:
Paradox and Integration

*Just as the wave cannot exist for itself, but is ever a part
of the heaving surface of the ocean, so must I never live
my life for itself, but always in the experience which is
going on around me.*
– Albert Schweitzer

*Walking, I am listening to a deeper way. Suddenly all
my ancestors are behind me. Be still, they say. Watch.
Listen. You are the result of the love of thousands.*
– Linda Hogan

IT IS TIME TO GO OUT TO PLAY.
This is what you have been after the whole time. Through the Nine Panes, you have a fluid range of perspectives on the complexity that surrounds you and is within you. The Panes help you differentiate elements of your swirling and perplexing reality, enabling you to find places of clarity and resilience from which you can mobilize. They also reveal a connectedness and a wholeness that is often lost to a myopic focus on results and the preservation of Identity at all costs.

277

You still don't have copy-and-paste solutions for addressing what you have found to be so perplexing. But now you recognize that those actually don't exist—and never did.

Rather, you find yourself present in the ongoing process of curiosity and experimentation. The Complexity of your leadership challenges provides both the conditions and the catalyst for your ongoing development as a leader and as a human.

Your practicing and your presence, applied over time in this way, will reveal that you can increasingly become internally self-correcting, a positive organizing principle in the system and a catalyst for the larger Context to practice self-correction and resilience.

THE GRAND STORY

This is the greatest discovery of the scientific enterprise:
You take hydrogen gas, and you leave it alone, and it
turns into rosebushes, giraffes, and humans.
– Brian Swimme

To be alive in this beautiful, self-organizing universe—
to participate in the dance of life with senses to perceive
it, lungs that breathe it, organs that draw nourishment
from it—is a wonder beyond words.
– Joanna Macy

I want to offer yet another perspective on your context. A new understanding of yourself and what you're up to. A story, if you will.

Pull up a chair by the fire.

This is simply another available view. Take it as literal truth, or as metaphor, as your own belief systems allow. I hope that this story will provide comfort and meaning for you. It does for me.

About 13.8 billion years ago, there was a flaring forth. From a singularity erupted inconceivably vast energies, creating time and space in the process. We call this the Big Bang.

While expanding through orders of magnitude, these energies began to cool, eventually forming hydrogen atoms that spread out as space itself was created. In the conditions of expanding hydrogen, giant swirls of hydrogen gas coalesced within slightly denser volumes of space. Gravity vortices of hydrogen concentrated this gas until the growing pressures ignited fusion reactions at the densest spots. Stars began to wink on. The universe came to light.

Many of these hydrogen vortices became galaxies: hundreds of billions of them, each containing hundreds of billions of stars. The early universe was a creative, violent and extraordinarily beautiful place!

In the specific conditions within certain kinds of stars, massive explosions called supernovae shred stars in some of the most violent events in the known universe. The intensity fuses simpler elements into heavier ones. In fact, many of the raw materials that make up your planet, your cars, your body and everything you recognize and love were born in a stellar explosion.

You and I are stardust.

Around 4.6 billion years ago, in a tiny little spot in the midst of the vast Milky Way imaginatively proximal to where your kitchen is now, the shock wave from a supernova pulsed out into space, rocking the cosmic debris and the new heavy elements formed in the explosion. In these disruptive conditions, some of the material accreted around a new star, coalescing as the planets and other objects you now affectionately refer to as your solar system. (For purposes of orientation: Your home, your loved ones, your office, and the book you're now reading are all located on the "third rock from the sun."[95])

Your Earth was initially a very hostile place. Volcanoes, crashing meteors, no oxygen… this was no Club Med! The first billion years were pretty rough and violent.

About 3.8 billion years ago, the first life arose from precursor chemicals, possibly at superheated thermal vents on the sea floor, but we don't really know.[96] Over time, these primitive life forms evolved, becoming more complex. Plants eventually arose, thriving in the carbon dioxide-rich atmosphere. Plants of course produced oxygen, which changed the composition of the atmosphere, creating the conditions for early animals to evolve.

As the evolutionary journey unfolded, the universe kept experimenting. ("Ha, let's try slime molds! Maybe dinosaurs? Hey, what if some could eat others? How about squirrels? A kangaroo sounds like fun!")

Then-current conditions always offered opportunities for experimental new species. Evolutionary branches split off as emerging conditions rewarded new capabilities. Species that couldn't adapt to changing conditions died off, having served their purpose in the Grand Story. From the perspective of dinosaurs, this was tragic. From the perspective of the universe, dinosaurs were simply another safe-to-fail experiment. From our perspective, we got birds out of the deal.

All species, still living or long extinct, are your cousins. You share about fifty percent of your genome with a banana. Yes, you and any old banana are literally cousins, albeit distant ones!

Your own species, *Homo sapiens*, emerged in East Africa around two hundred thousand years ago, in response to conditions that existed in that particular location and time in the universe. The particular safe-to-fail experiment that produced you combined a large brain, opposable thumbs, walking upright and an extraordinary capacity for socially driven collective learning. This experiment would prove to be astoundingly successful, and in particular conditions, our species scaled rapidly.

Your ancestors' survival instincts were, like yours, embodied as attachments, habits and drives that produced an ever-increasing dominance over "lesser" species. Over time, this led to rapidly growing populations, catalyzing migrations that would eventually circumnavigate the globe and populate nearly every environment and every continent but Antarctica.

The myths and stories generated by the psychobiologies of your ancestors drove the use of their accelerating capabilities. They competed with other species and other humans which they labeled as "less than," or whom they feared. They developed tools to aid this competition. Originally, these tools were spearheads, but tools rapidly evolved to language, plows, cotton gins, automobiles, factories, strip mining equipment, nuclear bombs, computers, spaceships and the Internet.

Our tools began as means of survival. Each tool was created in a particular set of conditions, in response to the evolutionary pressure for increasing the scale and efficiency of harvesting resources and dominating others. These, then, continued to evolve in response to our embodied attachments and organizing principles—including, notably, towards power and control in a complex world.

Of course, your ancestors didn't have available, in the way that you and I sometimes do, the realization that their stories were constantly and actively being generated by their nervous systems. They couldn't see, as we can, that our own nervous systems were more deeply committed to their personal pleasure and survival than to the survival of the species and the living systems of the planet. They simply experienced themselves as doing the best they could in a dangerous and confusing world. And, if they thought about it, they told themselves the convenient lie that bigger problems were up to others to solve.

This of course is the human condition: Your psychobiology and mine are elegantly designed to justify what you and I are attached to, to protect and defend the Identities that we believe ourselves to be.

This is our Bell Jar.

⤜❧ PRESENCE PAUSE ❧⤛

Fast forward to now. Collective actions driven by our all-too-human attachments are threatening the very survival of our planet. More precisely, we are disrupting the very tenuous conditions of relative abundance that enabled our historical flourishing until now. While poverty and suffering and violence are all too pervasive on our planet, there wouldn't be 7.5 billion of us without a rare and unique convergence of conditions.

We are becoming victims of our own success. And we are watching this happen before our very eyes!

While we suspect otherwise, as far as we actually know we are the most intelligent and evolved species in the universe. We arose in a set of conditions not of our making. We are the universe's safe-to-fail experiment.

The context we live in is precisely what we've inherited from this 13.8 billion-year history.

Getting the picture? The complex processes that created us are the very same processes that drove the entire 13.8 billion-year Grand Story. The process of creative emergence throughout the history of the universe follows this template.

A set of conditions exists. The creative impulse, the tendency towards differentiation and experimentation, reveals and amplifies what wants to emerge. Every experiment results in a new set of conditions, whether we are talking about cosmology, the differentiation and evolution of species, or the process of a leader acting amidst complexity. The insistent creative experimentation that produced galaxies and stars from hydrogen gas, heavy elements from stardust, and life from primal soup is the same creative experimentation that produced you, your dog, and this book. Everything that exists is the legacy of a previous safe-to-fail experiment in a particular set of conditions.

It took the universe 13.8 billion years to create you. It took every event along the path to give rise to this moment.

For the first time in our universe, as far as we know, a few very fortunate members of our species (including you and me) are able to sense, to actually realize in the fullest sense of the word, where we came from. We know the Grand Story. We understand our origins.

We can sense that we are the product of an evolutionary story that has unfolded over 13.8 billion years and counting. We can sense that we are literally the eyes of the universe seeing itself.

Perhaps most powerfully, after looking back and seeing where we came from, we also have the realization that the universal forces that produced us are still operating, still supporting us like the wind under outspread wings, still unfolding the Grand Story. You have been written into this story as a character by an intelligence not your own. And, with this realization, you cannot but recognize that you are also an author of it.

We have fleeting moments of realization, like waking from a dream before we go back to sleep again, hypnotized by the embodied automatic habits with which evolution endowed us for our own survival. The rest of the time, we enjoy the comforting dream that we are living in a world that is essentially stable, friendly and caring of us. In our brief moments of realization, we may actually startle at the recognition that we are collectively and unconsciously creating the conditions that will determine the fate of our species, the habitability of our planet and the fates of countless other species for millions of years to come. (Hmmm… Whoa! That IS A Big Responsibility!)

We know the truth of it. And, it's too much to continue to hold. So we go to the refrigerator for a sandwich, we check email, we make a phone call to resolve an oh-so-important issue. We drop back down from this big view into the reassuring but ultimately empty belief that our job is to bring home a paycheck, provide for our family and get the results that our organization intends.

CONTEXT AND MEANING

If humanity does not opt for integrity we are through completely. It is absolutely touch and go. Each one of us could make the difference.
– Buckminster Fuller

The most radical thing any of us can do at this time is to be fully present to what is happening in the world.
– Joanna Macy

This epilogue could feel like a bummer. I don't mean it to be so. But neither do I intend to insulate you from the impact of this perspective.

You have choices about how to respond. You could read this perspective and decide that this is too far removed from your daily imperatives to be either relevant or useful. Or, you could read this and conclude that doom is inevitable.

Or, you could experiment with staying present to this bigger perspective, allowing yourself to feel the fear and grief that may arise when you face the reality that all we love is at grave risk from our collective attachments and the myopic actions that result. Perhaps your safe-to-fail experiments begin with simply staying present to the overwhelming and tragic immensity of what we have wrought, or to the groundlessness you can feel when long-held beliefs get called into question.

When you allow yourself to Sense the largest possible Context, what your Identity might be within this, and for what your Soma most deeply longs—then and only then might a new way of stepping forward be revealed. Only then might you recognize your real contribution as a leader, grounded in staying present in this dynamic world, hurtling towards an as yet unwritten future.

I suggest that facing the reality of this view of the Context can inform every aspect of your leadership. This is Sensing your Context, writ large. This is the Context, really, in which you get to listen for what matters to you, and to choose what organizing principles will shape your leadership.

At the very least, this big view means that perhaps you can learn to not take yourself and your Complexity Challenges quite so seriously. Perhaps it makes it easier to try a few experiments. Perhaps "safe-to-fail" means something different from this perspective. (After all, that's what the entire universe has been doing for 13.8 billion years. How hard can it be?)

To me, this perspective is immensely liberating. It is a source of meaning and purpose. It's the reason I'm sitting here at my kitchen counter, writing, in my present moment at five o'clock on a cold December morning in North Carolina, United States, Planet Earth.

This perspective is profoundly reassuring after a tumultuous U.S. presidential election that has disrupted stasis in countless ways, reassuring even as research continues to substantiate that the probabilities of avoiding catastrophic climate change are small and dwindling. This perspective is the reason why I am speaking to YOU, in your particular time and location, you who are actively reading these precise words in what is precisely your present moment.

Listen…

Listen to me now…

Anything can happen. Anything can happen.

Yes, you are a character in this Grand Story. You have been written into this story by intelligences not your own. You arrived here, and you are reading these words.

Not only are you a character in this story, but you are also an author of it. Everything in the Nine Panes is at play, right now, in the very moment you are reading this. At the core, the Panes enable choices. Choices about how to make meaning of your particular moment in this Grand Story. Choices to declare who you are and what you stand for in each particular moment—choices to act in authorship, knowing that what you have to contribute is unique in all the world.

Nobody else in all the world can do what is uniquely yours to do. Nor can anyone else tell you what that might be.

It's really, truly, up to you.

❧ PRESENCE PAUSE ☙

THE PARADOX OF IDENTITY

How wonderful that we have met with a paradox!
Now we have some hope of making progress.
– Niels Bohr

It is not incumbent on you to complete the work,
but neither are you at liberty to desist from it.
– Avot 2:21, *Ethics of the Fathers*

It is an audacious thing to be an offer in the world. To claim that you can lead, that you have something to contribute, that you can make any kind of a difference in your short time on this hurtling complex world. Congratulations on the boldness and audacity that got you here! If you don't feel at least a bit of the "impostor syndrome," you are not paying sufficient attention.

To buttress your audacity requires the construction of a sense of self, a self-representation you have learned to call "Identity" that imagines and trusts that it has something unique that others want. People are seeking you out, paying you, exchanging some kind of energy for whatever they receive from you. The logic is inescapable that you have value in the eyes of others: it must therefore be true!

However, your audacity could be severely challenged by the realization that your Identity is simply an emergent property of a self-organizing psychobiology.

Whoa!

What's that again?

Yes, the source of your sense of Identity is actually impossible to locate. You understand that it arises as a felt experience from the unconscious interactions of billions of neurons in a disseminated biological system. But you have no idea whatsoever about how this chunk of meat somehow produces intelligence and the experience of agency.

This realization provides very little ground for your audacious offer! While your offer is essential for anything useful to happen, there's not much foundation under it. The more deeply you look, the flimsier the artifact of Identity becomes.

On your good days, you lead your life as an unfolding creative process. You fluidly move, like water, through the Nine Panes on somebody's map. You are Sensing, and Being, and Acting towards a future that, in your particular time and location, is a little bit better.

On bad days, you feel lost and stressed. You lose perspective, and you run around without purpose like a chicken with its head cut off.

You could cling to this future that you are constructing. You could celebrate successes, and you could judge yourself when you deem yourself to have failed or missed an opportunity. This roller coaster of emotions and experiences is Identity at play.

You also can remember that you are merely the safe-to-fail experiment of an intelligent universe. (Hey! Stop taking yourself so seriously!)

Life matters. And life is very, very short. You aren't in control of much, but what you are mostly in control of is simply what you do with your attention and energy in this moment...

And this one.

Moments, in fact, are all you get.

∿ PRESENCE PAUSE ∿

The work that you and I have done together through the vehicle of this book is partially about building an Identity, an embodied self that seems substantive and real enough to produce results that matter in the world. You are propelled by your Identity, which is how you organize yourself to get out of bed and do stuff. Through the device of Identity, you construct meaning and purpose, and you replenish your audacity to lead.

At the same time, another thread to our exploration is about recognizing and surrendering that same Identity, embracing fluidity and letting go of attachments, also in order to produce results that matter in the world! When you realize that the valuable neurological sleight-of-hand we are calling Identity is always and inevitably constricting, you begin to work at recognizing and loosening its grip. Over time, you come to take yourself less seriously. You have more fun, you become more free and spacious.

Herein lies paradox.

The Talmud teaches, "Carry two pieces of paper in your pocket. One should say, 'The universe was created just for me.' The other, 'I am nothing but dust and ash.' Wisdom is knowing when to read which piece of paper."

This transcendent perspective provides a fabulous way to live wisely through paradox; to harness the drive and agency of Identity while also seeing it for the illusion it has always been, and liberating yourself from its downsides. Within this luminous tension is revealed the perpetual possibility of choice.

You, reading this—you won the lottery! You have been given a precious human body—a temporary, self-organizing physical system blessed with consciousness—and an astonishingly short span of years. With this mysterious gift, though, come certain conditions: paradox, complexity, and the lonely responsibility to decide who you want to be, and when, and how.

In every single moment, you get to decide what you will sense, and what you will overlook or exclude.

In each moment, you can choose to shape the inner conditions of your own being towards what matters. Or, you can allow your precious experience to be hijacked by conditions around you, becoming a seamless component of what is inconsequential, or even destructive and toxic.

Any time you choose, you can act in service to what you really care about, or refrain from acting (which is sometimes the wisest action). Or, you can spend your precious life energy on stuff that doesn't actually matter to you at all.

Yes, the rumor is true! Moments are all you will ever get.

In this moment, what do you care about?

Your move.

⟡ PRESENCE PAUSE ⟡

Glossary of Terms

Below are short definitions of terms that have some particular meaning that may benefit from explanation. The page reference indicates the place in the text where the term is explained. Glossary terms are bolded in the index.

Acting: the meta-competency of extending our internal state outwards in order to evoke the results we care about most. (p. 19)

Action impulses: precursors in the body to specific actions. They are our body's neural mobilization of energy towards action, which can be directly experienced and inhibited with the support of presence. (p. 135)

Activation: an increased level of energy in the body, often in response to a trigger, and often observable as heightened sensation. (p. 135)

Anti-helpful: the state of actions that move the system away from the desired result or direction or produce unintended effects. (p. 80)

Attachments: pulls or urges towards experiences that are pleasant and affirming of our Identity and sense of self. (See Aversions.) (p. 112)

Aversions: the opposite of attachments, these are experienced as a resistance or revulsion, leading to an avoidance of experiences that are unpleasant, dangerous, or threatening to our Identity. (p. 112)

Awareness Map: a visual representation of our internal experience that helps us differentiate and observe the fabric of our experience, increasing our awareness of it. (p. 129)

Being: the meta-competency of self-regulation and mastery of our internal state, in service of resilience, creativity and resourcefulness. (p. 18)

Bell Jar: a metaphor for our unique constructed world, which inherently includes some information and precludes other information. Our Bell Jar represents the collective conditioning that holds our Identity structure in place and filters what we are able to sense and make meaning from. (p. 42)

Channels of awareness: four broad categories of experience, which I call cognition, emotions, sensations, and stillness. Together, these comprise the Awareness Map. (p. 129)

Chaotic: the domain in which events appear disconnected, random and out of any semblance of control. It's nearly impossible to identify patterns. (p. 22)

Clarity: the inner state of realization; a sharp cognitive understanding, along with the felt sense of truth. (p. 56)

Co-arising: the simultaneous arising of phenomena that may appear distinct but that are interdependent and linked. (p. 78)

Cognition: the "thinking" process of language, imagery, story, interpretation and meaning-making. In this work, cognition is one of four channels of the Awareness Map. (p. 130)

Complex: the domain in which cause and effect are not predictable due to invisible interactions between various elements of the system. There may be patterns, but they do not suggest an optimal solution. (p. 22)

Complicated: the domain in which cause and effect are predictable and knowable, and recognizable patterns suggest that there is an optimal solution. (p. 22)

Conditioning: the collective impact of the shaping forces that influence us and produce a unique personality and Identity. (p. 37)

Conditions: the nature and characteristics of the environment that shape what arises in that environment. Change the conditions, and different phenomena will arise; look at what is arising, and we can infer something about the conditions. (p. 20)

Congruence/internal congruence: an alignment of body, heart, thought and action that is coherent, present in the leader's inner state and palpable by others. (p. 192)

Connection: links between differentiated parts, whether internally through attention, through conversation between people or through creating relationships between different components of a system. Connection is a polar opposite of differentiation; both are key conditions in a Complexity-capable system. (p. 25)

Constriction: a holding or tightening in the body, often a bracing or defensive reaction to a trigger. They can be directly experienced. (p. 135)

Context: the human context in which you lead: your team, organization, community, agency, etc. (p. 69)

Decoupling: the differentiation of our Identity and Soma from the Context around us. (p. 170)

Development impulse: the innate urge to survive, learn, adapt and grow. (p. 36)

Differentiation: the distinguishing and labeling of parts allows observation and recognition. These differentiated parts can then be linked in new ways. Differentiation is a polar opposite of connection; both are key conditions in a Complexity-capable system. (p. 25)

Direction: the broad orientation in which we intend to lead the system. In Complexity, directions are often more useful than goals. (p. 95)

Disruptor: a person or force that pushes a system beyond its capacity to respond easily, forcing more fundamental changes. (p. 91)

Distinction: a set of labels for phenomena that allow them to be observed, named and described to others. (p. 24)

Embodied futures: explicit statements or visions about the future we intend, which are coupled with emotions and internal sensations, such that the future becomes incorporated into our Identity and our psychobiology as an inner state. (p. 193)

Embodied learning: the internalizing of learning into our physiology, such that it is readily available for instant and automatic use when conditions indicate. (p. 36)

Embodiment: the taking into ourselves of a value, a stand, a principle, a future or a commitment to the degree that it becomes literally part of who we are. (p. 36)

Emergence: the process through which unpredictable macro phenomena result from Complex and often invisible interactions between smaller phenomena. (p. 91)

Emotions: conditioned qualities of our internal state that we experience and that prime us to receive and act on information in particular ways. Emotions are one of four channels of the Awareness Map. (p. 130)

Executive control of attention: the capacity, built into our nervous system, to direct our attention where we choose. (p. 128)

Experiential neuroplasticity: the process of intentionally directing internal neuroplastic changes through the engagement of attention in experience. (p. 196)

Experiments: one-time experiences through which you make new meaning, inquire into yourself, and/or try out a new behavior or experience to see what happens. (See Safe-to-fail experiments.) (p. 9)

Feedback loops: system elements in which some component of the system creates secondary effects in other components that then influence the first. These can be **reinforcing loops**, where the effects accelerate change, or **balancing loops**, where the effects tend to cancel or attenuate change. (p. 91)

Felt sense: our gut feel or inner knowing about something; a somatic source of knowledge and understanding. (p. 125–126)

Fluidity: the capacity of a system to change, adapt and respond with a minimum of internal friction. Fluidity is a polar opposite of stability; both are key conditions in a Complexity-capable system. (p. 95)

Habit nature: the constellation of behaviors, meaning-making and reactions that we have embodied along the way and that now have become characteristically us. (p. 38)

Identification/dis-identification: when our sense of ourselves becomes fused with elements external to us, so our Identity is contingent. Dis-identification is the differentiation of our Identity from those external elements. (p. 115)

Identity: our self-image; our sense of our self in the world as an individual entity with particular characteristics that are uniquely ours. (p. 70)

Include and transcend: the essential process of development, described as an unfolding of ever-greater capacities and meaning-making; at each developmental stage, prior capabilities are both included and transcended into a new, more encompassing set. (p. 53)

Inner state: our Being, revealed by the constellation of internal experiences present at any given moment. This inner state can be both witnessed and intervened in through attention. (p. 59)

Internal conditions: the broad set of conditions—here in this book, listed as stasis, activation, resilience—that could include a nearly infinite variety of much more specific inner states. Recognizing and self-regulating the inner condition of activation is a key element of resilience. (p. 159)

Internal sensations: our sensory experience of our own bodies, revealing our inner state. Internal sensations are distinct from perceptions of the outside world. Internal sensations are one of four channels of the Awareness Map. (p. 130)

Leadership presence: the extension of our embodied inner state into the relational field of our interactions with others. Leadership presence is our inner state made palpable to others. (p. 216)

Meaning-making: our capacity to make sense of the energy and information we are taking in from outside ourselves; meaning-making is how we construct internal maps and representations of the world. (p. 26)

Meta-competency: a foundational capability that underpins, and provides access to, many other capabilities. Here, we address the meta-competencies of Sensing, Being, and Acting with presence. (p. 3)

Mindfulness: the practice of directing attention into our moment-by-moment experience. (p. 138)

Narratives: language-based internal stories, generated by our nervous system in order to perpetuate Identity, that we accept and mistake for the truth. (p. 132)

Nested systems: a hierarchy of systems in which concentric levels of systems are each contained within larger, more inclusive levels. (p. 68)

Neuroplasticity: the process by which the networks of associated neurons that embody our capacities and meaning-making can change over time; the key to embodied learning. (p. 195)

Obvious: the domain of predictable, straightforward action. (p. 21)

Organizing principle: forces, people or conditions that mobilize and focus people and energy in particular directions within a system. Also called *attractors* in Complexity literature. (p. 91)

Perspective: our vantage point on some phenomenon. It defines the relationship between us (the observer) and that phenomenon (the observed). Perspectives are always limited and subjective, yet we confuse them for truth. (p. 25)

Polarities: a pair of conditions, values or organizing principles that appear in tension but actually require each other over the long term. Polarities exist in dynamic tension. (p. 91)

Practices: experiences that are intended to be repeated over time in order to build embodied capacities. (p. 9)

Presence: the internal state of immediacy, stillness, inclusive awareness and possibility. Presence enables us to sense the world as it actually is and ourselves as we actually are. A rigorous embrace of reality supports clarity, resilience and results that matter. (p. XV)

Presence-Based Leadership: the commitment to, and rigorous practice of, presence in leadership situations demanding creativity, resilience, and new understandings of self. (p. XVI)

Psychobiology: the embodied structure of our lifelong learning, forming a unique, semi-permanent and conditioned physiological structure. (p. 37)

Realization: the experience of awakening that includes both cognitive insight and the felt sense of energy and clarity as we glimpse a reality that we had previously been blind to. (p. 50)

Relational field: the invisible, yet palpable field of energy and consciousness that connects us below the level of words when we are in relationship with someone. (p. 238)

Resilience: the capacity for choice, creativity, resourcefulness and skillful action, no matter what's going on around you. (p. 155)

Safe-to-fail experiments: small-scale, cheap, interesting experiments that probe how a system works. They can be amplified if they reveal something worthwhile, while having very low cost if not. (p. 222)

Self-observation: a structured practice of witnessing ourselves in action. We begin to develop a new perspective through observing the nuances of our behaviors and our inner experiences in daily life. (p. 118)

Self-organization: the manifestation within any system of results to internal and external conditions (even when not at all what we like or expect). (p. 20)

Self-regulation: the process of intervening in the workings of your own nervous system to change your inner state. (p. 150)

Sensing: the meta-competency of how we access information; doing so wisely and intentionally is essential to navigating the terrain of Complexity in new ways. (p. 18)

Soma: the psychobiological structures that, together with embodied functioning, preserve our Identity and produce our subjective experience. (p. 71)

Somatic literacy: the awareness, in the present, of the internal phenomena that comprise our experience. (p. 71)

Somatic practice: any ongoing practice, done over time, that explicitly includes attention to, and awareness of, internal experience in the service of the embodiment of new capabilities. (p. 159)

Stability: the capacity of a system to maintain stasis or to self-organize without overreacting in the face of disruption. Stability is a polar opposite of fluidity, and both are key conditions in a Complexity-capable system. (p. 95)

Stasis: a relatively stable state that persists over time in a given system. Usually, stasis is maintained through balancing feedback loops and strong organizing principles; however, the dynamics of stasis can also mean the system becomes resistant to change and not resilient. (p. 91)

State-shifting: a conscious fluidity of state, allowing the easy arising and passing of inner states, as well as the more intentional choosing of states in order to access the inner conditions of stability and resilience. (p. 161)

State: the detailed condition of any system at any point in time. The Awareness Map is a snapshot of the state of our experience at a moment in time. In this work, we primarily use state in reference to internal conditions. (See Inner state.) (p. 59)

Stillness: a quality of openness or lack of fixedness in a system. This can be in an external system, in which a direction or decision has not been made, or can be an internal experience, as in presence. (See Awareness Map for more on stillness.) (p. 91)

Triggers: external inputs that disrupt our internal sense of stasis. Triggers typically elicit anti-helpful reactions, driven by automatic and embodied Identity-preservation mechanisms. (p. 111)

Core Realizations of Sensing, Being and Acting

INSIDE THE BELL JAR OF SENSING	THE REALIZATIONS OF SENSING
We see the world through tinted glasses and think the world is that color.	We see the glasses themselves and that our lenses determine how we see the world.
We experience our Context as separate from us and ourselves as acting on it.	We experience ourselves as part of the Context and as participating with it.
Opportunities and threats are objective descriptors of the Context.	Opportunities and threats have meaning only in relationship to Identity.
The world is overwhelmingly Complicated, but if we just understood enough, we'd know what to do.	The world is inherently emergent and unpredictable. That's the deal! We can relax and marvel at it.
We feel competent that we have a basically reliable description of reality.	We realize that our lenses are sometimes unconsciously determined; therefore we can hold interpretations as tentative and partial.
We unconsciously assume that the most important data is external to us.	We realize that our interior is intrinsically connected to the whole, and we include internal data in our sensing.
We unconsciously filter out information that contradicts our view and attune to information that reinforces it.	Aware of our tendency to filter information, we consciously ask what we are missing or how we could be wrong.
We act automatically and tell ourselves a story afterwards that justifies what we did.	We sense the urges that precede action and consciously choose whether and how to act.

INSIDE THE BELL JAR OF BEING	THE REALIZATIONS OF BEING
We are "inside" our experience and can't identify, label, or have any perspective on it.	We track our experience and can label and describe our present-moment experience.
We believe that our experience is who we are; it has a sense of permanence and inevitability.	We recognize that all experience arises and passes, and we don't identify with it.
Our state is dependent on our Context, and we take on its stress and character.	We decouple our inner state from our Context, observing and self-regulating our state independently of Context.
We experience our body as separate from ourselves, to be cared for and acted upon.	We experience ourselves as a living body, recognizing all sensations, thoughts and feelings as experiences of our aliveness.
Our attention reacts to phenomena as they trigger us; we don't experience choice.	We recognize our executive control of attention and our inherent capacity to choose what we attend to.
We experience ourselves as energized and resilient by accident or as a product of an activity (e.g., yoga or running).	We access a centered, resourceful, resilient state at will; resilience is a natural state we have cultivated and chosen.
Our commitments are unconscious and unquestioned.	We embody what we care about, cultivating internal congruence with futures that matter.

INSIDE THE BELL JAR OF ACTING	THE REALIZATIONS OF ACTING
Our actions are driven by unconscious urges to protect and affirm our Identity.	We stay present to the urges that underpin and precede action.
We interact with others to motivate them to take actions of our choosing.	We are conscious of our leadership presence and the relational field. We interact to invite conditions of connection and creativity.
Actions have urgency and a future focus; our attention is down the road on results.	We are present in the moment, acting to foster curiosity and conditions conducive to the direction we intend.
Our actions arise spontaneously from an unregulated state triggered by our Context.	We self-regulate our state to cultivate internal conditions that naturally give rise to actions aligned with what we care about.
We learn in order to solve immediate problems and challenges.	We develop ourselves in order to create the internal conditions to meet the unforeseen.
We take actions in the belief that they are causal and are surprised and frustrated when things don't go according to plan.	We recognize the process of emergence. We act with an attitude of curiosity and experimentation, trusting that we can respond creatively to changing conditions.
We see leadership as an individual process, the results of which we are responsible for.	We see leadership as a collective, culture-shaping process in which we are participants.
We act to drive results.	We act to experiment, to learn and to create conditions.

Experiments at Levels of Scale

OKAY, YOU MANAGED TO FIND YOUR WAY BACK TO THIS APPENDIX HIDDEN IN THE DUSTY RECESSES OF THE BOOK! CONGRATULATIONS!

As warning to those who insist on reading further, this appendix offers multiple seductions. You may be particularly vulnerable if you bought this book thinking that this appendix is the gold and that you can skip the rest of the book and go directly to this fabulous toolbox! If this is you, you may be tempted to:

- Cherry-pick the easiest initiatives so you can check off the box but learn little.

- Get overwhelmed by the laundry list that follows and throw up your hands and say, "This is too complicated."

- Take several of them and integrate them into a robust change strategy.

- Seek solutions to problems and slide into an attitude of fixing rather than experimenting.

- See these ideas as ways to pilot something you could then scale and implement in a more definitive way.

All of these are Identity-driven traps. All are understandable, and all miss the point. If you recognize these reactions in yourself, go back and read Chapter 11! *These ideas represent a culmination and an expression of the work of the rest of the book, not a shortcut past it.* Any experimentation will be both more interesting and more useful if you integrate your Acting with the all-important Sensing and Being work that provides a stable foundation for leading with presence and intentionality.

With these caveats, I invite you to peruse these possibilities. But, please don't be content with copying-and-pasting these possibilities as simplistic solutions into your environment. That's unlikely to work, anyway.

Rather, consider them as seeds, available for your watering. Choosing which seeds to water depends on conditions in your own system. What seeds might open possibilities? Which are energizing and help reveal openings you haven't considered? What might be interesting and fun? What other possibilities do these seeds generate? Trust your sense of what might be useful, and water those seeds and let them grow. See what your imagination can do to change and adapt these in creative ways to your own unique Context. Use the five questions from Chapter 11 to explore how to work with this.

Stay present as you read. This, too, is practice.

Your own creativity and presence are the threads to follow, not the comforting structure of a bunch of words in a book. You are the leader, and it is your Complexity Challenge, not mine. Invite your creative energies to lead the way through curiosity and experimentation.

EXPERIMENTING WITH ATTITUDE

Tuning the Instrument experiments with *attitude in your Soma* might include:

- *Commit to a consistent curiosity practice.* There are countless ways to practice curiosity. Carry a tiny camera and take a photo, outdoors, of something you've never seen before. Do this daily for a month. Ask yourself, three times a day, why somebody might be doing what they're doing. Spend time looking at or creating art. I took a young goat named Phoebe for coffee. We hung out together for two hours at a table outside my favorite coffee shop, and Phoebe catalyzed the most interesting conversations with strangers! Curiosity is an innate capacity; awaken it.

- *Reminders in environment.* Place reminders in your environment and change them frequently (lest you tune them out). Post-It notes (e.g., "Be curious") are a super easy way. Or put an odd item on your desk and get curious about how people will react. Put evocative art where you will see it.

- *Practice spaciousness.* Do somatic practices (like tai chi) that develop spaciousness and flow. Practicing a physically more spacious attitude and way of Being will go a long way.

- *Practice being less responsible.* Cross a couple of items off your To-Do list that, really, you don't need to do. Renegotiate deadlines. Resign from a board or committee. Cancel a couple of meetings, or a business trip, or a social engagement. You may be surprised that the world doesn't end. The idea is to practice realizing that some of the things that fragment your time and attention simply aren't worth it.

- *Ask why.* Ask yourself why things are the way they are. Become genuinely curious: Why do people think the way they do? Why do the plans and performance metrics that drive your work provide reassurance to some, and why might they filter out important information? Why are particular processes done in a particular way?

- *Experiment constantly.* Try little experiments. Center before and during a meeting. Change the pitch or range of your voice slightly. Sit differently. Sit in a different chair than usual. Discover how you experience yourself differently and how others respond to you differently.

Extending Leadership Presence experiments with **attitude as an Identity** might include:

- *Invite others into curiosity activities.* Go with colleagues to art galleries, museums, walks in the park, or places you've never been. Be curious together. See how conversations shift, or what perspective being in a different environment offers on a current challenge.

- *Play with children.* Children, of course, are naturally curious. If yours are grown, borrow someone else's. Or, badger your kids to give you grandchildren (one of life's great gifts!). Spend time with them, but let them lead the activities. Learn about curiosity as you follow them through a forest. Play King of the Space Monsters. See the world through their eyes.

- *Ask more questions.* Practice extending curiosity into conversations and meetings by asking more questions than you make statements. Learn about questioning, and the value of questions, and experiment with new kinds of questions.[97] Ask questions with genuine curiosity.

- *Speak in groups and conversations* about what you are discovering about attitude and curiosity and experimentation. Start new conversations. Invite discovery. Teach something from this book.

- *Extend curiosity.* Bring your own attitude of curiosity and experimentation into meetings and conversations. Try new things. Meet outside, in new places, at different times, standing up, wearing hats.

Scaling Awareness experiments with *attitude with the Context* might include:

- *Have collective conversations about Complexity and attitude.* Semi-formal teaching and informal exchanges about Complexity, attitude and safe-to-fail experiments can be stimulating and inspiring. Time and again, people describe a palpable sense of physical relief from the realizations of this material and from recognizing "It's not me!" Not only will you enroll others to share the journey with you, but you also will provide them with palpable relief and amplify your own embodiment of the material by working with it.

- *Ask tough questions about plans*, and how they might be constricting creativity and resourcefulness. Widen your collective Sensing by engaging others to ask what the Bell Jar of your plan excludes. Having these conversations doesn't mean throwing out the plan, but it might reveal possibilities for information that should be gathered or experiments that could be tried. Get curious about what will be excluded by a narrow focus on the plan.

- *Use surprises as doorways.* When strange things happen, when people don't behave as you expect them to, or when perverse results arise that nobody predicted—get curious. Whatever happened arose from an underlying set of conditions that guaranteed it would happen. Explore, together, what might be present in the underlying conditions; a surprise is a certain indicator that there is something in those conditions that you never saw.

- *Experiment with meeting design and facilitation.* Everyone has meetings; most are relatively inefficient, and some are downright frustrating. Experiment together with different meeting structures, changing roles, active facilitation, or group agreements for meetings. These are safe-to-fail experiments with your own collective process.

EXPERIMENTING WITH CONNECTION

Tuning the Instrument experiments with **connection in your Soma** might include:

- *Commit to a consistent attention practice.* Any of the ongoing state-shifting practices from earlier chapters are possible. If you were well-intentioned, but fell off the wagon on these practices, recommit now. This is the best single investment in your capacity for presence that you can make.

- *Engage in a specific somatic practice* that is relevant and metaphorical to your commitment. Consider Pilates (to build core strength to make challenging moves), *tai chi* (to settle the nervous system and build ground), tennis (to be in strong, clear partnerships with requests and offers), or golf (to build focus and centeredness and acceptance). A client of mine facing retirement with trepidation went parachuting (to experience the freedom of jumping into the unknown).

- *Design and practice self-observations*[98] around behaviors that are problematic or that you wish to cultivate. Brief, frequent and rigorous observation builds strong internal awareness of when habit patterns are arising and supports embodiment of new capabilities.

- *Practice staying connected to yourself in action.* Before and during meetings and conversations, use the Awareness Map to direct attention inward, checking in with your emotions, sensations and thoughts to make them visible and explicit to yourself. (Recognize, of course, this will be diverting some attention from the conversation: Make this safe-to-fail by not trying this first in a high-risk presentation!) Using the prompt "I notice..." repeatedly with yourself is useful. There is always much to notice.

- *Eat well, exercise often, and sleep*. A healthy body has more energy and also provides the conditions for neuroplasticity and embodiment.

Extending Leadership Presence experiments with **connection as an Identity** might include:

- *Build connections and relationships* with people who embody qualities and understanding that you aspire to develop in yourself.

- *Make the invisible visible* in conversations with others. Asking provocative questions, surfacing sacred cows, naming what you see— these are speech acts that may feel risky but can strengthen the relational field and build trust and connection.

- *Center before speaking*. When you contribute, speak from an intentionally cultivated inner state. Organize yourself internally around the overall direction you care about and around your intention to connect (as distinct from your hope to persuade, cajole or convince).

- *Listen deeply.* Extension can be described as "a commitment to listening."[99] It is easy to think of leadership as sending our *energy* outward to affect others. This is part of the game. Experiment with extending your *attention* outward. Extend receptivity, as if you were unfurling an antenna so as to better attend to others with an active attitude of generosity and curiosity.

- *Connect transactions to context*. Link requests, offers or delegated tasks explicitly to the purpose and direction towards which you are jointly moving. This contextualizes the conversation, reminds others of the larger purpose, and connects both of you to the direction you are intending. It integrates distinct levels of system.

- *Ask for feedback from others*. They can see your Bell Jar in ways you, by definition, cannot. Getting reliable information about how you lead and affect others is absolutely essential. And the act of asking, when earnest and curious, builds trust and connection. Be specific in your request.

Scaling Awareness experiments with ***connection with the Context*** might include:

- ***Play with new meeting practices.*** Experiment with wholeness and immediacy. For example, allocate meeting time for topics of personal importance and meaning and the collective sharing of aspirations. Or begin regular meetings with a "check-in," in which each member in turn has the opportunity to share anything personal with the group.

- ***Normalize Complexity.*** Create new shared language that helps people legitimize and create new meaning about the Complexity around you. Invite colleagues to inquire into the implications and the attitude stepping stones of Chapter 11, or even do a book study group to explore the implications of the Nine Panes for your Context.

- ***Get outlier voices into the conversation.*** Invite connections to people with perspectives and voices often omitted from the conversation: customers, minority views, disruptors or people you're not serving (but could be!). Listen, connect, explore together.

- ***Get insiders out.*** Get people out of their collective Bell Jars. Do Outward Bound courses, visit end users of your products or services, get in touch with the purpose and benefits of what you do or have intensive learning experiences in which teams engage with thought leaders and outside stakeholders for insights that can shed new light.

- ***Convene communities of practice*** with peers and colleagues that can support the development of new ideas and practices. Connecting with others creates a social learning context that is deeply resonant and customized for development around shared interests.

EXPERIMENTING WITH FLUIDITY

Tuning the Instrument experiments with *fluidity in your Soma* might include:

- ***Take multiple perspectives.*** In a meeting, see how many perspectives you can access. These might include the perspective of the whole room, the point of view of another person, the point of view of someone not present, the perspective of someone hearing about this conversation a year from now, etc. See how many perspectives you can access during the meeting.

- *Nourish and express your creativity.* Sing out loud in the shower or driving. Improvise music. Read poetry. Create art. Play with kids or grandkids. Take a ballroom dancing or improvisational theater class. Learn to juggle. Really! Have fun! All of these, superficially unrelated to leadership, engage your nervous system in different ways. They build the muscles for sensing and following intuition in the moment.

- *Ask how you might be wrong.* A characteristic of living in the Bell Jar is that we filter out information that contradicts our mental models. We unconsciously seek confirmation that stabilizes our Identity, but isn't ideal for Sensing reality as it is. Asking how you might be wrong directs you to contrarian data and perspectives, increasing fluidity.

- *Hang out with creative people.* Fostering relationships with people who think differently than you and spending time with creative people is stimulating. This is developmental, and will increase your own creativity and capacity to access multiple perspectives.

Extending Leadership Presence experiments with *fluidity as an Identity* might include:

- *Experiment with roles.* Recall the discussion about multiple roles. (p. 254) List the various roles you play as a leader, and consciously experiment with shifting between these different roles during the course of a meeting or conversation. Connect each role you shift into with a particular purpose or intention for that point in the conversation.

- *Share what you are Sensing.* Being transparent about what you notice in the moment, both within yourself and in the room, brings immediacy to a conversation. Share without an agenda, just offering your data. Ask what the other person is Sensing, inviting transparency in the other. Fluidity is increased when we are present with each other.

- *Make disruptive moves in conversations.* Ask questions about how a different person or constituency might see the situation, or someone looking back on this decision from the future. Offer a different perspective yourself, without insisting that it's right or better. Ask new questions, based on any of the Nine Panes, that invite new Sensing.

- *Vary vocal tone and physical stance in public settings.* Experiment with changing the pacing and depth of your voice, and bringing attention to how you are sitting, facing, standing in conversations. Notice how these changes affect your experience in the conversation, and how it might be affecting others. Play with your leadership presence.

Scaling Awareness experiments with *fluidity with the Context* might include:

- *Remove a constraint and see what happens.* Allow everyone access to new information, a tool crib, increased levels of authority, etc. Yes, there usually will be boundaries, but often existing boundaries were created for reasons that are no longer relevant, and eliminating anti-helpful constraints frees up energy.

- *Reconfigure office space.* Create co-working spaces, move furniture, take down walls, co-locate functions that are at odds but need each other. Create magnets that draw people: espresso machines, ice cream, or a bonsai garden and koi pond with places to sit.

- *Allow broken processes to fall apart.* Lots of organizational energy goes into creating workarounds and propping up dysfunctional processes that might be better off collapsing. Band-aids can prolong the draining of energy, and prevent the organization from having to address more fundamental issues. Experiment with allowing safe-to-collapse breakdowns that trigger short-term disruption, and can also increase fluidity.

- *Break a rule.* It is generally an uphill battle to work to change rules that are controlled by those with more organizational power, or on changing those who control the rules. Rather, focus on what's in your power to do. You can experiment with a limitation or rigidity and see what might happen. Choose an anti-helpful (but safe-enough-to-break) rule or restriction or process and break it. See what happens.

- ***Create new facts on the ground*** that are disruptive and require the system to adjust on the fly. Changing dates of project milestones (in either direction), providing flex time, offering 20% of work time for employees to focus on whatever they want, regardless of benefit to the company.[100] New facts on the ground alter the conditions within which culture develops. They shift the field within which we make decisions; new risks appear, as do new opportunities.

- ***Experiment with creative meeting designs.*** There are all kinds of ways to design and facilitate meeting designs in ways that encourage participation, creativity and ownership. Professional facilitation can help, and bold leaders can experiment with structures as well. Try things out; meeting designs leverage the creativity and wisdom in the room.[101]

Experimenting With Stability

Tuning the Instrument experiments with **stability in your Soma** might include:

- ***Stabilize your inner state***. Use grounding and stabilizing breath practices before and during conversations and meetings. See what happens!

- ***Engage in somatic practices*** like rock-climbing, Pilates or martial arts that require you to build stability in the midst of intense experience. Building ground in the Soma in this way carries over into other Contexts as well.

- ***Spend time in nature.*** There are clear physiological and psychological benefits from being in nature, and the natural environment supports inner states of ground and stability. Of course, we are not going to have all our meetings in the woods, but spending regular time in nature is a powerful stabilizing antidote to the stress and fragmentation of most professional lives.

- ***Use triggering stimuli as practice.*** Daily life presents endless opportunities. A clueless driver cuts you off in traffic or sits at a green light, texting. A needle is inserted into your vein to draw blood. Two people you care about argue. Someone gives you tough feedback. You get the idea. All these, and more, are practice opportunities for you to organize attention around internal stability rather than what's going on "out there."

Extending Leadership Presence experiments with **stability as an Identity** might include:

- *Ask what is known.* In ambiguity and confusion, it's most helpful to parse what is really known and reliable, differentiating that from what is unknown or even unknowable.

- *Share your internal stability through the relational field* in conversations and meetings. Experiment with grounding yourself and extending stability into the room or conversation. Your way of being, stabilized through directed attention, will touch and affect the states of others. Discover how your leadership presence can amplify stability in interactions with others.

- *Make public declarations* about values, direction and organizing principles. Speak in a centered, embodied way about articulating direction, not goals. Articulating an overall direction, without specifying how you intend to get there, can be reassuring and stabilizing.

- *Make promises you can keep, and keep promises you make.*[102] Create experiments about making and asking for promises, which are the currency of coordination in relationships and teams. The reliability and clarity of human relationships are a major source of stability in Complexity and Chaos.

Scaling Awareness experiments with **stability with the Context** might include:

- *Introduce Complexity language.* Perhaps a new leadership program or self-organizing interest group can begin to normalize Complexity and create shared language that allows different kinds of conversations to happen. Foster a collective Complexity attitude (per Chapter 11) and an informed, intentional, collective approach to playing with experiments together. Do a book study and see what experiments might emerge. Facing and engaging with Complexity makes it reassuringly more knowable.

- *Resolve low-hanging fruit.* Not everything is Complex. Differentiate what is Complex from what is not. Where there are Obvious things that can be fixed, fix them. Where there are Complicated things that need additional expertise, find it. Delay a nonurgent decision that introduces unnecessary anxiety. Increase stability by managing the business, freeing up energy for the elusive stuff.

- ***Establish rituals that evoke meaning and purpose.*** Create regular collective practices that invite people to bring their full selves to the table. These might include time to explore topics of personal importance, beginning meetings with a "check-in" where each member shares something personal, or sharing responsibility by rotating meeting facilitation. These practices humanize the workplace, and their consistency creates stabilizing traditions.[103]

- ***Put guardrails on experiments and innovation.*** Create agreements about early warning signals or thresholds beyond which an experiment will be reevaluated or cancelled. Put time frames on experiments. Boundaries and escape hatches increase the felt sense of stability and make innovation and fluidity feel more contained and therefore "safe enough to try."

A Resource for Coaches

Coaches: EVERYTHING in this book is for you!

Here are a few perspectives on how this book might support you as a coach.

Of course, you are a work in progress. Like nearly every coach I know, you are engaged in your own learning, or you would not be interested in this book. (This material selects for learners!) Most certainly, you are living your own version of Complexity.

The book is first and foremost a map. It offers new distinctions, practices and perspectives. In working with some of the places you yourself get stuck and by double-clicking to learn through specific Panes, you deepen your mastery of self and of your own navigation of Complexity.

This earns you the right to offer to support others.

CAVEATS

I want to offer a few considerations as you think about how to bring this work to clients.

First, *realize that your coaching relationship is itself a Complex system.* There are at least two Identities involved, multiple levels of Context, two Somas and likely other stakeholders with their own agendas. Everything in this book applies to the Complex system of the coaching partnership. You will likely trigger each other, avoid saying things that should be said and face the entanglement of both your Identities with the success of the engagement. Recognizing and working with these dynamics as they arise makes the coaching relationship itself a real-time practice laboratory in Complexity, and your relationship will assuredly reveal much of relevance for the client's leadership.

Second, ***watch out for the "toolkit mindset!"*** Yes, the book offers plenty of specific frameworks, experiments and practices. Many can be incorporated directly into your coaching work, and I encourage you to do so. I also caution you against becoming attached to a set of leading-edge tools from which to select to move your client where she wants to go! However tempting, this is the same mindset we sought to inoculate against in Chapter 11, and the same caveats apply here. Having simplistic Identity-affirming answers smothers the creativity of what might emerge in the moment. Being present and spacious will reveal the most elegant and useful possibilities!

Third, ***cultivate conditions of attitude, connection, fluidity and stability in the coaching partnership*** itself. Consider every coaching conversation to be a safe-to-fail experiment in which you and your client jointly seek to create the conditions in which something useful can emerge. Your curiosity and embodiment of connection, your own fluidity and stability and your full capacity for deep presence and receptivity are the absolute best you have to offer. The loveliest coaching interventions are likely to be jointly designed, arise out of the creativity of the present moment and be related to the overall direction that the client intends to move in.

Last, ***do your own work.*** The best coaches, in my experience, are those who venture deeply into their own development process. We all have Bell Jars, and you, by definition, are unable to see important aspects of the dynamics of your coaching relationship with clients and the ways in which your Identity gets hooked. Working with a skilled supervisor, doing your own practices, and being actively and consistently engaged in your own development are essential foundations for being able to support others.

Use yourself, and your own journey, as a laboratory for curiosity and experimentation.

SOME SEEDS

With these caveats, here are some seeds. They are organized around the Nine Panes, but of course there are other perspectives that could be included. These seeds are pragmatic ways to engage with the work revealed by double-clicking each of the Panes. Some of these might be client "fieldwork"; others you might do together during the coaching session itself.

I intend these seeds to be vague enough to imply neither a polished and complete methodology nor a menu of copy-and-paste tools looking for the right application.

Rather, I hope these seeds will inspire your own curiosity and willingness to experiment in partnership with clients, and to self-organize with presence and compassion in the unique and Complex emergent system that includes you, your client and her Complexity Context.

Observe the System
- Map polarities in the system
- Identify system elements dynamics
- Identify and map stakeholders
- Scan for weak signals, surprises, and perverse unanticipated effects that might reveal something new
- Inquire about perspectives of others in the system

Recognize Identity at Stake
- Name and acknowledge the multiple roles the client plays in any situation, as well as conflicts between these
- Work with the dis-identification questions in Chapter 6
- Self-observe Identity in action and challenges to Identity
- Self-observe attachments and aversions
- Write about Identity and sense of self
- Reflect on feedback via 360s, psychometrics and leadership assessments

Attend to Experience
- Work with the Awareness Map to describe present experience in the moment
- Work with specific channels of the Awareness Map within sessions and as fieldwork via mood checks, body scans and other practices
- Commit to ongoing sitting and attention practices
- Direct attention into client's inner state during coaching sessions
- Self-observe internal states during the course of the day
- Self-observe triggered states

Regulate Inner State
- Observe executive control of attention
- Work with state-shifting practices in session and as fieldwork

- Direct attention into client's inner state during sessions, and ask client to track shifts
- Self-observe state-shifting during the course of the day, including working with triggered states
- Practice state regulation in particular situations, building capacity to stay present alongside triggers

Decouple State from Context
- Work with decoupling in a specific situation
- Look for historical evidence of resilience and decoupling
- Inventory resilience-supporting strategies
- Do regular resilience practices
- Work with differentiating where client has control and where not
- Work with accepting where there is little control

Embody What Matters
- Articulate future and direction
- Design embodiment practices for incorporating this intended future into way of Being
- Make public declarations
- "Take in the good" practice
- Design somatic practices to embody values, directions and organizing principles

Extend Leadership Presence
- Practice centering and grounding in conversations and meetings
- Get feedback from others on presence in public settings
- Experiment with attention to the relational field in conversations and meetings
- Experiment with body stance, voice and internal awareness

Scale Awareness
- Experiment in the system with new collective practices of Sensing, Being and Acting
- Conduct safe-to-fail experiments with others, fostering conditions of connection, fluidity and stability
- Use prototyping approaches for fast-cycle learning
- Create a book study group

- Open shared conversations about Complexity dynamics, and build shared language around experiments

Tune the Instrument
- Commit to somatic and embodiment practices
- Participate in, or create, a community of practice
- Get support from allies, mentors, etc.
- Take good care of the physical instrument: diet, exercise, meditation and sleep
- Hang out with people who inspire and energize

Further Reading

Adams, Tony. *Agile Leadership.*

Anderson, Kathy. *Polarity Coaching.*

Beinhocker, Eric. *The Origin of Wealth.*

Berger, Jennifer Garvey. *Growing on the Job.*

Berger, Jennifer Garvey, and Johnston, Keith. *Simple Habits for Complex Times.*

Blake, Amanda. *Your Body Is Your Brain.*

Boyatzis, Richard, and McKee, Annie. *Resonant Leadership.*

Burton, Robert. *A Skeptic's Guide to the Mind.*

Cashman, Kevin. *Leadership from the Inside Out.*

Cashman, Kevin. *The Pause Principle.*

Catmull, Ed. *Creativity, Inc.*

Claxton, Guy. *Intelligence in the Flesh.*

Coleman, Peter. *The Five Percent.*

Davidson, Richard, and Begley, Sharon. *The Emotional Life of Your Brain.*

Flaherty, James. *Coaching: Evoking Excellence in Others.*

Gazzaniga, Michael S. *Who's in Charge?*

Gendlin, Eugene. *Focusing.*

Goldsmith, Marshall. *Triggers: Creating Behavior That Lasts.*

Goldsmith, Marshall. *What Got You Here Won't Get You There.*

Goldstein, Hazy, Lichtenstein. *Complexity and the Nexus of Leadership.*

Goleman, Daniel. *Emotional Intelligence.*

Gunaratana, Henepola. *Mindfulness in Plain English.*

Hanson, Rick. *Hardwiring Happiness.*

Kegan, Robert and Lahey, Lisa. *Immunity to Change.*

Laloux, Frederic. *Reinventing Organizations.*

Leonard, George. *Mastery: The Keys to Success and Long-Term Fulfillment.*

Levine, Peter A. *Waking the Tiger: Healing Trauma.*

Lewis, Thomas, and Armini, Fari. *A General Theory of Love.*

Maclean, Pamela. *The Handbook of Coaching: A Developmental Approach.*

McChrystal, Stanley. *Team of Teams.*

Meadows, Donella. *Thinking in Systems.*

O'Connor, Joseph. *The Art of Systems Thinking.*

O'Neill, Mary Beth. *Executive Coaching with Backbone and Heart.*

Ramalingam, Ben. *Aid on the Edge of Chaos.*

Rinpoche, Yongey Mingyur. *The Joy of Living.*

Siegel, Daniel J. *Pocket Guide to Interpersonal Neurobiology.*

Silsbee, Doug. *The Mindful Coach.*

Silsbee, Doug. *Presence-Based Coaching.*

Strozzi-Heckler, Richard. *The Leadership Dojo.*

Sull, Donald, and Eisenhardt, Kathleen. *Simple Rules.*

Swimme, Brian, and Berry, Thomas. *The Universe Story.*

van der Kolk, Bessel. *The Body Keeps the Score.*

Wilber, Ken. *A Brief History of Everything.*

Notes

1. Robert Kegan and Lisa Laskow Lahey, *Immunity to Change: How to Overcome It and Unlock the Potential in Yourself and Your Organization* (Boston, MA: Harvard Business Press, 2009). C. Otto Scharmer, *Theory U: Leading from the Future as It Emerges*, 2nd ed. (Oakland, CA: Berrett-Koehler, 2016). Robert J. Anderson and William A. Adams, *Mastering Leadership: An Integrated Framework for Breakthrough Performance and Extraordinary Business Results* (Hoboken, NJ: Wiley, 2016). Richard Strozzi-Heckler, *The Leadership Dojo: Build Your Foundation as an Exemplary Leader* (Frog Books, 2007).

2. Sensing, Being, and Acting are closely related to the Sensing, Presencing, and Prototyping elements of Theory U, a powerful approach to social and organizational transformation. Although the two bodies of work are unrelated, they work at mapping similar territories. C. Otto Scharmer, *Theory U: Leading from the Future as It Emerges*, 2nd ed. (Oakland, CA: Berrett-Koehler, 2016). The meta-competencies also reveal echoes of Darya Funches' "ways of seeing, being, and doing." Darya Funches, *Three Gifts of the Organization Development Practitioner* (Seattle, WA: REAP Gallery Unlimited Corporation, 1989).

3. Kevin Cashman writes about the importance of pauses as a way to step back and to transform one condition into another. *The Pause Principle: Step Back to Lead Forward* (San Francisco, CA: Berrett-Koehler, 2012).

4. Seth Godin, *Poke the Box: When Was the Last Time You Did Something for the First Time?* (London: Portfolio, 2015), 13.

5. Jerry Brown initiatives: "Governor's Drought Declaration," California Department of Water Resources, http://www.water.ca.gov/waterconditions/declaration.cfm.

6. Future drought predictions: Daryl Fears, "California's terrifying climate forecast: It could face droughts nearly every year," *Washington Post*, March 2, 2015, http://wapo.st/2vtielS.

7. Drought fatigue: Taylor Goldenstein, "When it comes to saving water, Southern Californians are tapped out—or are they?" *Los Angeles Times*, February 10, 2016, http://www.latimes.com/local/california/la-me-drought-survey-20160210-story.html.

8. Paul Batalden, after Arthur Jones, "Every organization...."

9. Jennifer Garvey Berger and Keith Johnston, *Simple Habits for Complex Times: Powerful Practices for Leaders* (Stanford, CA: Stanford Business Books, 2015). Jeffrey Goldstein, James K. Hazy, and Benyamin B. Lichtenstein, *Complexity and the Nexus of Leadership: Leveraging Nonlinear Science to Create Ecologies of Innovation*, 2010 ed. (New York: Palgrave Macmillan, 2011). Bill Joiner and Stephen Josephs, *Leadership Agility: Five Levels of Mastery for Anticipating and Initiating Change* (San Francisco, CA: Jossey-Bass, 2006).

10. David J. Snowden and Mary E. Boone, "A Leader's Framework for Decision Making," *Harvard Business Review,* November 2007, https://hbr.org/2007/11/a-leaders-framework-for-decision-making.

11. Genesis 1:1–5.

12. Dan Siegel writes that "integration is the linkage between differentiated parts of a system." This intimate relationship between connection (linkage) and differentiation has a strong basis in neuroscience and is fundamental to the functioning of complex systems. Daniel J. Siegel, *Pocket Guide to Interpersonal Neurobiology: An Integrative Handbook of the Mind* (New York: W. W. Norton, 2012), 10.

13. This is Hebb's postulate, which describes the process of "long-term potentiation," in which neurons that are frequently energized together acquire a predisposition to do so in the future. This is the basis for learning and for neuroplastic change, and explains why it is so darned hard to change a habit! It is described well by Michael Gazzaniga in *Who's in Charge?: Free Will and the Science of the Brain*, reprint (New York: Ecco, 2012).

14. This process of embodying environmental influences is articulated well in a social justice context by Staci Haines and Richard Strozzi-Heckler in the Sites of Shaping model. See *The Art of Somatic Coaching: Embodying Skillful Action, Wisdom, and Compassion* (Berkeley, CA: North Atlantic Books, 2014).

15. Kevin Cashman, *Leadership from the Inside Out: Becoming a Leader for Life*, 2nd revised and updated edition (Oakland, CA: Berrett-Koehler, 2008). Daniel Goleman, *Emotional*

Intelligence: Why It Can Matter More Than IQ, 10th anniversary edition (New York: Bantam Books, 2005). Roger Walsh, *Essential Spirituality: The 7 Central Practices to Awaken Heart and Mind* (New York: Wiley, 2000).

16. David Rooke and William R. Torbert, "Seven Transformations of Leadership," *Harvard Business Review,* April 2005, https://hbr.org/2005/04/seven-transformations-of-leadership. Robert Kegan, *The Evolving Self: Problem and Process in Human Development,* reprint (Cambridge, MA: Harvard University Press, 1982). Ken Wilber, *A Brief History of Everything,* 2nd revised edition (Boulder, CO: Shambhala, 2001).

17. "Transcend and include" is Ken Wilber's language for the transitions between stages of development. *Brief History,* 5.

18. This exercise was designed by Carolyn Coughlin for a retreat that we were leading together.

19. Dan Siegel defines mind as "a process that regulates the flow of *energy and information* within our bodies and within our relationships, an emergent and self-organizing process that gives rise to our mental activities such as emotion, thinking, and memory." The three meta-competencies of sensing, being, and acting support this foundational understanding of mind as a process. *Pocket Guide,* 65.

20. Wilber describes nested systems as holarchies, and this universal structure figures centrally in integral theory. *Brief History,* 32.

21. Guy Claxton, in his profound and delightful book, describes us humans as "confections constantly being whipped up by a combination of the Super-Systems in which we are participating, and the Sub-Systems of which we are composed." This is precisely context, identity, and soma. *Intelligence in the Flesh: Why Your Mind Needs Your Body Much More Than It Thinks,* reprint (New Haven, CT: Yale University Press, 2016), 54.

22. *Soma* ... from the Greek. The term *somatic,* coined by Thomas Hanna, is "the field of study dealing with somatic phenomena; i.e., the human being as experienced by himself (or herself) from the inside." Somatics Educational Resources website, http:// www.somaticsed.com/whatIs.html.

23. Names and examples have been anonymized, as mentioned earlier.

24. A. H. Almaas, *Runaway Realization: Living a Life of Ceaseless Discovery* (Boston, MA: Shambhala, 2014), 22.

25. For more language about system dynamics, see Peter M. Senge, *The Fifth Discipline: The Art & Practice of The Learning Organization,* revised and updated (New York: Doubleday, 2006). Joseph O'Connor and Ian McDermott, *The Art of Systems Thinking: Essential*

Skills for Creativity and Problem Solving (London: Thorsons, 1997). Donella H. Meadows, *Thinking in Systems: A Primer* (White River Junction, VT: Chelsea Green Publishing, 2008). Berger and Johnston, *Simple Habits for Complex Times.*

26. Much of the complexity literature refers to *attractors* and *attractor basins.* I am using *organizing principle* with a very similar meaning, because I find that people get confused about the idea of attractors, especially when an attractor is sometimes a thing that repels. Organizing principle simply seems more intuitive to more people.

27. I am using the term *polarities* as a general term for the system dynamic wherein two organizing principles (commitments, values, interests) appear in opposition and both are important to take care of. This is a general term; some readers will be familiar with *competing commitments* from Kegan and Lahey's important book ***Immunity to Change.*** Barry Johnson has built a life's work around polarities and their application in personal and system change. (See Polarity Partnerships at http://polaritypartnerships. com.) Both competing commitments and polarities offer language and change models around this specific dynamic; I am using the term *polarities* because it is highly inclusive. I also want to focus on the underlying system dynamic rather than on the powerful change methodologies that Kegan, Lahey, and Johnson and others have developed around this crucial dynamic.

28. Patrick O'Sullivan, Mark Smith, and Mark Esposito, eds., *Business Ethics: A Critical Approach: Integrating Ethics Across the Business World* (London: Routledge, 2012).

29. Google's founders famously questioned why they even needed managers; Eric Schmidt was eventually brought in as CEO in an effort to leverage both radical innovation and the structures needed to scale. See Steven Levy, *In The Plex: How Google Thinks, Works, and Shapes Our Lives* (New York: Simon & Schuster, 2011).

30. This process of constructing social identity is described well by James Flaherty, *Coaching: Evoking Excellence in Others*, 3rd ed. (London: Routledge, 2011).

31. Doug Silsbee, *Presence-Based Coaching: Cultivating Self-Generative Leaders Through Mind, Body, and Heart* (San Francisco, CA: Jossey-Bass, 2008). Doug Silsbee, *The Mindful Coach: Seven Roles for Facilitating Leader Development* (San Francisco, CA: Jossey-Bass, 2010).

32. *Awakening the Buddha Within: Tibetan Wisdom for the Western World*, reprint, by Lama Surya Das (Broadway Books, 1998) is a good starting point.

33. The term *felt sense* was first introduced by Eugene Gendlin in his classic book. He makes a strong case that someone's access to their own felt sense is a primary determinant of when efforts at personal change will be successful and when they will not. This supports the

notion of somatic literacy as being a key component of development and change. Eugene T. Gendlin, *Focusing*, 2nd (revised) ed. (Bantam Books, 1982).

34. The notion of *competing coalitions of neurons* was first articulated by Francis Crick, the co-discoverer of DNA and researcher into the neurological correlates of consciousness, along with Christof Koch. Susan Blackmore, *Consciousness: An Introduction*, 2nd ed. (New York: Oxford University Press, 2011).

35. Actually, there are many additional ways awareness can be parsed. Buddhism, neuroscience, and psychology all offer far more elaborate taxonomies. I am lumping for the sake of accessibility and pragmatism.

36. Guy Claxton offers a lucid exploration of how emotions essentially serve to prime the nervous system for particular kinds of actions; an emotional state is in essence a predisposition toward specific sets of behaviors, and from a certain perspective, a skillful and pragmatic response to whatever is going on around us. *Intelligence in the Flesh: Why Your Mind Needs Your Body Much More Than It Thinks*, reprint (New Haven, CT: Yale University Press, 2016).

37. Somatic Experiencing, developed by Peter Levine, is one of many somatic-based therapeutic modalities which are uniquely well developed to address underlying trauma. See the website of the Somatic Experiencing Trauma Institute at https://traumahealing.org/about-us/. For more background on somatics and trauma, see Bessel van der Kolk, *The Body Keeps the Score: Brain, Mind, and Body in the Healing of Trauma*, reprint (New York: Penguin Books, 2015).

38. Morning Pages is a wonderful creativity practice from Julia Cameron that makes this an ongoing daily practice. See *The Artist's Way: A Spiritual Path to Higher Creativity*, 10th ed. (New York: Tarcher/Putnam, 2002).

39. "How Many Basic Emotions Are There? Fewer Than Previously Thought," Psyblog website, February 4, 2014, http://www.spring.org.uk/2014/02/how-many-basic-emotions-are-there-fewer-than-was-previously-thought.php.

40. Dr. Andrew Weil; keynote address, Psychotherapy Networker Symposium, 2012.

41. See Guy Claxton, *Intelligence in the Flesh: Why Your Mind Needs Your Body Much More Than It Thinks* (Yale University Press, 2016), and Bruce Tift, *Already Free: Buddhism Meets Psychotherapy on the Path of Liberation* (Boulder, CO: Sounds True, 2015).

42. Daniel Goleman, *Emotional Intelligence: Why It Can Matter More Than IQ*, 10th anniversary ed. (New York: Bantam Books, 2005).

43. For our purposes, we will simply call this channel *sensation*, though a purist would argue that touch and proprioception are also sensations. These groupings are somewhat approximate. The literature describes many other senses, and not all sources agree on what really constitutes a sense to begin with. Also, other species have senses without human analogues; e.g., echolocation in dolphins and magnetic guidance in sea turtles. Close enough.

44. Robert Burton describes mental sensations in a couple of relevant and important books. The notion of these self-generated "green lights" that justify the actions our bodies have already decided to take is powerful and fascinating. There simply isn't the space in this book to address it in more depth. See *On Being Certain: Believing You Are Right Even When You're Not*, reprint (New York: St. Martin's Griffin, 2009), and *A Skeptic's Guide to the Mind: What Neuroscience Can and Cannot Tell Us About Ourselves* (New York: St. Martin's Griffin, 2014).

45. A *body scan* is a commonly used and widely available practice for cultivating somatic literacy and access to the sensations that are always available to you. See Jon Kabat-Zinn, or do an online search for body scan audio resources. Jon Kabat-Zinn, *Full Catastrophe Living*, revised ed. (New York: Bantam Books, 2013).

46. For more on the benefits of mindfulness, see Daniel Goleman and Richard J. Davidson, *Altered Traits: Science Reveals How Meditation Changes Your Mind, Brain, and Body* (New York: Avery, 2017), and Yongey Mingyur Rinpoche and Eric Swanson, *The Joy of Living: Unlocking the Secret and Science of Happiness*, reprint (New York: Harmony, 2008).

47. Mindfulness-Based Stress Reduction courses are widely available, as are beginning meditation classes. If you choose to experiment on your own, Sharon Salzberg's book is an excellent resource: *Real Happiness: The Power of Meditation: A 28-Day Program* (New York: Workman Publishing, 2010).

48. Richard J. Davidson and Sharon Begley, *The Emotional Life of Your Brain: How Its Unique Patterns Affect the Way You Think, Feel, and Live—and How You Can Change Them* (New York: Avery, 2012), and Daniel Goleman, *Focus: The Hidden Driver of Excellence*, reprint (New York: Harper, 2015).

49. With presence and attention, strong emotions and sensations related to trauma history can sometimes surface, unbidden. This can be disturbing and even destabilizing. If you have, or suspect you may have, such a history, it is wise to work with a trauma-informed practitioner to ensure adequate support. Somatic Experiencing, developed by Peter Levine, is one of many somatic-based therapeutic modalities uniquely well suited for addressing underlying trauma. See the Somatic Experiencing Trauma Institute website at https://traumahealing.org/about-us/. Also see Bessel van der Kolk, *The Body Keeps the Score: Brain, Mind, and Body in the Healing of Trauma*, reprint (New York: Penguin Books, 2015).

50. See my previous books for detailed explorations of self-observation: *Presence-Based Coaching: Cultivating Self-Generative Leaders Through Mind, Body, and Heart* (San Francisco, CA: Jossey-Bass, 2008), and *The Mindful Coach: Seven Roles for Facilitating Leader Development* (San Francisco, CA: Jossey-Bass, 2010).

51. This definition of resilience is from my collaboration with Bev Wann in the development of a somatically-based resilience program we taught at the Federal Executive Institute and in a number of federal agencies in the United States and Africa.

52. Following the logic of conditioning and cognitive neuroscience raises real questions about whether we have free will at all. And, if not, how can we be held responsible for actions taken by our nervous systems, even if those actions are criminal? These fascinating and pragmatic questions are richly explored elsewhere: Michael S. Gazzaniga, *Who's in Charge?: Free Will and the Science of the Brain*, reprint (New York: Ecco, 2012). Robert A. Burton, *A Skeptic's Guide to the Mind: What Neuroscience Can and Cannot Tell Us About Ourselves* (New York: St. Martin's Griffin, 2014). Sam Harris, *Free Will* (Free Press, 2012).

53. For more on this process of witnessing your executive control of attention, Dan Siegel has wonderful guided experiences on what he calls the Wheel of Awareness (which informs our Awareness Map). http://www.drdansiegel.com/resources/wheel_of_ awareness/.

54. The three-dimensional body is one of many approaches to centering, all of which gather attention into the body and the realm of sensation. This practice and the grounding practice that follows are adapted from Richard Strozzi-Heckler; more detailed descriptions can be found in *The Leadership Dojo: Build Your Foundation as an Exemplary Leader* (Frog Books, 2007).

55. Kevin Cashman, *The Pause Principle: Step Back to Lead Forward* (San Francisco, CA: Berrett-Koehler, 2012).

56. Viktor Frankl, *Man's Search for Meaning* (Boston, MA: Beacon Press, 2006), 37.

57. Ibid., 66.

58. These conversations informed the resilience work I developed with Bev Wann. Interviewees included F-16 pilots, military special forces trainers, people facing terminal illness, priests, people living in abject poverty, and leaders of change in overwhelmingly dire circumstances.

59. Pema Chodron, *Start Where You Are: A Guide to Compassionate Living* (Boston, MA: Shambhala, 2001).

60. Steven Hayes and Bruce Tift both provide practical tools and practices for this fundamental approach to staying present to our own experience. Steven Hayes and

Spencer Smith, *Get Out of Your Mind and Into Your Life* (Oakland, CA: New Harbinger, 2005). Bruce Tift, *Already Free: Buddhism Meets Psychotherapy on the Path of Liberation* (Boulder, CO: Sounds True, 2015).

61. See previous notes on Somatic Experiencing. https://traumahealing.org/about-us/.

62. Frankl, *Man's Search for Meaning.*

63. Robert Gass, and the Social Transformation Project, have built a very useful library of leadership and mastery practices. A practical toolkit recognizing and managing triggers and for shifting state can be downloaded here: http://stproject.org/toolkit_ tool/managing-your-triggers-toolkit/.

64. This iconic incident was described later by Rory Steyn (Kevin McCallum, 'That was the start of Madiba Magic,' *Saturday Star*, 7 December 2013). The leadership dynamics of this very difficult moment in history, and Mandela's extraordinary grasp of the importance of acting with moral authority and embodying the future are also illustrated in the excellent movie *Invictus.*

65. Ed Catmull and Amy Wallace, *Creativity, Inc.: Overcoming the Unseen Forces That Stand in the Way of True Inspiration* (New York: Random House, 2014).

66. It should be noted that the science of neuroplasticity is a relatively new field. Nearly miraculous (and untested) claims are made daily about what is possible. While it is truly amazing what is possible, and the implications are profound, it is also important to remember that it is both easy and profitable to make unsubstantiated claims. As of yet, the research doesn't support some of what is being touted. Robert A. Burton, *A Skeptic's Guide to the Mind: What Neuroscience Can and Cannot Tell Us About Ourselves* (New York: St. Martin's Griffin, 2014).

67. Jefrey Schwartz and Sharon Begley, *The Mind and the Brain: Neuroplasticity and the Power of Mental Force* (New York: HarperCollins, 2002), 107.

68. Richard Strozzi-Heckler, *The Leadership Dojo: Build Your Foundation as an Exemplary Leader* (Frog Books, 2007).

69. Rick Hanson, *Hardwiring Happiness: The New Brain Science of Contentment, Calm, and Confidence* (New York: Harmony Books, 2016), 11–12.

70. These kinds of somatic practices are profoundly helpful in developing self and others. Somatic practices engage the whole nervous system in integrated developmental learning, and support embodiment. For more depth on these practices, see Silsbee, *Presence-Based Coaching,* and Strozzi-Heckler, *The Leadership Dojo.*

71. Richard Strozzi-Heckler, *Being Human at Work: Bringing Somatic Intelligence Into Your Professional Life* (North Atlantic Books, 2003).

72. The tension between tradition and innovation is a classic polarity. Along with other polarities, this tension was very present in Susan's situation. Barry Johnson and Roy Oswald co-authored a book on working with polarities in churches; many of the principles can be extrapolated to other change initiatives. *Managing Polarities in Congregations: Eight Keys for Thriving Faith Communities* (Lanham, MD: Rowman & Littlefield, 2009).

73. "The Story of Little Black Sambo," Wikipedia, last modified October 19, 2017, https://en.wikipedia.org/wiki/The_Story_of_Little_Black_Sambo. The 1899 children's book tells the story of a South Indian boy who outsmarts a tiger. Some later editions of the book have graphics that were interpreted as racist, but these are not implicit in the story itself, which was one of the earliest depictions of a black hero.

74. Safe-to-fail experiments were advocated by David Snowden: "Safe-to-Fail Probes," Cognitive Edge website, http://cognitive-edge.com/methods/safe-to-fail-probes/. Jennifer Garvey Berger explains more about their applications in fostering complexity-capable cultures. *Simple Habits for Complex Times: Powerful Practices for Leaders* (Stanford, CA: Stanford Business Books, 2016).

75. Carolyn Coughlin, through personal communications with me, and her New Zealand-based consulting firm, Cultivating Leadership, have been instrumental in shaping my own work with safe-to-fail experiments. https://www.cultivatingleadership.co.nz. Also see Jennifer Garvey Berger and Keith Johnston, *Simple Habits for Complex Times: Powerful Practices for Leaders* (Stanford, CA: Stanford Business Books, 2015).

76. "Safe-to-Fail Probes," Cognitive Edge website, http://cognitive-edge.com/methods/safe-to-fail-probes/.

77. These criteria draw from Cultivating Leadership's guidelines for safe-to-fail experiments. https://www.cultivatingleadership.co.nz.

78. Those with an eye for polarities will likely recognize connection and differentiation as a polarity. For the sake of bounding our discussion, I am not analyzing this as a dynamic polarity system. However, the application of polarity theory is highly relevant here. Barry Johnson's work, in particular, provides a rich set of lenses on polarities in general. See the Polarity Partnerships website, http://polaritypartnerships.com.

79. Stephen Gilligan and Dvorah Simon, eds., *Walking in Two Worlds: The Relational Self in Theory, Practice, and Community* (Phoenix, AZ: Zeig, Tucker & Theisen, 2004).

80. Richard Strozzi-Heckler, *The Leadership Dojo: Build Your Foundation as an Exemplary Leader* (Frog Books, 2007), 148.

81. David Despain, "Early Humans Used Brain Power, Innovation and Teamwork to Dominate the Planet," *Scientific American*, February 27, 2010, https://www.scientificamerican.com/article/humans-brain-power-origins/.

82. Adam Kahane writes from deep experience about a closely related polarity dynamic using different language. Power (the drive for self-actualization and results) and love (the yearning for connection and relationship) are both necessary to create real change. Yet, they often appear in tension with each other. *Power and Love: A Theory and Practice of Social Change* (San Francisco, CA: Berrett-Koehler, 2010).

83. General Stanley McChrystal, Tantum Collins, David Silverman and Chris Fussell, *Team of Teams: New Rules of Engagement for a Complex World* (New York: Portfolio, 2015).

84. Bhante Henepola Gunaratana, *Mindfulness in Plain English*, revised and expanded edition (New York: Wisdom Publications, 1996), 75.

85. Fluidity and stability are, of course, another polarity. A chapter could usefully be written on navigating the polarity of fluidity and stability itself, as well as the polarity of connection and differentiation. But that would make this a different book. For more, I again refer the reader to Barry Johnson's excellent work on polarities: http:// polaritypartnerships.com

86. *The Mindful Coach: Seven Roles for Facilitating Leader Development* (San Francisco, CA: Jossey-Bass, 2010).

87. Noel Tichy and Ram Charan, "Speed, Simplicity, Self-Confidence: An Interview with Jack Welch," *Harvard Business Review*, September–October 1989, https://hbr.org/1989/09/speed-simplicity-self-confidence-an-interview-with-jack-welch.

88. "Minimum critical specifications" is an engineering term for the essential parameters for a design process. When these are provided, without specifying detail, there is maximum space for innovation and creativity by those actually doing the work. Marvin Ross Weisbord, *Discovering Common Ground: How Future Search Conferences Bring People Together to Achieve Breakthrough Innovation, Empowerment, Shared Vision, and Collaborative Action* (San Francisco, CA: Berrett-Koehler, 1992).

89. Frederic Laloux, *Reinventing Organizations: A Guide to Creating Organizations Inspired by the Next Stage of Human Consciousness* (Brussels: Nelson Parker, 2014).

90. Charles Casto, personal communication, and Ranjay Gulati, Charles Casto, and Charlotte Krontiris, "How the Other Fukushima Plant Survived," *Harvard Business Review*, July–August 2014, https://hbr.org/2014/07/how-the-other-fukushima-plant-survived.

91. Personal communications with Red Cross staff; conversations took place in context of leadership programs, and leadership presence was one of the topic areas.

92. Riva Richmond, "Mayor Muriel Bowser on Heatwaves and Local Leadership," The Story Exchange website, July 13, 2017, http://thestoryexchange.org/mayor-muriel-bowser-heatwaves-local-leadership/.

93. C40 Cities website, http://www.c40.org/about; Sydney, http://thestoryexchange.org/sydney-mayor-clover-moore-heat-trees-women-charge/; Paris, http://thestoryexchange.org/paris-mayor-anne-hidalgo-resilient-cities-resilient-women; Washington, DC, http://thestoryexchange.org/mayor-muriel-bowser-heatwaves-local-leadership/; Cape Town, http://thestoryexchange.org/cape-town-mayor-patricia-de-lille-protecting-societys-vulnerable/.

94. Polarity Partnerships website, http://polaritypartnerships.com.

95. *Third Rock from the Sun* was an American sitcom that ran from 1996 to 2001.

96. Nick Lane, *Life Ascending: The Ten Great Inventions of Evolution*, reprint (New York: W. W. Norton, 2010).

97. Marilee Adams, *Change Your Questions, Change Your Life: 12 Powerful Tools for Leadership, Coaching, and Life*, 3rd ed. (Oakland, CA: Berrett-Koehler, 2016).

98. Much more on the theory and practicalities of this essential practice can be found in *Presence-Based Coaching: Cultivating Self-Generative Leaders Through Mind, Body, and Heart* (San Francisco, CA: Jossey-Bass, 2008)

99. Richard Strozzi-Heckler, personal communication. Also in his book, *The Leadership Dojo: Build Your Foundation as an Exemplary Leader* (Frog Books, 2007).

100. Pioneered at 3M, made famous at Google. Jeffrey Goldstein, James K. Hazy, and Benyamin B. Lichtenstein, *Complexity and the Nexus of Leadership: Leveraging Nonlinear Science to Create Ecologies of Innovation*, 2010 ed. (New York: Palgrave Macmillan, 2011).

101. Rodney Napier and Matti Gershenfeld, *Making Groups Work: A Guide for Group Leaders* (Boston, MA: Houghton Mifflin, 1983).

102. Donald Sull and Charles Spinosa, "Promise-Based Management: The Essence of Execution," *Harvard Business Review*, April 2007, https://hbr.org/2007/04/promise-based-management-the-essence-of-execution.

103. Frederic Laloux, *Reinventing Organizations: A Guide to Creating Organizations Inspired by the Next Stage of Human Consciousness* (Brussels: Nelson Parker, 2014).

Index

Page numbers in bold indicate detailed explanations of terms

About the Author

DOUG SILSBEE IS A PREEMINENT AUTHOR, executive coach and thought leader in the fields of Presence-Based Coaching, leadership development and resilience.

Doug's groundbreaking work integrates deep pragmatic experience with organization and leader development on five continents with mindfulness, interpersonal neurobiology, somatics, complexity and developmental psychology. His influential books provide the foundation for a leading-edge coach certification program, accredited by the International Coach Federation (ICF). Doug's work is grounded in a deep commitment to the development of human beings that can be a stand for a future world that works for everyone.

Doug is a Master Somatic Coach with the prestigious Strozzi Institute. He is a sought-after speaker for ICF and many other international conferences, and has taught at the Brookings Institution, UCLA Executive Education, Georgetown University's Institute for Transformational Leadership, George Mason University, and the Federal Executive Institute. Doug is a 2018 winner of the prestigious International Thought Leader of Distinction Award, presented annually by the MEECO Leadership Development Institute and the Association of Corporate Executive Coaches.

Doug's personal interests have included a geology research trip in West Greenland, the second canoe descent of a river in Labrador, and a climb of Mt. Rainier. With his wife Walker, Doug has explored many spiritual and personal growth lineages, and created a carbon neutral mountain retreat center near Asheville, North Carolina. They enjoy traveling with dogs in their cozy Airstream trailer named Hobbes. Doug and Walker have three grown children, two very loved grandsons, and a Quechua god-daughter in Peru.

Most of all, Doug has lived fully, recognizing that self-knowledge and contribution arise through aliveness and attention. His current experiences with stage 4 cancer are serving as a potent sandbox for discovery.

Doug can be reached at dksilsbee@gmail.com.

Previous Books by Doug Silsbee

Doug's pioneering book, *The Mindful Coach* (2004, 2010) explores the intersection of mindfulness and coaching. This groundbreaking book integrates self-awareness into a logical and pragmatic approach to developing coaching skills. Here are seven "Voices" that a coach uses, and how to orient these Voices to the client's learning, rather than the unconscious needs of the coach. Extensive coaching dialogues illustrate a pragmatic road map for coaching conversations that work. Foreword by Marshall Goldsmith.

"Success in business is predicated on eliciting the best from people. *The Mindful Coach* clearly articulates the essentials of how to do this. As someone who believes deeply in the potential of all people, I found Silsbee's approach both practical and profound. This is a must-read for everyone concerned with people and learning."
—Arthur M. Blank
Philanthropist; Co-founder, The Home Depot; and Owner & CEO, Atlanta Falcons

"*The Mindful Coach* is not just another coaching model. It is a frame of reference for anyone involved in developing people. This highly readable book should serve as a reference for anyone genuinely concerned about helping others. It has had a significant impact on the way I approach coaching and developing others."
—James N. Bassett, M.Ed.
Employee Development, Institute of Nuclear Power Operations

"Doug's analysis of the coaching process is clear and intuitive. Its simplicity allows it to be easily used, yet it's rich in detail, making it a powerful analytical tool for the professional. Wrapped in a holistic framework that accounts for the coach, the client, and the process of coaching, it will enrich the insight and practice of every interested reader."
—Christopher C. Dennen, Ph.D.
President, Innovative Healing Inc.

Presence-Based Coaching (2008) reveals the essential contribution of presence as a meta-competency for human development. Doug's second book offers concrete models and approaches for becoming, and for coaching, the resilient leaders that our times require. Business examples, actual coaching dialogues and pragmatic practices integrate mind, body and heart into a robust toolkit for building your own presence and extending it to others. With a foreword by Richard Strozzi-Heckler.

"*Presence-Based Coaching* is a masterful treatise on coaching in the consciousness age. This book brings structure and strategy to accelerating the evolution of leaders."

—Richard Barrett

Author, *Liberating the Corporate Soul* and *Building a Values-Driven Organization*

"Doug Silsbee has written a powerful guide for those who believe that *presence* has moved to the forefront as one of the most important qualities that leaders need. This is a must-read for coaches and anyone else doing the work of developing themselves and others."

—Alfred L. Cooke, PhD. Director, Center for Organizational Performance,
Federal Executive Institute

"Finally, a truly great book that develops the *being* of a coach. Nothing else offers such clear and practical tools. A must-read for professional coaches and leaders using a coaching approach."

—Henry Kimsey-House Cofounder of The Coaches Training Institute,
and coauthor, *Co-Active Coaching*

"Doug Silsbee nails it, giving us a doorway to experience the power of presence, and to bring it to bear on the development of authentic, purpose-driven leaders. This book is a sensible, grounded must-read!"

—Richard J. Leider
Founder, The Inventure Group, and author, *The Power of Purpose*

Lightning Source UK Ltd.
Milton Keynes UK
UKHW040352080920
369523UK00002B/69/J